THREE RIVERS
COOKBOOK II

"The Good Taste of Pittsburgh"

Cover Design and Illustrations by Susan Gaca.

CHILD HEALTH ASSOCIATION OF SEWICKLEY, INC.

Sewickley, Pennsylvania

1981

Our grateful appreciation to the following companies and foundations for their generosity in helping to underwrite the first printing of THREE RIVERS COOKBOOK II.

Alcoa Foundation
Derby & Company, Inc.
H. J. Heinz Company Foundation
Jones & Laughlin Steel Corporation
The Pittsburgh Foundation
Rockwell International
United States Steel Corporation
Westinghouse Electric Corporation

First Printing	40,000	May, 1981
Second Printing	40,000	July, 1981
Third Printing	40,000	November, 1981
Fourth Printing	30,000	March, 1985
Fifth Printing	10,000	June, 1990
Sixth Printing	10,000	November, 1992
Seventh Printing	10,000	January, 1996
Eighth Printing	2,500	September, 2010

For additional copies, use the order blanks in the back of the book or write directly to:

THREE RIVERS COOKBOOK II
Child Health Association of Sewickley, Inc.
1108 Ohio River Boulevard
Sewickley, Pennsylvania 15143
(412) 741-3221   or   (800) 624-8753

Printed in the United States of America
by
Geyer Printing Company, Inc.
Pittsburgh, Pennsylvania

  ISBN 0-9607634-1-4

CHILD HEALTH ASSOCIATION
OF SEWICKLEY

Since its founding in 1923 as a community service organization of concerned area women, the Child Health Association of Sewickley has compiled a most impressive record of accomplishments. The statistics of dollars and volunteer hours given to child-oriented projects within Allegheny County are staggering enough: $636,500 in allocated funds and over 41,000 hours given in volunteer service to local needs.

The strength behind these figures is an Active and Associate membership dedicated to the organization's commitment to child welfare, and one which has enthusiastically supported a wide variety of innovative projects. Golf Exhibitions, twenty House Tours, a Jazz Concert with Sarah Vaughan and Count Basie, and annual Balls are sources of funds. An on-going dental hygiene program in area elementary schools (represented throughout this book by Chappy, a beloved puppet), support of Pittsburgh's Three Rivers Arts Festival, the D.T. Watson Home, Sewickley Valley Hospital, community drug and alcohol abuse workshops, parenting courses and Parents Anonymous, and an innovative Cultural Enrichment program bringing artistic and dramatic experiences to area schools - these are but a few of our varied endeavors. As a catalyst group with seed money and a willingness to explore or finance new ideas, Child Health can often identify a need and move to meet that need.

The financial success Child Health enjoys today in large part results from the phenomenal success of THREE RIVERS COOKBOOK I, first published in October, 1973. Our volunteer membership has, to date, processed fifteen printings of 265,118 books, and we have allocated in charitable funds $269,118 from Cookbook proceeds alone.

THREE RIVERS COOKBOOK I is found in homes across this country and abroad, and is sold currently in over 450 stores. The public's acceptance of our first book has been nothing short of a love affair - we are confident that this, our new effort, THREE RIVERS COOKBOOK II, will meet with the same enthusiastic reception. The Child Health Association of Sewickley is proud of its past record of service to Pittsburgh and looks forward to a bright future of community involvement.

Eleanor H. Friedman

May, 1981
Eleanor H. Friedman
President

3

Our special thanks to our friends, old and new, who shared their favorite and finest recipes with us and with you. Without their generosity this, the second THREE RIVERS COOKBOOK, would not have been possible. We most sincerely regret that it was not feasible, because of space, to include all of the outstanding recipes received and tested.

We have endeavored to make this volume a fitting complement to THREE RIVERS COOKBOOK I, and to present all recipes in their simplest and most practical form. Editorial adjustments have been made in order to standardize measurements and procedures, and to provide you with appropriate guidelines in preparation. We trust that liberties taken will meet with the approval of our contributors.

Finally, we are most grateful to the members, families and friends of Child Health who responded with their customary exuberance during the production of this book. We hope you, your families and guests find the recipes excellent and the results marvelously good to eat.

Carolyn Smyser Hammer.............................Chairman
Doris H. Paul.....................................Co-Chairman
Susan Gaca..Artist
Mary Anne Trenchard Riley...................Testing Chairman
Margaret R. Zimmerman......................Testing Chairman
Anne F. Dithrich...............................Commentaries

CONTENTS

INDEX OF ILLUSTRATIONS

FOREWORD 1

OPENERS 7

BREADS 45

ENTREES 61

VEGETABLES 145

SALADS 167

SWEETS 183

NATIONALITY FAVORITES 227

OPENERS

"CITY OF CHAMPIONS"

In 1980, Pittsburgh became a "City of Champions" when the Pittsburgh Pirates won the World Series in a dramatic come-from-behind finish against the Baltimore Orioles; and the Pittsburgh Steelers brought a fourth Super Bowl Championship trophy home to the Steel City.

Additional illustrations in this section:

Rare 18th Century famille noire teapot and cover from a private collection.

Opal ware fish pitcher.*

Early blown glass pieces.

Former entrance to the William Thaw house on Beechwood Boulevard in Squirrel Hill.

Pittsburgh lead glass pieces, courtesy of the Historical Society of Pennsylvania.

Whale oil lamps and clear lead candlesticks.

Pittsburg (sic), Knoxville and St. Clair Railway - 1888.

Free blown glass vases.

The Liberty Theater, designed by Edward Lee, was a part of the Pittsburgh scene from 1915 until 1968 when it was razed.

Double glass dolphin candlesticks and tumbler.

Carnegie Mellon University.

*All glassware is early Pittsburgh unless otherwise indicated.

JOY COCKTAIL
"Whamo!"

1½ oz. dry light Rum
1½ oz. Triple Sec
½ oz. lemon juice

Mix ingredients in a cocktail shaker; shake and strain into a sugar-rimmed cocktail glass. Can be varied by adding Grenadine or Creme de Menthe.

Preparation: 10 min.　　Easy　　Serves: 1

Diana Morrow

MELON BALL
"Try this in place of Bloody Marys."

½ oz. Midori
½ oz. Vodka
½ oz. orange juice
1½ oz. sweetened lemon juice
　　or frozen lemonade

Mix ingredients and serve in a sour glass with a cube of ice. Can also be mixed in a blender with ice included.

Preparation: 5 min.　　Easy　　Serves: 1

Arnold J. Stevens, Jr.

HOLIDAY PUNCH
"A different Bloody Mary"

12 cups clamato juice
1 tsp. Tabasco sauce
2-3 tbsp. lemon or lime juice
2 tsp. basil, crumbled
2-3 cups Vodka
ice ring
celery stalks

Blend first 5 ingredients. Pour over ice ring in a punch bowl. Garnish glasses with stalks of celery. Can substitute 6 cups tomato and 6 cups clam juice for the clamato juice.

Preparation: 10 min.   Easy   Serves: 24 4-oz. servings
                          Can do ahead

Doris H. Paul

EGG NOG

6 eggs, beaten
1 can Eagle Brand milk
1 tsp. vanilla
½ tsp. salt
1 qt. milk
½ pt. whipping cream, whipped
nutmeg

Beat eggs; mix in both milks, vanilla and salt. Fold in the whipped cream and sprinkle with nutmeg.

Preparation: 15 min.   Easy   Serves: 8-12

Mrs. Lee Huizenga

STRAWBERRY SPARKLER
"Refreshing summer drink"

½ cup lemon juice
1 cup orange juice
½ cup superfine sugar
1 pt. strawberries, washed, hulled & quartered
1 750 ml. bottle Rosé wine
1 750 ml. bottle Champagne, chilled
2 7-oz. bottles carbonated water, chilled

Place lemon juice, orange juice and sugar in pitcher and stir to dissolve sugar. Add strawberries and Rosé wine and refrigerate several hours. Just before serving, add Champagne and carbonated water.

Preparation: 15 min.   Easy   Yields: 3 qts.
                          Must do ahead

Mrs. Roy M. Eckstrom

HOT RUM DRINK
"A holiday favorite"

½ lb. butter
1 lb. dark brown sugar
¼ tsp. cinnamon
¼ tsp. nutmeg
¼ tsp. cloves
dark Rum
boiling water

Cream butter with sugar. Sprinkle the cinnamon, nutmeg and cloves over the sugar mixture and mix thoroughly. Refrigerate in covered container to store.

To serve: Place 1 heaping tablespoon of mixture into mug, add 1½ ounces of Rum and fill with boiling water. Stir and serve, garnished with a cinnamon stick and lemon slice.

Preparation: 10 min.　　**Easy**　　　　**Serves: 30**
　　　　　　　　　　　　　Do ahead

Carolyn K. Kastroll

SUMMER PUNCH
"A real summer cooler"

1 cup sugar
5 cups water
1 6-oz. can frozen lemonade
1 12-oz. can frozen orange juice
1 46-oz. can unsweetened
　　pineapple juice
4 bananas, mashed
1 32-oz. bottle 7-UP
1-2 cups Vodka

Mix first 5 ingredients and freeze 24 hours. Take from freezer 1½ hours before serving. Mash 4 bananas and add to the above mixture. Add 7-UP and 1-2 cups Vodka, depending on how strong you want it to be. This will be slushy when served.

Preparation: 15-20 min.　　**Must do ahead**　　**Yield: 12 cups**
　　　　　　　　　　　　　　Must freeze

Phyllis Hurley

CHAMPAGNE PUNCH
"Perfect for a wedding"

1 qt. strawberries
⅔ cup sugar
1 750 ml. bottle Moselle
2 750 ml. bottles Champagne
½ 750 ml. bottle Claret
ice ring with strawberries

Chill all wines 1 day. Wash and hull strawberries; if large, quarter. Put into large punch bowl and sprinkle with sugar. Add bottle of Moselle and let stand at least 1 hour. Add Champagne, Claret and ice ring.

Preparation: 10 min.　　**Easy**　　　　**Serves: 15**
　　　　　　　　　　　　　Must do ahead

Carolyn S. Hammer

EXPANDING PUNCH

"Use this without Rum for kids."

1 46-oz. can pineapple juice
1 46-oz. can apricot nectar
1 12-oz. can frozen orange juice
1 6-oz. can frozen lemonade
1 qt. gingerale
1 qt. mint gingerale
1 qt. water
½ to ¾ cup sugar
1 qt. orange sherbet
Rum to taste, start with ½ pt. to
   2 gals. punch

Mix all ingredients except Rum. Add Rum to taste and serve. Use pale mint gingerale, not green.

Preparation: 5-10 min.   Easy   Yield: 2 gals.
                         Can do ahead

Mrs. John Ireland

CRANBERRY FLOAT

"Great for kids"

2 qts. cranberry juice cocktail
1 qt. ginger ale
½ gal. lemon sherbet

Combine the chilled cranberry juice and ginger ale in punch bowl. Spoon lemon sherbet to cover the surface of the punch. Serve immediately.

Preparation: 5 min.   Easy   Yield: 5 qts.

Mrs. Charles Dithrich

FROSTY GOLDEN PUNCH

"Great summertime drink"

2 20-oz. cans crushed pineapple,
   with juice
2 6-oz. cans frozen lemonade
   concentrate
¼ cup sugar
1 28-oz. bottle club soda
1 tray ice cubes
1 750 ml. bottle Champagne,
   optional

10 minutes before serving, blend pineapple with juice at high speed 15-20 seconds until thickened. In chilled punch bowl, stir blended pineapple, lemonade concentrate and sugar. Stir in soda, add ice cubes and serve at once. Add 1 bottle Champagne after soda - then it serves 26 ½-cup servings.

Preparation: 10-15 min.   Easy   Serves: 20 4-oz. servings

Doris H. Paul

FRESH AND FROSTY LEMONADE
"Delicious - like Grandma used to make"

1 cup freshly squeezed lemon
   juice
¾ cup sugar
4 cups cold water
ice cubes
1 lemon, sliced
Grenadine, optional

Combine lemon juice and sugar. Add water, stirring. Serve over ice in glasses and garnish with lemon slices. May add Grenadine for pink lemonade.

Preparation: 15 min.   Easy   Yield: 2 qts.
                                Can do ahead

Chappy's Choice

ORANGE SLUSH
"Nutritious and popular drink for children (and adults)"

1 egg
⅓ cup frozen concentrated
   orange juice
1 cup milk
1 tsp. honey
4-6 ice cubes, partially crushed

Combine all ingredients in a blender and blend just until slushy. *Do not overblend.*

Preparation: 5 min.   Easy   Yield: 1 pt.

Kathy Stewart

BRANDY ALEXANDER FRAPPÉS
"So smooth"

1 qt. vanilla ice cream
½ cup Brandy
½ cup Creme de Cacao
chocolate curls

Refrigerate 4 to 6 champagne or sherbet glasses several hours to chill well. One half hour before using, remove ice cream from freezer to refrigerator, let soften.

Just before serving, combine ice cream, Brandy and Creme de Cacao in blender. Blend at high speed until smooth. Turn into chilled glasses and decorate with chocolate curls.

Preparation: 5 min.   Easy   Serves: 4-6

Carol Anne Boumbouras

CHRISTI'S MINT CHOCOLATE CHIP FLIP
"Combination dessert - after dinner drink all rolled into one."

ice, 2 cups, approx.
1 ½ oz. Gin
1 ½ oz. Kahlua
1 ½ oz. Creme de Cacao
2-3 scoops mint chocolate chip
ice cream, can use chocolate
chip, chocolate or coffee

Put approximately 2 cups of ice in a blender; add Gin, Kahlua and Creme de Cacao. Blend well, add ice cream and blend until the consistency of a milk shake.

Preparation: 5 min.　　　　Easy　　　　Serves: 2-3

Christiana Hays

"NO STING" STINGERS
"Still beware - these are sneaky."

1 ½ oz. Brandy
1 ½ oz. White Creme de Menthe
2 drops Holland House foamy
head

Mix equal parts of Brandy and White Creme de Menthe in a blender. Add two drops of Holland House foamy head and blend. Add crushed ice and blend again. Serve in cocktail glass.

Preparation: 5 min.　　　　Easy　　　　Serves: 1

J. William Paul

JON'S IRISH COFFEE
"Serve with pride."

¾ cup coffee
1 oz. Bushmillers Irish Whiskey
1 tbsp. brown sugar
whipped cream
¼ tsp. brown sugar

Pour freshly brewed coffee into mug. Add Whiskey and sugar, stirring twice. Place dollop of whipped cream on top and sprinkle with brown sugar.

Preparation: 5 min.　　　　Easy　　　　Serves: 1

Jon E. McCarthy

APPETIZERS

RHEA'S CHILI CHEESE CUBES
"Olé Amigos"

8 eggs
½ cup all-purpose flour
1 tsp. baking powder
¾ tsp. salt
3 cups Monterey Jack cheese, shredded
1 ½ cups cottage cheese
2 4-oz. cans whole green chilies, drained, seeded and chopped

Beat eggs until light and fluffy. Stir together flour, baking powder and salt. Add to eggs. Fold in cheese, cottage cheese and chilies. Turn into 9x9x2" greased baking dish. Bake 40 minutes at 350°. Remove from oven and let stand 10 minutes. Cut into cubes and serve hot.

| Preparation: | 15-20 min. | Easy | Yield: 3-4 doz. |
| Baking: | 40 min. | Can do ahead | |

Rhea Lynch

CHEESE BALLS
"The Queen loved these."

6 oz. Blue cheese
2 5-oz. jars Cheddar cheese
2 tbsp. onion, grated
1 tbsp. Worcestershire
½ tbsp. Accent
1 cup pecans, finely chopped
parsley, snipped

Mix first five ingredients well. Add ½ cup chopped pecans. Form into one large or two small balls. Chill. Roll in chopped parsley and remaining chopped pecans on plastic wrap. Chill. Serve with crackers.

| Preparation: 20 min. | Easy | Yield: 2 small cheese balls |
| | Can do ahead | Can freeze |

Dorothy Clark Schmidt

MOCK BOURSIN
"Tastes like the real thing"

1 8-oz. pkg. cream cheese, softened
½ stick (¼ cup) butter
½ tsp. Beau Monde seasoning
1 clove garlic, minced
¼ tsp. Herbes de Provence*
1 tsp. water
1 tsp. parsley, fresh or dried, finely chopped
¼ tsp. red wine vinegar
¼ tsp. Worcestershire sauce

*Herbes de Provence: equal parts of sage, rosemary, marjoram, basil and thyme

Beat all ingredients with an electric mixer and pack into a container. Refrigerate at least 12 hours. Bring to room temperature before serving.

Preparation: 5 min.   Easy   Yield: 2 cups
                          Must do ahead

Phyllis R. Grine

CHEESE COCKTAIL STRIPS
"Get your kids to help with these."

1 large loaf Pepperidge Farm sliced white bread
½ cup butter, melted
2 8-oz. pkgs. Philadelphia cream cheese, room temp.
6 tbsp. Hellmann's mayonnaise
4-6 green onions chopped, including tops
6-8 drops Tabasco sauce
1 cup Parmesan cheese, freshly grated

Stack 4 slices of bread on top of one another and remove crusts. Cut each slice into 4 strips. Repeat until all bread is sliced. Brush melted butter on 1 side of each strip and place on cookie sheet. Toast under broiler lightly and on both sides. Mix other ingredients together except the Parmesan. Spread mixture on buttered side of bread. Put Parmesan in shallow bowl and dip each coated piece of bread so that Parmesan adheres to coating. At this point the strips may be frozen to use whenever you wish. When serving, broil until golden brown and bubbly. Must be watched carefully.

Preparation: 30 min.   Easy   Yield: 120 strips
Cooking: 4 min.   Can do ahead   Can freeze

Cordelia Jacobs

SESAME CHEESE BALL
"Sesame Cheese Ball opens door to fine taste"

¼ cup sesame seeds
2 tbsp. instant minced onion
1 tsp. beef stock base or 1 beef
   bouillon cube
2 tbsp. lemon juice
½ lb. med. sharp Cheddar
   cheese, finely grated
2 tbsp. mayonnaise
1 tsp. Worcestershire sauce
1 tsp. dry mustard
1 tbsp. ketchup

Toast sesame seeds in 350° oven for 15 minutes. Soak instant minced onions and beef stock base in lemon juice. Combine mayonnaise, Worcestershire, ketchup and dry mustard. Mix soaked onions, grated cheese and mayonnaise mixture until well blended. Shape into ball and roll in sesame seeds which have been spread on wax paper. Coat well. Chill.

Preparation: 30 min.   Easy   Yield: 1 cup plus
    Can do ahead

Mrs. Kenneth N. Myers

TOASTED PARMESAN CANAPÉS
"Don't leave the oven while broiling"

1 loaf white bread, cut into small
   rounds
white onions, sliced
3 tbsp. Parmesan cheese
1 cup mayonnaise
Parmesan cheese for topping

Cut tiny rounds of sliced bread. Cut small white onions into ⅛" slices and place a slice on each bread round. Mix 3 tablespoons freshly grated Parmesan cheese with 1 cup mayonnaise and top each bread round with a little mound of cheese mixture. Place canapés on cookie sheet and sprinkle with a little more grated Parmesan. Keep in refrigerator until ready to broil; broil until tops are brown and serve hot.

Preparation: 20 min.   Easy   Yield: 80
Cooking: 3 min.   Must do ahead

Mrs. M.G. Patton

HERB CURRY DIP
"Try this with your crudités"

1 cup mayonnaise
1 tsp. mixed herbs or fines
   herbes
¼ tsp. salt
⅛ tsp. curry powder
1 tbsp. parsley, snipped
1 tbsp. onion, grated
1½ tsp. lemon juice
½ tsp. Worcestershire sauce
2 tsp. capers

Mix ingredients together and serve with raw vegetables.

Preparation: 10 min.   Easy   Yield: 1 cup
    Must do ahead

Mrs. Malcolm Hay, Jr.

SOUR CREAM CLAM DIP
"You'll want to double this, it's so good"

1 cup sour cream
½ cup minced clams, drained
½ tsp. ground basil leaves
½ tsp. garlic powder
½ tsp. onion powder
½ tsp. salt
dash of black pepper
paprika for garnish

Combine ingredients and garnish with paprika. Serve with raw zucchini slices, mushrooms, radishes, cauliflower, cherry tomatoes, etc.

Preparation: 10 min.   Easy   Yield: 1½ cups
                         Can do ahead

Barbara Gaudio

CRABMEAT DIP

3 8-oz. pkgs. cream cheese,
   softened
2 6½-oz. cans crabmeat,
   broken into bits
garlic salt
1¼ cups mayonnaise
1 tsp. mustard
¼ cup dry Sherry
1 tbsp. confectioners' sugar
1 tsp. onion juice
Lawry's seasoned salt, to taste

Heat all ingredients in a double boiler until cheese is melted and dip is thoroughly blended. Serve in a chafing dish or an electric fondue pot. Bugles are great scoops for this dip.

Preparation: 20 min.   Easy   Serves: 25
                         Can do ahead

Mrs. Walter F. Parker

LOBSTER SPREAD OR DIP
"The smooth sweet taste of lobster"

1 8-oz. pkg. Philadelphia cream
   cheese
1 14-oz. can frozen lobster
1½ tsp. salt
5 tsp. lemon juice
1 tsp. Zest or Accent
Tabasco sauce, to taste
cream

Let cheese come to room temperature. Thaw lobster, remove from can, and drain thoroughly. Remove hard cartilage from meat. Chop finely or grind meat. Combine with cream cheese. Add salt, lemon juice, Accent and Tabasco sauce to taste (about 5-6 dashes). Thin to desired consistency with cream, as necessary. Could be varied by adding finely diced chives or other seasonings for those who like a stronger flavor.

Preparation: 5-10 min.   Easy   Yield: 2½ cups
                           Can do ahead

Mrs. Leon Thomson

18

CURRY DIP FOR RAW VEGETABLES
"Very pleasant - not too hot."

2 cups mayonnaise
3 tsp. curry powder
3 tbsp. chili sauce
1 tbsp. Worcestershire sauce
½ tsp. salt
pepper
½ tsp. garlic salt
1 tsp. instant onion

Combine all ingredients and refrigerate. Serve with assorted raw vegetables such as carrots, string beans, cauliflower, green pepper, etc.

Preparation: 5 min.

Easy
Can do ahead

Yield: 2 cups

Mrs. Dick Thornburgh

MEXICAN DIP
"Low calorie, different dip"

3 fresh tomatoes
3 green onions
1 can black olives
1 small can green chili peppers, "mild," chopped
3 tbsp. olive oil
1½ tsp. wine vinegar
½-1 tsp. garlic salt

Dice the tomatoes, onions, olives and chili peppers by hand. Add the oil, vinegar and salt, mixing thoroughly. Refrigerate several hours or overnight and serve with corn chips.

Preparation: 20 min.

Easy
Must do ahead

Yield: 2 cups

Heather Dills

CHUTNEY GLAZED CHEESE PATÉ
"Attention curry lovers"

6-oz. cream cheese, softened
4-oz. Cheddar cheese, grated
3 tbsp. dry Sherry
2-3 tsp. curry powder, or to taste
¼ tsp. salt
½ cup chutney, finely chopped
1 bunch scallions, finely chopped

Mix the two cheeses thoroughly. Add Sherry, curry powder and salt and mix. Spread mixture ½ " thick on serving platter. Chill until firm. At serving time, spread top with chutney and sprinkle with scallions. Serve with sesame rounds.

Preparation: 30 min.

Easy
Must do ahead

Yield: 2 cups

Mayo Moore

ESCARGOT IN MUSHROOMS

"Something special for snail lovers."

1 lb. fresh mushrooms, cleaned, stems removed
lemon juice
36 canned snails, drained
½ lb. butter
3 tbsp. fresh parsley, finely chopped
2 tbsp. shallots, finely chopped
1 large clove garlic, crushed
1 tbsp. Parmesan cheese
¼ tsp. salt
black pepper, freshly ground
fresh French bread

Dip mushroom caps in lemon juice, drain and set aside. Rinse snails in hot water; dry on paper towels. In small bowl, cream butter and remaining ingredients except bread. Insert snail into each cap; spread generously with butter mixture. Place in baking pan and cover. Bake in 425° oven 10-12 minutes until hot and bubbling. Serve immediately with thick slices of bread.

Preparation: 25 min.   Easy   Yield: 36 appetizers
Baking: 12 min.   Can do ahead

Beth Adams

CREAMY CRABMEAT IN TOAST CUPS

"A crowd pleaser"

3 loaves white bread, 1 lb. each, firm texture
1 cup butter, melted
3 tbsp. butter
¼ cup flour
1½ cups milk
8-oz. Cheddar cheese, shredded
2 7½-oz. cans crabmeat
2 tbsp. scallions, minced
1 tsp. lemon rind, grated
1½ tbsp. lemon juice
3 tbsp. parsley, minced
1 tsp. Worcestershire sauce
1 tsp. prepared mustard
½ tsp. salt
dash Tabasco

Cut crusts from bread. Cut slices into 2½″ rounds. Brush with melted butter on both sides and press into tiny muffin pans. Bake at 450° for 5 minutes until golden.

In saucepan, melt 3 tablespoons butter, stir in flour and cook until blended. Add milk gradually and cook over low heat, stirring constantly, until thickened. Stir in cheese until melted. Bone and flake crabmeat. Add sauce and remaining ingredients. Mix. Fill each toast cup with 1-2 tablespoons of crab mixture. Bake at 400° for 10 minutes until piping hot. Can freeze by placing unbaked cups with crab on cooking sheet; freeze solid, then layer in rigid plastic containers, separating layers with plastic wrap. Bake 15-20 minutes at 400°

Preparation: 45 min.   Moderately difficult   Yield: 80
Baking: 10 min.   Can freeze

Carolyn K. Kastroll

20

CAVIAR MOUSSE
"A most attractive presentation."

¼ lb. butter, unsalted preferably, melted
2 7-oz. cans water packed tuna
1 tsp. green onion tops, chopped
1 4-oz. jar black caviar, drained
1 6-oz. jar herring tidbits in wine
¼ tsp. garlic powder
½ tsp. sugar
1 4-oz. jar red caviar, drained
lemon slices

Using a food processor or blender, combine melted butter with tuna until it becomes the consistency of paste. Add the green onion tops, herring, 1 heaping teaspoon of the black caviar, garlic powder and sugar and blend until lump-free. Pack into a 1 pint mold and refrigerate. 1 hour before serving, unmold onto a bed of lettuce; if mold breaks, reshape with a knife. Spread sides with remaining black caviar and the top with red caviar. Decorate with lemon slices and serve with pumpernickle or rye bread.

Preparation: 15 min.   Easy   Serves: 20
Must do ahead

Mrs. Jon E. McCarthy

RIBBON PATÉ
"A pleasing blend"

Aspic layer:
1 env. unflavored gelatin
2 beef bouillon cubes
1 cup water
1 tbsp. lemon juice

Cheese layer:
2 8-oz. pkgs. cream cheese
½ cup sour cream
1 tbsp. onion, grated

Ham layer:
2 4½-oz. cans deviled ham
¼ cup sweet mustard relish, or hot dog relish

Liver layer:
2 4½-oz. cans liver paté
¼ cup mayonnaise
2 tbsp. parsley, chopped
½ small jar olives, sliced, optional

Aspic layer: Combine gelatin, water and bouillon cubes in saucepan; heat until gelatin dissolves. Pour ½ cup gelatin mixture into a six cup mold; stir in lemon juice. Retain remaining aspic. Set mold in bowl of ice water.

Cheese layer: Combine cheese and sour cream and onion with ¼ cup reserved aspic. Beat until creamy smooth.

Ham layer: In small bowl combine ham, relish and ¼ cup reserved aspic.

Liver layer: In small bowl combine liver, mayonnaise, parsley and ¼ cup aspic.

When aspic is sticky firm in mold, arrange a ring of olives, ripe or stuffed, on top. You may do this before making ham and liver mixtures so it will be ready for next layer. Spoon half of cheese mixture on aspic layer. Dab small spoonsful around to minimize spreading; spread very gently. Repeat with all of ham mixture, then remaining cheese mixture, then all of liver mixture. Chill several hours. Unmold onto tray, decorate to suit your fancy, and serve with crackers.

Preparation: 45 min.   Must do ahead   Serves: 25

Audrie Borchardt

21

CORNED BEEF PATÉ
"A tasty change from the usual paté"

2 tsp. instant minced onion
⅔ cup water
12 oz. can corned beef
8 oz. braunschweiger
½ cup mayonnaise
1 tbsp. vinegar
½ tsp. dry mustard
parsley for garnish

Soften onion in water for 5 minutes. Flake corned beef with fork, add braunschweiger, mayonnaise, vinegar, dry mustard and onion. Blend at medium speed in food processor, ½ cup at a time. Turn into a 3½ cup mold and chill. Turn out on plate; decorate with parsley and serve with crackers or party rye bread. Can be mixed by hand.

Preparation: 5 min.   Easy   Yield: 3 cups
                      Can do ahead

Joanne Taylor

MARINATED SHRIMP
"A simple delight"

1 lb. shrimp, cleaned & cooked
1 cup Miracle Whip
1 onion, thinly sliced
juice of ½ lemon

Pat shrimp dry to remove all moisture. Combine marinade and marinate the shrimp, refrigerated, at least 24 hours. Serve with toothpicks.

Preparation: 15 min.   Easy   Serves: 8
                       Must do ahead

Anna Rae Kitay

BAKED CLAMS
"These have a nice texture, look great."

1 stick butter
2 cloves garlic, minced
1 10-oz. can minced clams
1 4-oz. can water chestnuts, drained, rinsed, & finely chopped
½ cup coarse bread crumbs
salt & freshly ground pepper, to taste
paprika
12 clam shells, thoroughly cleaned

Sauté garlic in melted butter until golden. Place clams in a large bowl; remove and reserve half of the liquid. Add all but 2 tablespoons of the garlic butter to the clams. Mix the water chestnuts, bread crumbs, salt and pepper with the clam mixture. Let rest 5 minutes to thicken. Spoon into clam shells; sprinkle with paprika. Combine reserved liquid with remaining garlic butter and drizzle over the clams. Broil until bubbling hot and lightly browned.

Preparation: 15 min.   Easy   Yield: 12-14 med. shells
Cooking: 5-8 min.   Can do ahead   Can freeze

Mrs. Howard LeVine

MRS. SMITH'S SCALLOPS
"A delicate surprise"

2 lbs. bay scallops, or sea
   scallops cut into bite-size
   pieces
¼ cup lime juice
¼ cup Gulden's mustard
¼ cup olive oil
dash MSG
purple onion, thinly sliced rings

Poach scallops in simmering water for 2 minutes. Rinse in cold water. Combine the juice, mustard and olive oil; pour on top of the scallops. Add the MSG and onion rings. Chill at least 3 hours. Serve with toothpicks.

| Preparation: | 10 min. | Easy | Serves: 12 |
| Cooking: | 2 min. | Must do ahead | |

Mrs. F. Gordon Kraft

SALMON BALL
"Very quick and easy"

1 16-oz. can salmon
1 8-oz. cream cheese
1 tbsp. lemon juice
2 tsp. onion, grated
1 tsp. horseradish
1 tsp. salt
½ cup pecans, chopped
3 tbsp. parsley, snipped

Drain salmon, remove skin, bones. Flake salmon and combine with all ingredients except pecans and parsley. Chill several hours. Roll into ball. Roll in nuts and parsley. Serve surrounded by crackers.

| Preparation: | 15 min. | Easy | Serves: 16-20 |
| | | Can do ahead | |

Dorothy Clark Schmidt

EVERYDAY PATÉ
"A lovely mild paté"

1 cup water
1 med. onion, chopped
3 whole ribs celery with leaves,
   chopped
1 lb. veal or chicken liver
1½ " cube of salt pork
2 eggs
1 tsp. salt
¼ tsp. pepper
1 cup cracker or bread crumbs
½ tsp. marjoram
milk, if necessary

Preheat oven to 350°. Boil together 1 cup water, onion and celery for 5 minutes. Add liver and simmer for 2 minutes. Drain, reserve liquid. Purée liver and vegetables in processor with salt pork. Add the eggs, salt, pepper, cracker or bread crumbs, marjoram and 1 cup reserved liquid and blend well; add milk if necessary. Pour into a greased loaf pan and bake 40 minutes. Cool, turn out on serving plate and garnish.

| Preparation: | 20 min. | Easy | Serves: 15 |
| Cooking: | 40 min. | Must do ahead | |

Jackie Holz

ARTICHOKE APPETIZERS
"A Cheddar cheese delight"

8 oz. Cheddar cheese, grated
2 6-oz. jars marinated
 artichokes, drained &
 chopped
4 eggs, beaten
2 tsp. parsley
1 bunch green onions, chopped
1 clove garlic, minced
3 drops Tabasco sauce

Mix all ingredients together and bake in greased 9" pan at 325° for 35 minutes. Cool for 15 minutes, cut and serve.

Preparation:	15 min.	Easy	Yield: 20 appetizers
Baking:	35 min.	Can do ahead	

Melissa Booth Moore

APPETIZER-LEEK PIE

16 sheets phyllo dough
¾ cup butter, melted
1 lb. leeks, sliced
1 small onion, sliced
1 small clove garlic, minced
3 tbsp. butter
5 large eggs, beaten
1 tsp. salt
several grinds fresh nutmeg
1 tbsp. parsley, minced
1 tsp. dill
1 lb. large curd cottage cheese
½ cup Swiss and Parmesan
 cheeses, grated & combined

Heat oven to 400°. Bring phyllo to room temperature. Cover sheets with damp (not wet) towel. Sauté leeks, onions and garlic in 3 tablespoons of butter. Remove from heat; cool slightly and add eggs. Combine remaining ingredients.

Butter a jellyroll pan. Place one sheet of phyllo on pan; brush with melted butter. Place second sheet of phyllo on top of first. Brush with butter. Repeat until you have 8 layers. Spread remaining combined ingredients on stack of phyllo. If it seems wet, sprinkle with ¼ cup fine dry bread crumbs. Cover with remaining phyllo sheets using same procedure as above. Fold sides under. Score in triangles with very sharp knife. Brush with more butter.

Bake at 400° for 10 minutes; lower temperature to 350° and continue baking for 25 minutes. Can freeze before baking.

Preparation:	30 min.	Easy	Serves: 15
Baking:	35 min.	Can do ahead	

Mrs. Timothy J. Leveque

GREEK STUFFED MUSHROOMS
"You don't have to be Greek to love these."

1 10-oz. pkg. frozen chopped
  spinach
½ cup Parmesan cheese, grated
4-oz. crumbled Feta cheese,
  rinsed
½ cup green onions, finely
  chopped
½ cup parsley, finely chopped
12 large fresh mushrooms,
  stems removed & saved for
  another use

Cook spinach, drain well. Combine with next 4 ingredients. Fill mushroom caps and bake at 350° for 10-15 minutes.

Preparation: 15 min.	Easy	Yield: 12 appetizers
Baking: 10-15 min.	Can do ahead	

Mrs. Dana M. Friedman

MUSHROOM BITES
"Fun with phyllo"

1 med. onion, finely chopped
¼ cup butter or margarine
8-oz. can mushroom pieces or 1
  cup fresh mushrooms
2 tbsp. flour
2 tbsp. dry Sherry
½ tsp. salt
⅛ tsp. pepper
6 frozen phyllo leaves, thawed
½ lb. unsalted butter, melted &
  clarified
1 egg, beaten

Preheat oven to 350°. Sauté onion in butter in large skillet over medium heat until tender, about 8 minutes. Stir in mushrooms, flour, Sherry, salt and pepper. Cook and stir until mixture is thickened, about three minutes. Cool slightly.

Cut phyllo dough lengthwise into 4 strips, about 3-3½" wide. Stack and place strips between lightly dampened paper towels to prevent drying. Melt approximately ½ pound butter in saucepan. Remove foamy layer on top and pour clear yellow liquid into a cup, being careful not to include the salty residue from bottom of pan. You now have clarified butter.

Place 1 strip of dough on a cookie sheet and, using a pastry brush, brush with butter. Place 1 tablespoon of mushroom mixture on one corner of strip and fold up to adjacent corner, forming a triangle. Continue folding in triangles the length of the strip. Seal end seam with butter and place seam side down on lightly greased sheet. Brush tops with melted butter, then with beaten egg. Bake 25 to 30 minutes or until brown. Serve warm.

Preparation: 1 hour	Moderately difficult	Yield: 24 appetizers
Baking: 30 min.	Can do ahead	

Marianne Caspary

ASPARAGUS ROLLS

1 1½ lb. loaf sandwich bread
1 8-oz. pkg. Philadelphia cream
    cheese
3 tbsp. bottled horseradish
14½ oz. can asparagus spears
butter, melted
paprika

Remove crusts from bread; roll bread in both directions with rolling pin to flatten. Mash the cream cheese and horseradish together; blend thoroughly. Spread mixture thinly on bread. Place one asparagus spear on each slice and roll tightly. Cut into thirds and place on greased baking sheet. Brush lightly with butter and sprinkle with paprika. Refrigerate. Bake 10-12 minutes at 350°.

Preparation: 15 min.	Easy	Yield: 40-60 pieces
Baking: 12 min.	Can do ahead	

Mrs. Edward I. Sproull, Jr.

MUSHROOM-ANCHOVY SPREAD

"Anchovies add zest to this spread"

1 lb. mushrooms
3 tbsp. oil
1 clove garlic, crushed
4 anchovy fillets, crushed
2 tbsp. parsley, minced
2 tbsp. lemon juice

toast rounds

Clean mushrooms and slice thinly. Sauté garlic in hot oil until brown; remove garlic. Sauté the mushrooms. Use several tablespoonsful of the mushroom liquid to make a thick paste with the crushed anchovy fillets. Add the paste to the mushrooms and mix thoroughly. Cook 5 minutes or until liquid is absorbed. Add lemon juice and parsley and toss lightly. Serve on toast rounds.

Preparation: 15 min.   Easy
Cooking: 10 min.   Do ahead

Gerry Armstrong

26

"HOT" AVOCADO DIP

"Try this in a pretty clear glass bowl."

1 soft avocado, chopped
1 8-oz. container sour cream
½ 7-oz. can Green Chile Salsa
  (Ortega, if possible)
1 8-oz. pkg. Monterey Jack
  cheese, shredded
1 pkg. Fritos

Chop the soft avocado and cover bottom of serving bowl. Spread with sour cream and cover with half can of Salsa. Cover with the shredded Monterey Jack cheese and pat down over all. Refrigerate overnight. Serve with Fritos.

Preparation: 20 min. Easy Serves: 10-12
  Must do ahead

Kathleen Pearson

STUFFED MUSHROOMS

"Tasty cheese treats."

1 lb. fresh mushrooms
1 cup Progresso bread crumbs
½ cup Swiss cheese, grated
¼ cup butter, melted
2 tbsp. onions, minced
½ tsp. salt
dash pepper

Clean mushrooms and remove stems. Cut half the stems into little pieces and mix with Progresso bread crumbs, Swiss cheese, butter, onions, salt and pepper. Stuff mushrooms and broil 5-8 minutes.

Preparation: 20-30 min. Easy Yield: 24 appetizers
Cooking: 5-8 min. Can do ahead

Cissy Stalling

STUFFED MUSHROOM CAPS

"Everyone's favorite-just like coming home"

24 fresh mushrooms
½ cup butter
1 env. Lipton onion soup mix
¾ cup bread crumbs
½ cup blanched almonds,
    chopped
⅓ cup Sherry
2 tbsp. butter, melted
¼ cup Parmesan cheese, grated

Remove stems from mushrooms, chop finely and set aside. In skillet, melt butter, add stems and cook until tender. Add onion soup mix, bread crumbs and almonds; mix well. Stir in Sherry. Fill mushrooms with mix and place on well greased pan; brush with melted butter and sprinkle with cheese. Broil 5 minutes and serve on toast rounds if desired.

Preparation:	20 min.	Easy	Will freeze
Cooking:	5 min.	Do ahead	Yield: 24

Mrs. David Yasko

MUSHROOM APPETIZER

"Even non-mushroom lovers like this"

2 lbs. fresh mushrooms
¼ lb. butter
1 pkg. garlic "Good Seasons"
    mix

Sauté cleaned mushrooms in butter for 5 minutes. Sprinkle with the package of garlic dressing mix. Simmer covered, do not boil, for 1½ hours. Serve hot with toothpicks.

Preparation:	15 min.	Easy	Serves: 10
Cooking:	1½ hours	Can do ahead	

Mrs. Thomas R. Wright

SPINACH CHEESE SQUARES

4 tbsp. butter
3 eggs
1 cup flour
1 cup milk
1 tsp. salt
1 tsp. baking powder
1 lb. sharp Cheddar cheese,
    grated
2 pkgs. chopped spinach, thawed
    & drained

Preheat oven to 350°. In a 9x13x2" pan, melt the butter in the oven; remove. In bowl, beat the eggs, add flour, milk, salt and baking powder; mix well. Add cheese and spinach and blend. Pour into buttered pan and bake at 350° for 35 minutes. Remove and cool 10 minutes to set. Cut into bite-size squares.

Can freeze by placing squares on cookie sheet; freeze solid. Place in plastic bags and store. To serve: heat 12 minutes at 325°.

Preparation:	15 min.	Easy	Yield: 32 squares
Baking:	35 min.	Can do ahead	Can freeze

Mrs. John Carter

SPINACH IN RYE ROUND
"Looks different - tastes great"

2 pkgs. frozen chopped spinach, thawed
1 pkg. Knorr's dry vegetable soup mix
1½ pts. sour cream
½ bunch green onions, chopped
1 8-oz. can water chestnuts, drained & chopped
1 env. Lipton beefy dry onion soup mix
Lawry's seasoned salt
3 lb. rye round loaf

Mix all ingredients, except bread, until smooth. Scoop out center of rye round forming a bowl. Fill with spinach dip.

Cut or tear remaining rye into bite-sized pieces. Dip rye chunks in vegetable mixture.

The spinach dip can be made ahead of time and refrigerated.

Preparation: 20 min.   Easy   Serves: 8-10
                              Can do ahead

Marjorie Ganter Scholtz

MINI-SPINACH SOUFFLÉS
"Think big and make your own pastry shells"

1 pkg. frozen Stouffer's spinach soufflé
2 pkgs. pre-baked miniature pastry shells
nutmeg
Parmesan cheese
paprika

Partially thaw spinach soufflés and cut to fit pastry shells. Sprinkle with cheese, nutmeg and paprika. Bake at 375° for 15 minutes or until puffed. You can spoon the spinach into the shells if it has thawed too much.

Preparation: 15 min.   Easy   Yield: 36-48
Baking: 15 min.   Can do ahead

Doris H. Paul

SPINACH BALLS
"So tasty"

2 pkgs. frozen chopped spinach, cooked & well drained
2 cups Pepperidge Farm herb dressing
2 onions, minced
5 eggs, beaten
1½ sticks butter, softened
½ cup Parmesan cheese, grated
1 tsp. garlic salt
1 tsp. pepper
½ tsp. thyme

Combine all ingredients. Refrigerate before making balls. Roll into small balls. At this point, the balls may be frozen. Bake on cookie sheet at 350° for 20 minutes. Serve with toothpicks.

Preparation: 45 min.   Easy   Yield: 60-72 balls
                              Can do ahead   Can freeze

Mrs. Jon E. McCarthy

TOMATO-CRAB BITES
"A bite of heaven"

1 pt. cherry tomatoes (25-30)
¼ cup low-calorie mayonnaise-
 type dressing
1 tsp. lemon juice
¼ tsp. salt
bottled hot pepper sauce, few
 drops
2 tbsp. green onion, chopped
7½-oz. can crabmeat, drained
 with cartilage removed

Using melon baller or grapefruit knife, hollow out the cherry tomatoes; invert and drain. Blend remaining ingredients. Stuff tomatoes with crab mixture. Refrigerate. Serve on lettuce and chopped ice. Low calorie—about 16 calories per piece.

Preparation: 30 min.   Easy   Yield: 30 appetizers
Can do ahead

Barbara Gaudio

HAM STUFFED TOMATOES
"This is even better if you have grown your own tomatoes."

1½-2 pts. cherry tomatoes
2 2¼-oz. cans deviled ham
2 tbsp. sour cream
1½ tbsp. horseradish
parsley

Choose the best of the cherry tomatoes. Thinly slice tops and remove pulp; drain shells upside down on paper towels. In a small bowl, combine ham, sour cream and horseradish. Fill tomatoes, garnish with parsley and refrigera

Preparation: 30 min.   Easy   Serves: 10
Can do ahead

Mrs. John G. Zimmerman, Jr.

CHICKEN SALAD IN CHERRY TOMATOES
"Everyone loves these"

cherry tomatoes
2-3 cups cooked chicken,
 chopped in processor
1 cup celery, chopped in
 processor
1 cup almonds, chopped in
 processor
1 cup mayonnaise
1 tsp. curry powder
1 tsp. soy sauce
1 tbsp. fresh lemon juice
⅛ tsp. ground black pepper
¾ tsp. salt
paprika

Hollow cherry tomatoes with sharp knife. Combine remaining ingredients except paprika for salad. Fill tomatoes and sprinkle with paprika.

Preparation: 20 min.   Easy   Yield: 2-3 doz.
Do ahead

Nancy F. Lawton

ANTIPASTO SPREAD
"Cold in the summer, hot in the winter"

2 raw carrots, diced
½ head cauliflower, diced
½ cup olive oil
2 green peppers, diced
½ stalk celery, diced
½ lb. mushrooms, sliced
½ can tuna fish
½ lb. crabmeat
2 cloves garlic, crushed
1 ½ tsp. Accent
1 12-oz. bottle chili sauce
1 12-oz. bottle catsup
½ cup pitted green olives, sliced
½ cup pitted whole black olives, sliced

Sauté the carrots and cauliflower for 5 minutes in hot olive oil. Add the remaining raw vegetables and continue sautéeing until tender. Add remaining ingredients and simmer 10 minutes. Serve hot or cold with crackers.

Preparation: 30 min.   Easy   Serves: 20-24
Cooking: 25 min.   Do ahead

Mrs. William C. Ormiston

MARINATED VEGETABLES

8 cups assorted vegetables*
¾ cup lemon juice
¾ cup vegetable oil
3 tbsp. sugar
1 tbsp. salt
1 ½ tsp. oregano leaves
½ tsp. pepper

*any combination of:
cauliflowerets, sliced
mushrooms, radishes,
zucchini, carrots, etc.

Use food processor to slice vegetables. Place all vegetables in shallow 3 quart glass serving bowl. In small bowl, combine remaining ingredients. Pour over vegetables and refrigerate, covered, 6 hours or overnight. Stir occasionally. Serve with toothpicks.

Preparation: 15-30 min.   Easy   Serves: 12 or more
                           Must do ahead

Woodene Merriman

SOUPS

CHILLED CUCUMBER SOUP

2 cups chicken broth or 2
   bouillon cubes dissolved in 2
   cups water
2-4 cucumbers, peeled, seeded
   & cut in strips
1 tbsp. onion flakes or freshly
   chopped onion
salt & freshly ground pepper, to
   taste
1 tsp. dillweed
2 cups sour cream or yogurt
chopped cucumber & dill for
   garnish

Combine broth, cucumbers and
onion and cook over low heat
until cucumbers are just tender.
Whirl in blender with seasonings.
Chill. Combine with sour cream.
Serve in chilled cups sprinkled
with chopped cucumber and dill.

Preparation:	10 min.	Easy	Serves: 4
Cooking:	10-15 min.	Must do ahead	

Kathy Stewart

32

LENA'S CREAM CHEESE SOUP
"A sophisticated soup"

1 8-oz. pkg. cream cheese
2 cans Crosse & Blackwell
  chicken Madrilene, reserve ½
  can
1 tsp. Sherry
1 tbsp. Worcestershire sauce
mayonnaise
paprika

Blend first 4 ingredients in blender until smooth. Pour into individual cups or bowls. Refrigerate 1 hour. Skim foam from top of soup; discard foam. Pour reserved half can evenly on top of each serving and refrigerate. Serve cold with a dollop of mayonnaise and sprinkle with paprika or parsley.

Preparation: 5 min.   Easy   Serves: 6
                           Must do ahead

Mrs. William Penn Snyder, IV.

COLD BEET SOUP
"Dieter's delight"

1 can Campbell's chicken broth
1 20-oz. can beets, with juice
1 med. cucumber, peeled &
  seeded
4 tbsp. vinegar
sour cream

Mix in blender. Chill. Serve with dab of sour cream on top.

Preparation: 10 min.   Easy   Serves: 4
                           Can do ahead

Mrs. F. W. Okie, Jr.

RHUBARB SOUP
"Think Spring"

1 cup sugar
1 cup dried apricots, diced
1 3" stick cinnamon
4 cups water
3 cups rhubarb, diced
2 tbsp. cornstarch

Simmer sugar, apricots and cinnamon with water for 10 minutes. Add rhubarb and simmer until rhubarb is tender. Mix cornstarch with 2 tablespoons cold water to make a paste; add to mixture and simmer, stirring, until thickened. Serve either hot or well chilled. Can be used as an appetizer or dessert.

Preparation: 15 min.   Easy   Serves: 4-6
Cooking: 30 min.   Can do ahead

Clara Obern

RED GAZPACHO SOUP
"Start this the day before"

1 bell pepper, chopped
3 med. tomatoes, peeled &
   chopped
1 cucumber, peeled & chopped
1 small onion, chopped
2 tbsp. olive oil
4½ tsp. vinegar
2 tsp. salt
dash pepper
dash paprika
shake of Tabasco
2½ cups V-8 juice
1 tsp. chives
2 tsp. parsley
½ clove garlic, minced

Mix all ingredients together and refrigerate at least 12 hours.

Preparation: 30 min.   Easy   Serves: 6-8
                           Must do ahead

Mrs. Roger E. Wright

CHILLED STRAWBERRY SOUP
"Something special for a summer luncheon"

2 pts. fresh strawberries,
   washed & hulled
1 cup orange juice
1¼ tsp. instant tapioca
⅛ tsp. allspice
⅛ tsp. cinnamon
½ cup sugar
1 tsp. grated lemon peel, or to
   taste
1 tbsp. lemon juice, or to taste
1 cup buttermilk

Set aside 6 perfect strawberries. Purée remaining berries in food processor or blender; strain into 4-quart saucepan. Add orange juice. In a small bowl, mix tapioca with 4 tablespoons puréed strawberry mixture. Add to saucepan with allspice and cinnamon. Heat, stirring constantly, until mixture comes to a boil. Cook 1 minute or until thickened. Remove from heat.

Pour soup into large bowl; add sugar, lemon peel, juice and buttermilk and blend well. Cover and chill at least 4 hours. Serve in your prettiest tea cups garnished with a sprig of mint and one perfect strawberry on the saucer.

Preparation: 1 hour   Easy   Serves: 6
Cooking: 10 min.   Must do ahead

Marlene Parrish

WATERCRESS SOUP
"For summer time, when the living is easy"

2 tbsp. butter
2 leeks or 1 bunch green onions, chopped
3 med. potatoes, peeled & diced
2 cans Campbell's chicken broth
2 cans water
1 bunch watercress
salt & pepper
1 cup heavy cream

Sauté leeks or onions in butter until translucent. Simmer potatoes, broth and water for 30 minutes. Add watercress, salt and pepper and simmer 2 more minutes. Cool soup and whirl in a blender. Add cream and refrigerate.

Preparation: 10 min.   Easy   Serves: 4-6
Cooking: 30 min.   Can do ahead

Mrs. Charles Dithrich

CREAM OF ZUCCHINI SOUP
"A dream of a cream of zucchini soup"

2 tbsp. butter
1 lb. zucchini, sliced
2-3 scallions or shallots, chopped
1 clove garlic, minced
½ tsp. salt
½ tsp. curry powder
½ cup heavy cream
1 ¾ cups chicken broth
chives or dill, garnish

Melt butter, add scallions, garlic and zucchini. Cover and simmer 10 minutes. Stir occasionally - don't let it brown. Spoon into blender. Add curry, salt, cream and ¾ cup broth. Blend, then add last cup of chicken broth. Serve hot or cold and sprinkle with chopped chives or dill.

Preparation: 20 min.   Easy   Serves: 4-6
Cooking: 10 min.   Can do ahead

Bonnie Wood

ZUCCHINI SOUP
"Gardener's delight"

¼ cup butter
1 cup onions or leeks, sliced
1 cup potatoes, diced
2 cups zucchini, grated
½ cup carrots, grated
1 qt. chicken stock
1 tsp. salt
¼ tsp. pepper, freshly ground

Sauté onion or leeks in butter until translucent; add vegetables, chicken stock, salt and pepper. Simmer ½ hour or longer until potato is tender. Purée in food processor or blender; correct seasoning. Serve hot or cold. To serve cold, thin with a little cream, oversalt slightly.

Preparation: 15-20 min.   Easy   Serves: 6
Cooking: 30-45 min.   Can do ahead

Dina Fulmer

ARTICHOKE SOUP
"Could also be called Oyster Soup"

½ cup butter
1 large onion, chopped
2 cloves garlic, pressed
2 tbsp. parsley, chopped
2 dozen oysters
2 16-oz. cans artichoke hearts
1 cup oyster liquid or water
1 10¾-oz. can cream of
  mushroom soup
1 bay leaf
salt & pepper, to taste

Sauté onions in hot butter until translucent. Add garlic and parsley and cook 2 to 3 minutes. Add oysters and cook 3 to 4 minutes. Add drained, quartered artichoke hearts and cook for a few more minutes. Blend oyster liquid, cream of mushroom soup and bay leaf into soup. Cook for 20 minutes. Prepare 30 minutes or so before serving to allow flavors to penetrate. Add salt and pepper to taste.

Preparation: 15 min. Easy Serves: 4-6
Cooking: 30 min. Can do ahead

Mrs. Paul J. McKenzie

SUN CHOKE SOUP
"Different and tasty"

1 lb. Jerusalem artichokes
2 qts. water
2 tsp. lemon juice
4 stalks celery, sliced
3 tbsp. butter
½ cup onion, chopped
1 clove garlic, minced or pressed
¼ tsp. marjoram leaves
¼ tsp. pepper
3 chicken bouillon cubes
3½ cups water
1 cup half & half
salt
parsley

Scrub and peel chokes and cut into ½ " pieces. Bring water and lemon juice to a boil, add chokes and celery; cover and simmer until chokes are tender, about 15 minutes. Set aside.

In 5 quart pan, melt butter. Add onion and garlic and cook, stirring, until onion is limp. Add marjoram, pepper and bouillon dissolved in water and cooked vegetables. Purée all in blender; return to pan, stir in cream and salt to taste. Heat to boiling and serve hot, garnished with parsley.

Preparation: 35 min. Easy Serves: 6-8
Cooking: 5 min. Can do ahead

Mrs. John G. Zimmerman, Jr.

BLOODY MARY SOUP
"Great to take to a football game"

2 tbsp. butter or margarine
1 med. onion, diced
3 stalks celery, diced
2 tbsp. tomato purée
1 tbsp. sugar
5 cups tomato juice
1 tbsp. salt
1 tbsp. lemon juice
Worcestershire sauce, to taste
pepper, to taste
4 oz. Vodka
lime slices

Sauté onions and celery in butter until light brown. Add tomato purée and sugar; sauté 1 minute. Add tomato juice and simmer 8 minutes. Add remaining ingredients and strain; bring to a boil. Serve hot with a slice of lime on each serving.

Preparation: 10 min.	Easy	Serves: 6
Cooking: 10 min.	Can do ahead	

Mrs. William C. Crampton, Jr.

DELICIOUS BOUILLON
"Just as delicious as the name suggests"

2 qts. tomato juice
2 10½-oz. cans beef bouillon
2 cans water
2 tbsp. Jane's Krazy Salt
2 6-oz. cans tangerine juice, thawed & undiluted
Sherry, optional

Combine in saucepan, tomato juice, bouillon, water and salt. Simmer for 15 minutes. Cool slightly, then add tangerine juice and Sherry. Serve in small mugs.

Preparation: 5 min.	Easy	Serves: 10-12
Cooking: 15-20 min.	Can do ahead	

Mrs. Richard H. Greene

MAGIC MONGOL SOUP
"Good, elegant and so easy"

1 can Crosse & Blackwell's black bean soup with Sherry
1 can tomato soup
1 can onion soup
thin lemon slices
Sherry, to taste

Combine the 3 soups and whisk well; heat in a saucepan. Top each cup or bowl of soup with a lemon slice. Serve with a cruet of Sherry.

Preparation: 5 min.	Easy	Serves: 6
Cooking: 10 min.	Can do ahead	

Mrs. Richard W. Friday

37

CREAMY CAULIFLOWER SOUP
"A good appetizer soup"

1 med. head cauliflower,
separated into flowerets
¼ cup butter
1 small onion, chopped
2 tbsp. flour
3 chicken bouillon cubes
dissolved in 3 cups reserved
liquid (add water if necessary)
2 cups light cream
1 tsp. Worcestershire sauce
½ tsp. salt
1 cup Cheddar cheese, grated
chives, chopped

Simmer cauliflower in water to cover until done, about 15 minutes. Drain, reserving liquid. Melt butter in 4 quart pan, stir in onions and cook until soft. Add flour and blend. Gradually stir in bouillon, cream, Worcestershire sauce and salt. Add cauliflower. Bring to a boil; remove from heat. Stir in cheese until it melts. Serve hot, sprinkled with chives.

Preparation: 15 min. Easy Serves: 6
Cooking: 45 min. Can do ahead

Mrs. James P. O'Malley

CREAM OF CAULIFLOWER SOUP
"Creamy texture, but not too thick"

2 tbsp. butter
1 onion, sliced
1 stalk celery, sliced
2 cups boiling water
1 cup cauliflower, coarsely
chopped
1 env. Lipton chicken noodle
soup mix
⅛ tsp. caraway seeds
2 cups milk
whipped cream
curry
celery salt

Melt butter and sauté onion and celery about 3 minutes. Stir in water, cauliflower, soup mix and caraway seeds. Bring to a boil. Cover and simmer until cauliflower is tender, about 10 minutes. Pour enough soup into blender to cover blade. Cover and blend at high speed about 1 minute. Remove cover and gradually pour in remaining soup. Cover again and blend until smooth, about 2 minutes. Stir blended soup into milk. Serve

hot, but do not boil. Season whipped cream with curry and celery salt. Serve soup with cream on top.

Preparation: 10 min. Easy Serves: 4-6
Cooking: 20 min. Can do ahead

Frances Merryman Rollman

CROCKPOT CHEESE SOUP
"Even crackpots like this soup"

2 slices ham, cubed
8 slices bacon, crisp
3 carrots, diced
6-8 potatoes, diced
4 stalks celery, sliced
1-2 onions, chopped
½ cup green pepper, chopped
3 cups water with 6 beef bouillon
　　cubes, or equal amount of
　　canned broth
1 4-oz. can mushrooms, reserve
　　liquid
1 16-oz. can corn
¼ cup flour
1 16-oz. jar Cheez Whiz

Combine first 8 ingredients in crockpot. Cook for 3-4 hours. Add the mushrooms and corn. Mix a little broth with the flour and add the mushroom juice and stir. Cook on high until slightly thickened. Add cheese and cook on low until ready to serve.

Preparation: 30 min.　　　Easy　　　Serves: 10-12
Cooking: 　　5 hours

Mrs. Lee M. Huizenga

SWISS CHEESE SOUP
"Excellent, easy soup"

2 cans condensed chicken
　　bouillon
1 can condensed beef bouillon
3 cups water
2 large onions, sliced
4 large potatoes, diced
2 cups celery, chopped
8 mushrooms, sliced
½ cup parsley
⅓ cup margarine
⅓ cup flour
salt & pepper, to taste
6-oz. Swiss cheese, shredded

Combine broth, water, onions, potatoes, celery, mushrooms and parlsey. Cover and simmer 30 minutes until tender. Melt butter in skillet, add flour and stir until golden brown. Add to soup and stir until thickened. Season with salt and pepper. Sprinkle with shredded cheese when ready to serve.

Preparation: 15 min.　　　Easy　　　Serves: 4-6
Cooking: 　　45 min.　　　Can do ahead

Frances Merryman Rollman

CREAM OF LETTUCE SOUP
"Peas add a nice surprise"

½ stick butter
½ cup scallions, thinly sliced
4 heads Boston lettuce
1½ cups Béchamel sauce
5 cups chicken broth, canned
1 cup light cream
1 cup green peas, cooked
chopped mint for garnish

Béchamel Sauce:
3 tbsp. butter
3 tbsp. flour
1½ cups milk

Melt butter and add scallions. Cover and cook for 10 minutes or until wilted. Wash, quarter, core and shred lettuce. Add to pan, toss to coat with butter and cook 5 minutes until wilted. Add Béchamel sauce and chicken broth and stir. Cook 10 minutes and then purée in blender or food processor. Return purée to pan, add cream and peas and cook until heated. Salt and pepper to taste. Garnish.

Preparation: 1 hour   Easy   Serves: 10-12
Cooking: ½ hour   Can do ahead

Susan Gasparich

ONION SOUP BAVARIAN

7 tbsp. butter or margarine
2-3 med. Spanish onions, thinly
   sliced
1½ qts. beef stock
2 tbsp. sugar
1 tsp. onion salt
1 tbsp. white pepper
1¼ cups quality beer
1⅓ cups flour
2 cups fresh cream
⅛ tsp. Gravy Master

Melt butter in 2 quart saucepan over medium heat. Add onions and simmer, covered, stirring occasionally, until onions cook down and are semi-soft. While stirring onions, add sugar. Stir about 1 minute until sugar dissolves. Add stock, pepper and onion salt. Heat to boiling, stirring occasionally and skimming surface as needed. Add beer. As soup returns to a boil, more skimming will be required. When soup cooks down and skimming is no longer required, remove from heat. Whip flour and cream together until smooth. Beat into soup, add Gravy Master so soup has medium brown hue. Best kept hot in crockpot or double boiler

Preparation: 1 hr.   Easy   Serves: 8-9
Cooking: 45 min.   Can do ahead

Arthur's

SHERRIED MUSHROOM SOUP
"A little extra Sherry for the cook"

1 lb. fresh mushrooms, sliced
3 tbsp. butter
2 tbsp. flour
2 cups College Inn chicken broth
¼ cup dry Sherry

Place mushrooms in soup pot *without* water or oil. Cover, cook over very low heat for 15 minutes until only a small amount of mushroom liquid remains. Add butter; when melted, sprinkle with flour. Cook, stirring, a few minutes to blend. Slowly add chicken stock, stirring; simmer 10 minutes. With slotted spoon, transfer mushrooms to blender or food processor. Add Sherry, blend until smooth. If needed, use ¼ cup of soup liquid to achieve a smooth purée. Stir puréed mushrooms into soup, reheat.

Preparation: 5 min.   Easy   Serves: 4
Cooking: 35 min.   Can do ahead

Mrs. Dana M. Friedman

MUSHROOM POTATO SOUP
"A light soup - good as an appetizer"

½ lb. fresh mushrooms
3 tbsp. butter or margarine
1 small onion, finely chopped
3 tbsp. flour
5 cups boiling water
2 cups raw potato, cubed
1½ tsp. salt
⅛ tsp. pepper
2 tsp. Worcestershire sauce
2 tbsp. parsley, chopped
3 tbsp. lemon juice
sour cream
parsley, garnish

Clean mushrooms, remove stems and chop; slice mushroom caps. Sauté mushrooms and onions in hot butter in a 4 quart pan until mushrooms are lightly browned. Add flour and stir continually until flour is light brown. Gradually add water and stir until blended. Add potatoes, salt, pepper, Worcestershire sauce, parsley and lemon juice. Cover and cook for 30 minutes over low heat. Serve hot, topped with sour cream and a sprinkle of parsley.

Preparation: 30 min.   Easy   Serves: 8
Cooking: 30 min.   Can do ahead

Trudy Hetherington

ONION SOUP AU GRATIN

1 stick margarine
1½ cups onions, thinly sliced
½ cup flour
2 13¾-oz. cans beef broth
1½ tsp. salt
dash cayenne pepper
1 egg yolk
2 tbsp. cream
Parmesan cheese, grated

Melt margarine in pan. Sauté onions until translucent. Blend in flour and cook for 5 minutes, stirring often. Add beef broth, salt and pepper; simmer for 15 minutes. In small bowl, beat egg yolk with cream. Blend ½ cup of hot liquid into the egg mixture, and then gradually mix into soup. Serve with cheese.

Preparation: 15-20 min.　　Easy　　　　Serves: 4
Cooking:　　30 min.　　Can do ahead

Linda Payne

"MY SISTER EILEEN'S" SOUP

1 can Campbell's condensed
　　green pea soup
1 can Campbell's condensed
　　consommé
2 tsp. curry powder
salt & pepper
1½ cups half & half
½ apple, peeled & grated

Bring pea soup, consommé and curry to a boil. Cool; season with salt and pepper. Blend 1½ cups half and half into soup. Chill. Top with grated, peeled apple before serving.

Preparation: 20 min.　　Easy　　　　Serves: 4-6
　　　　　　　　　　Can do ahead

Mrs. Frank L. Seamans

CIOPPINO — SEAFOOD SOUP

1 cup onion, chopped
1 med. green pepper, chopped
1 carrot, shredded
½ cup celery, sliced
3 cloves garlic, minced
3 tbsp. olive oil
2 1-lb. cans tomatoes
1 8-oz. can tomato sauce
1 tsp. leaf basil, crumbled
1 bay leaf
1 tsp. salt
¼ tsp. pepper
2 tbsp. parsley
1 lb. white fish, flounder or sole
1½ cups dry white wine
1 8-oz. pkg. frozen shrimp
½ lb. scallops
1 7-oz. can chopped clams,
　　drained

Sauté onion, green pepper, celery, carrots and garlic in olive oil. Stir in tomatoes, tomato sauce, basil, bay leaf, salt, pepper and parsley. Heat to boiling. Reduce heat and simmer 2 hours. Cut fish into small pieces. Stir in wine. Add fish, shrimp and scallops. Add clams at the end. Simmer, covered, 10 minutes. Can do ahead to point of adding fish.

Preparation: 25 min.　　Can do ahead　　Serves: 6
Cooking:　　2¼ hours

Amy Cohen

SEAFOOD CHOWDER

2-4 tbsp. butter, divided
2 yellow onions, chopped
½ lb. mushrooms, sliced
½ lb. scallops
1 qt. fish stock
½ lb. crabmeat, cleaned
½ lb. cooked shrimp
1 qt. half & half
Sherry, to taste
salt, to taste
pepper, to taste

Sauté onions and mushrooms in 2 tablespoons butter. Sauté scallops in 2 tablespoons butter. Add to boiling fish stock. Add crabmeat and cut-up shrimp. Boil ½ hour, then add cream and Sherry. Season to taste. If you want to stretch this, you can add cooked, cut-up potatoes.

Preparation: 20 min.   Easy   Serves: 10-12
Cooking: 30 min.   Can do ahead

Richard Arrigo
Allegheny Country Club

TOMATO & SAUSAGE SOUP
"Tastes like Pittsburgh"

2 cans tomato soup
1 large Polish sausage, browned,
    drained & cut into 1" pieces
1 cup cooked rice
1 15-oz. can stewed tomatoes
1 30-oz. can kidney beans
Italian spices

Combine all ingredients in a large pot and simmer until mixed and thoroughly heated. Salt and pepper to taste.

Preparation: 30 min.   Easy   Serves: 10-12
Cooking: 15 min.   Must do ahead

Becky Smith

MEATBALL SOUP
"Archie Bunker's favorite"

Meatballs:
1½ lbs. ground chuck
1 egg, lightly beaten
3 tbsp. water
1 slice soft bread, crumbled
¼ tsp. salt
1 tbsp. parsley, chopped

In medium bowl, combine beef, egg, water, bread crumbs, salt and parsley; shape into small balls. In hot butter in a 4½ quart kettle, sauté meatballs until brown. Remove and set aside. In

Soup:
1 10½-oz. can bouillon
1 1 lb. 12-oz. can tomatoes, undrained (or 3½ cups V-8 juice)
1 env. onion soup mix
2 cups carrots, sliced
½ cup celery, sliced
¼ tsp. pepper
¼ tsp. dried oregano
¼ tsp. dried basil
1 bay leaf
1½-2 cups water

same kettle, combine soup ingredients. Simmer 20 minutes. Add meatballs, and simmer 30 minutes longer.

Preparation: 30 min.   Easy   Serves: 6
Cooking: 50 min.   Can do ahead

Mrs. John L. Baldwin

DAN'S VEGETABLE SOUP
"Very good and different"

1-1½ lbs. stew meat, chopped
2 onions, chopped
3 potatoes, chopped
4 carrots, chopped
4 ribs celery, sliced
1 10-oz. pkg. frozen peas*
1 10-oz. pkg. frozen corn
1 10 oz. pkg. frozen limas
1 10-oz. pkg. frozen green beans
2 46-oz. cans V-8 juice
1 tsp. butter or margarine

* fresh vegetables may be used

Trim fat from meat and cut into small pieces. Cook meat in pot with 2 cups water and 1 chopped onion at least 30 minutes. Add salt and pepper. Cook vegetables in a separate pot with water and 1 teaspoon butter until tender. Drain; add V-8 juice and let simmer 10 minutes. Add the cooked meat and simmer 15 to 30 minutes.

Preparation: 1½ hours   Easy   Serves: 8
                         Can do ahead

Mrs. F. Gordon Kraft

SUSAN'S SUPER VEGETABLE SOUP
"For a cold winter's evening"

3 med. onions, chopped
2 tbsp. butter
1 lb. lean ground chuck
1 garlic clove, minced
3 cups beef stock or bouillon
2 large cans tomatoes
1 cup small whole potatoes
1 cup celery, sliced
1 cup green beans, sliced
1 cup carrots, sliced
1 cup dry red wine

Cook onions in butter until golden and tender. Stir in ground chuck and minced garlic; cook until brown. Drain excess fat. Add remaining ingredients and bring to a boil. Immediately reduce heat and simmer for 1¼ to 1½ hours.

Preparation: 30 min.   Easy   Serves: 6-8
Cooking: 1½ hours   Can do ahead

Mrs. John M. Gilmore

BEEF BARLEY SOUP
"Lovely delicate flavor"

2 lbs. beef short ribs
2 tbsp. cooking oil
5 cups water
1 16-oz. can tomatoes, cut up
1 large onion, sliced
½ tbsp. salt
2 cups carrots, sliced
1 cup celery, sliced
½ cup green pepper, chopped
⅔ cup quick-cooking barley
¼ cup parsley, snipped

In dutch oven, brown beef ribs in hot oil. Add water, tomatoes, onion and salt. Simmer, covered, for 1½ hours. Add carrots, celery, green pepper, barley and parsley. Simmer, covered, 45 minutes. Remove from heat. Drain ribs; cut meat from bones. Skim fat from broth, return meat to soup and heat thoroughly.

Preparation: 3-3½ hours   Can do ahead   Serves: 6-8

Mrs. John G. Zimmerman, Jr.

Pittsburgh's GREAT RACE
START

BREADS

PITTSBURGH'S "GREAT RACE"

Pittsburgh's "Great Race" is sponsored by the City's Department of Parks & Recreation. Begun in 1976 with 1,100 entrants, this 6.2 mile event grew in just 4 years to the second largest 10,000 meter race in the country. 1980 saw an entry of 10,000 from 12 states and 3 foreign countries.

Additional illustrations in this section:

This mud and log cabin, which once stood on Penn Avenue, was one of the city's first homes.

Loop Compote - Covered Dish - Lead Candlestick.*

Porcelain base toaster and food grinder, courtesy of the Pittsbburgh History and Landmarks Foundation.

*All glassware is early Pittsburgh unless otherwise indicated.

BREADS

CRANBERRY BREAD
"A festive holiday bread"

2 cups flour
1 cup sugar
1½ tsp. baking powder
½ tsp. baking soda
juice & grated rind of 1 orange,
  or ½ cup orange juice & 1
  tsp. of dehydrated orange
  rind
2 tbsp. shortening
boiling water
1 egg, beaten
1 cup raw cranberries, halved
1 cup pecans, broken into
  pieces

Sift together the flour, sugar, baking powder and soda. Set aside. Combine orange juice, rind and shortening added to boiling water to make ¾ cup. Add beaten egg and liquid mixture to the dry ingredients and stir until moist. Add cranberries and nuts. Place mixture in a well-greased loaf pan. Set aside for 20 minutes. Bake at 350° for 60-70 minutes.

Preparation: 20 min.   Easy   Yield: 1 loaf
Cooking: 60-70 min.   Can do ahead Can freeze

Mrs. David F. Yasko

BEER BREAD
"Fun in the making"

3 cups self-rising flour
3 tbsp. sugar
1 can warm beer, minus 2 sips

Mix ingredients together and bake at 350° for 45 minutes in a greased loaf pan.

| Preparation: 5 min. | Easy | Yield: 1 loaf |
| Baking: 45 min. | Can do ahead | Can freeze |

Becky Smith

AUNT ROSE'S "TOP SECRET" DATE AND NUT BREAD
"Fresh dates are a must"

1 8-oz. pkg. dates, pitted
1 tsp. baking soda
¾ cup boiling water
1½ cups flour
1 cup sugar
½ tsp. salt
1 egg
1 tsp. vanilla
1 tbsp. butter, melted
½ cup walnuts, chopped

Cut dates in half lengthwise - a must for a moist loaf. Add baking soda to water, bring to a boil and pour over dates. Let stand until you mix the dry ingredients. Mix dry ingredients; add date mixture, egg, vanilla, butter, nuts. Bake at 350° for 45-60 minutes in a floured loaf pan.

| Preparation: 20 min. | Easy | Yield: 1 loaf |
| Cooking: 45-60 min. | Can do ahead | Can freeze |

Mrs. Richard Jamison, Jr.

ONION-CHEESE SUPPER BREAD
"Good for winter supper with soup"

½ cup onions, chopped
1 tbsp. butter
1 egg, lightly beaten
½ cup milk
1½ cup Bisquick
1½ cup sharp Cheddar cheese, grated
1 tbsp. poppy seeds
2 tbsp. butter, melted

Heat oven to 400°. Sauté onions in butter until tender and light brown. Combine egg and milk; add Bisquick and stir until blended. Add onion and 1 cup of the cheese. Spread in butter-greased 8" baking dish. Sprinkle top with remainder of cheese, poppy seeds and drizzle butter over all. Bake 20 to 25 minutes at 400°. Do not overcook.

| Preparation: 30 min. | Easy | Serves: 8 |
| Cooking: 25 min. | Can do ahead | Can freeze |

Mrs. Gerald C. Kitch

SECKEL PEAR BREAD

½ cup butter
1 cup sugar
2 eggs
1 tsp. vanilla
2 cups flour, sifted
½ tsp. salt
½ tsp. baking soda
1 tsp. baking powder
¼ tsp. pumpkin pie spice
⅓ cup plain yogurt or
  buttermilk
1½ cups pears, peeled &
  coarsely chopped*

Cream butter, sugar, eggs and vanilla. Combine dry ingredients and add alternately to the first mixture with yogurt. Stir in pears. Pour into loaf pan and bake at 350° for 1 hour. Cool, remove from pan and let sit 6 hours before slicing.

*If using processor, be careful to only chop and not to over process.

Preparation: 35 min.
Cooking: 60 min.

Easy
Must do ahead

Serves: 6-8
Can freeze

Mrs. George H. Craig, Jr.

RHUBARB BREAD

1½ cups brown sugar, packed
⅔ cup butter
1 egg
1 cup buttermilk
1 tsp. vanilla
1 tsp. baking soda
2½ cups flour
1½ cups rhubarb, diced
½ cup nuts, chopped
½ cup sugar
½ tsp. cinnamon
1 tbsp. butter, melted

Combine brown sugar and butter. Stir in egg, buttermilk and vanilla. Mix well. Sift soda and flour together; stir into butter mixture. Stir in rhubarb and nuts. Pour into 2 well-greased loaf pans. Combine remaining ingredients; sprinkle over top. Bake at 325° in pre-heated oven for 40 minutes. Do not overbake. Let stand 2-3 minutes. Remove from pan and cool on rack.

Preparation: 15 min.
Cooking: 40 min.

Easy
Can do ahead

Serves: 10
Can freeze

Mrs. Raymond Egler

PINEAPPLE-GINGER MUFFINS

1¾ cups flour, sifted
¾ tsp. salt
¼ cup sugar
2 tsp. baking powder
2 eggs
4 tbsp. butter, melted
¾ cup milk
3-oz. candied ginger, diced
6-oz. candied pineapple, diced

Sift first 4 ingredients together. Beat eggs, then combine with milk and butter. Mix lightly with dry ingredients: mixture will be lumpy. Add ginger and pineapple. Spoon into muffin tins with paper liners. Bake at 350° for 20 minutes. Serve warm.

Preparation: 20 min.
Baking: 20 min.

Easy
Serve warm

Yield: 12 large or 24 small
Can freeze

Mrs. K. B. Mellon

STRAWBERRY BREAD
"Surprise your family with this moist bread"

2 cups sugar
1 tsp. baking soda
¼ tsp. salt
4 eggs
3 cups flour
1 tsp. cinnamon
1¼ cups oil
1 16-oz. pkg. frozen
   strawberries, thawed
1 cup pecans, chopped

Mix all ingredients thoroughly using an electric mixer. Grease two 9 x 5 x 3" loaf pans. Pour batter into pans and bake at 350° for 1 hour. Use unsweetened berries.

Preparation:	15 min.	Easy	Yield: 2 loaves
Cooking:	1 hour	Can do ahead	Can freeze

Nancy Penney

ZUCCHINI BREAD
"Wonderful flavor and texture"

3 eggs
1 cup cooking oil
2 cups sugar
2 cups zucchini, grated
3 tsp. vanilla
3 cups flour
1 tsp. salt
1 tsp. baking soda
3 tsp. cinnamon
1 cup nuts, chopped

Mix first 5 ingredients together. Set aside. Mix dry ingredients together. Add to first mixture and blend. Stir in nuts, if desired. Pour into 2 greased and floured loaf pans. Bake at 350° for 50-60 minutes. Cool before slicing.

Preparation:	20 min.	Easy	Yield: 2 loaves
Cooking:	50-60 min.	Can do ahead	Can freeze

Karen Maloney

PINEAPPLE ZUCCHINI BREAD

zucchini bread batter
1 8-oz. can crushed pineapple,
   with syrup

Follow directions for zucchini bread, above; add the pineapple and syrup to batter and blend. Pour into 2 loaf pans and bake at 350° for 40-60 minutes.

Preparation:	20 min.	Easy	Yield: 2 loaves
Baking:	60 min.	Can do ahead	Can freeze

Mrs. Thomas M. Potter

BRAN MUFFINS FOR MULTITUDES
"A delicious, nutritious start on the day"

5 cups flour, unsifted
3 cups sugar
5 tsp. baking soda
2 tsp. salt
1 cup oil
4 eggs
1 qt. buttermilk
1 16-oz. box Raisin Bran or
   11-oz. 40% Bran Flakes

Toss dry ingredients together lightly. Add oil, eggs and buttermilk and mix well. Fold in Raisin Bran until blended. Can store batter, refrigerated, 4-6 weeks. Bake desired amount in greased muffin tins at 350° for 15-20 minutes. Or bake and freeze, reheat in foil and serve warm.

Preparation: 10 min.   Easy   Yield: 4-5 doz.
Cooking: 15-20 min.   Can do ahead   Can freeze

Mrs. Dennis L. Leonetti

CARROT CAKE MUFFINS

1 cup carrots, grated
1¼ cups wholewheat flour
1 egg
½ cup honey
½ cup butter, melted
½ tsp. cinnamon
2 tsp. baking powder
1 tsp. baking soda
¼ cup lemon juice
½ cup nuts, chopped, optional

In large bowl, combine all the ingredients and mix well. Pour into buttered muffin tins. Bake at 350° for 20 minutes.

Preparation: 10 min.   Easy   Yield: 12 muffins
Cooking: 20 min.

Guen Larson

ZUCCHINI PANCAKES
"Another great way to use zucchini"

3 med. zucchini
2 eggs, beaten
2 tbsp. Parmesan cheese
1½ tsp. chives, chopped
¼ tsp. parsley
¼ tsp. garlic powder
4 tbsp. flour
salt & pepper

Grate zucchini and drain thoroughly. Stir in remaining ingredients, then drop batter onto well-oiled griddle or skillet. Brown well on both sides. Can be garnished with sour cream.

Preparation: 15-20 min.   Easy   Serves: 8
Cooking: 3 min.

Mrs. Robert Grigsby

OATMEAL MUFFINS

1 cup rolled oats, uncooked
1 cup buttermilk
1 cup flour, sifted
½ tsp. salt
½ tsp. baking soda
1½ tsp. baking powder
½ cup vegetable oil
½ cup brown sugar, firmly
  packed
1 egg, beaten
1 cup raisins or dates

Combine oats and buttermilk and let sit 30 minutes or longer. Sift flour, salt, soda and powder together. Add oil, brown sugar and egg to oatmeal mixture; blend thoroughly. Stir in dry ingredients and raisins, mixing just enough to moisten. Spoon into muffin tins and bake at 350° for 25 minutes or until brown.

| Preparation: | 35 min. | Easy | Yield: 12-16 |
| Baking: | 25 min. | Can do ahead | Can freeze |

Mrs. Clifford Early

DUTCH BOY PANCAKES
"Great for a holiday breakfast"

½ cup milk
2 eggs
½ cup flour
dash nutmeg
2 tbsp. margarine
confectioners' sugar
fresh lemon juice

Mix the first 4 ingredients until blended. Melt margarine in a pyrex pie plate. Pour in batter and bake 12-15 minutes at 400° or until cake rises very high. Remove from oven, sprinkle with sugar and juice or maple syrup.

| Preparation: | 5 min. | Easy | Serves: 2-4 |
| Cooking: | 15 min. | Serve warm | |

Mrs. Robert L. Purvis

BUTTERMILK PANCAKES
"For an army"

5 large eggs
4 cups flour
4 tsp. baking powder
2 tsp. baking soda
2 tsp. salt
¼-½ cup sugar
1 qt. buttermilk
½ cup plus 1 tbsp. butter or
  margarine, melted

Beat eggs until lemony. Add flour, baking powder, soda, salt and sugar. Mix well. Add buttermilk and melted butter and blend. Batter gets better as it ages. Can easily be done ahead and batter kept in refrigerator.

| Preparation: | 10 min. | Easy | Serves: 10 |
| Cooking: | 5 min. | Can do ahead | |

Chris Gaburi

WHOLEWHEAT PANCAKES
"Wholesome wholewheat"

2 eggs
2 tbsp. margarine, melted
2 cups buttermilk
1 cup wholewheat flour
1 cup flour
1 tsp. baking powder
½ tsp. baking soda
4 tbsp. sugar
½ tsp. salt

Beat eggs, margarine and milk. in large bowl until well blended. Add flours, baking powder, baking soda, sugar and salt to liquid ingredients, and mix just enough to make a creamy batter with some lumps. For electric skillet, use setting of 400°.

| Preparation: | 10 min. | Easy | Serves: 6 |
| Cooking: | 5 min. | Can do ahead | Can freeze |

Mrs. Thomas M. Garrett

APPLE FRITTERS

1 cup flour
1½ tsp. baking powder
3 tbsp. powdered sugar
¼ tsp. salt
⅓ cup milk
1 egg, beaten
2 med. tart apples, thinly sliced
cooking oil

Sift dry ingredients together and set aside. Add milk to beaten egg and combine thoroughly. Add to the dry mixture and beat well. Add apple slices. Drop batter by spoonsful into hot fat and fry until golden. Serve warm with a sauce or syrup.

| Preparation: | 15 min. | Easy | Serves: 4 |
| Cooking: | 5-10 min. | Can do ahead | |

Mrs. John E. Ruane

BREAKFAST ROLLS
"Yummy & Oh! so easy."

butter
1 cup walnuts or pecans, chopped & divided
1 pkg. Rhodes frozen dinner rolls
1 3-oz. pkg. butterscotch pudding mix
¼ cup butter, melted
½ cup brown sugar

Butter a bundt cake pan heavily and then cover the bottom with ¾ cup chopped nuts. Place frozen rolls around the pan and sprinkle with the dry pudding mix. Combine the butter and brown sugar; drizzle with mixture over the rolls and sprinkle with remaining chopped nuts.

Place in a cold oven overnight. Remove pan, heat oven to 325°, return pan to oven and bake for 30 minutes. Remove from oven and let rolls sit in pan 2 minutes, then invert onto serving plate.

| Preparation: | 10 min. | Easy | Yield: 12-15 rolls |
| Cooking: | 30 min. | Must do ahead | |

Phyllis R. Grine

53

CINNAMON DOUGHNUT HOLES
"Very quick, very easy, very tasty"

1 cup complete buttermilk
  pancake mix
1 tbsp. sugar
1 tbsp. vanilla
½ cup milk
¼ cup sugar
1 tsp. cinnamon

Heat oil before making batter, fry at once. Combine pancake mix, sugar, vanilla and milk, stirring until blended. Drop rounded half-teaspoons into hot fat, 375°, frying 4-6 balls at a time. Fry until brown and drain on paper towels. Roll warm doughnut balls in mixture of sugar and cinnamon. For large amounts, mix and fry consecutive batches. Do not double the recipe; the longer the batter stands, the more leavening power it loses.

Preparation: 5 min.   Easy   Yield: 24-30
Cooking: 10-15 min.

Mrs. Charles Dithrich

DANISH PASTRY APPLE BARS
"Elegant, sweet fruit bars"

2½ cups flour
1 tsp. salt
1 cup shortening
1 egg yolk
milk, to make ⅔ cup with egg
  yolk
2 handsful cornflakes
8-10 apples, peeled & thinly
  sliced
1 cup sugar
1 tsp. cinnamon
1 egg white

Combine flour and salt, cut in shortening with pastry cutter until crumbly; combine egg and milk and add to flour mixture all at once. Mix well. Roll out half of the dough and place on a greased cookie sheet with sides. Sprinkle with crushed cornflakes. Peel and slice apples; place evenly on top of cornflakes. Sprinkle with cinnamon sugar mixture.

Frosting:
1 tbsp. water
1 cup powdered sugar
vanilla

Roll out second half of pastry and cover apples; pinch edges as for a pie. Beat egg white until stiff and brush over crust. Bake 60 minutes at 400°. Make frosting by combining the water, sugar and vanilla. Frost pastry while warm. Cool and cut into bars.

Preparation: 35 min.   Moderately difficult   Yield: 24 bars
Cooking: 60 min.   Must do ahead

Barbara Gaudio

MOM'S EASTER COFFEE CAKE
"Good any time of year"

Cake mixture:
½ cup milk, scalded
2 tbsp. sugar
¼ cup Crisco oil
½ tsp. salt
1 pkg. dry yeast
½ cup lukewarm water
1 egg, lightly beaten
2¾ cups flour
butter, melted

Sugar mixture:
2 cups sugar
½ cup cinnamon
1 cup nuts, finely chopped

Cool milk. Then add sugar, salt and Crisco. Dissolve yeast in warm water. Add yeast, egg and 2 cups flour. Beat well. Add the remaining flour and blend well. Let rise in warm place 1½ hours or until doubled in bulk.

Beat dough down. Form into balls the size of walnuts. Dip into melted butter, and then into sugar mixture. Drop in buttered tube pan in uneven layers. Let rise 20 minutes. Bake at 350° for 50-60 minutes. Turn out at once.

Preparation: 40 min.   Moderately difficult   Serves: 8-12
Baking: 50-60 min.

Mrs. William Kirmeyer

GERMAN COFFEE CAKE
"A moist, dark coffee cake"

Cake:
2 cups flour
¾ cup sugar
¼ tsp. nutmeg
¼ tsp. cinnamon
1 tsp. salt
2 eggs, unbeaten
4 tsp. baking powder
¼ cup Crisco
1 cup milk

Topping:
4 tbsp. flour
½ tbsp. cinnamon
⅛ tsp. salt
¼ cup Crisco
1 cup brown sugar

Combine cake ingredients and mix until smooth. Blend topping ingredients with a fork. Pour two-thirds of cake batter into an 8 x 12" greased pan. Sprinkle one-half of the topping over the batter. Spread remaining batter and cover with second half of the topping. Bake 30 minutes at 350°.

Preparation: 20 min.   Easy   Serves: 8
Cooking: 30 min.   Can do ahead   Can freeze

Roselyn M. Allison

MOTHER EARTH BREAD
"Heavenly aroma"

1 cup rolled oats
2 cups boiling water
3 pkgs. yeast
½ cup warm water
½ cup honey
1 tbsp. salt
2 tbsp. shortening, melted
6-6½ cups flour
1 egg yolk
few drops water
poppy seeds, optional

Pour boiling water over rolled oats in large bowl and allow to sit at least ½ hour. Soften 3 packages yeast in ½ cup warm water. Add honey, salt and shortening to oat mixture, then add yeast mixture. Gradually add flour until a soft dough is formed. Knead until elastic on floured surface. Place in buttered bowl and allow to rise until doubled, about 1 hour. Punch down and cut into either 2 or 4 loaves. Place in greased pans and brush tops with egg yolk mixed with water. Sprinkle with poppy seeds. Cover and allow to rise until doubled. Bake at 325° for 40-45 minutes.

Preparation: 30 min.   Easy   Yield: 2 large or
Cooking: 45 min.   Can do ahead   4 small loaves
                                            Can freeze

Jean Pensyl

NO-KNEAD WHOLEWHEAT BREAD

4 cups wholewheat flour
⅔ cup warm water
2 envs. dry yeast
⅓ cup honey
½ cup wheat germ
1 tsp. salt
¼ cup molasses
1¼ cup water
sugar

Heat wholewheat flour in a 9 x 13″ pan at 250° for 20 minutes. While flour is heating, dissolve yeast in water. Add honey to yeast mixture. When flour is done, put in large bowl and add wheat germ, salt, molasses, water and yeast mixture. Mix *thoroughly*. Line loaf pan with foil; grease foil lightly. Put dough in pan and sprinkle lightly with sugar on top, press in. Let rise until a little above rim of pan. Bake 30-40 minutes at 400°.

Preparation: 30 min.   Easy   Yield: 1 loaf
Cooking: 30-40 min. Can do ahead

Ralph Wilson
"Willow Inn"

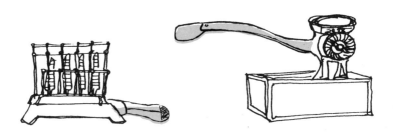

SOUR DOUGH BREAD
"Have fun feeding your starter"

Starter: use only glass or
plastic
2 cups flour
2 cups warm water
1 pkg. dry yeast

Bread:
1 pkg. active dry yeast
1 cup warm water
3 tbsp. sugar
2 eggs
1½ cups starter
4 cups flour
2 tsp. salt

Starter: Mix all ingredients. Let stand in warm place overnight or up to 48 hours. After fermenting, starter is ready to use or to store in refrigerator. "Feed" once or twice a week with 1 cup milk, 1 cup flour, ¼ cup sugar.

Bread: In a large bowl, sprinkle yeast over water. Let stand for 5 minutes. Stir in sugar, eggs and 1½ cups starter. Gradually add 4 cups flour mixed with 2 teaspoons salt; mix well. Cover bowl with damp cloth and let rise until doubled in bulk. Knead on a floured board until satiny. Make a rectangle and place in bread pan. Make diagonal slashes in top of loaf. Cover with towel and let rise until doubled in bulk. Bake at 400° for 35 minutes.

Preparation: 40 min.	Difficult	Yield: 1 loaf
Cooking: 35 min.	Can do ahead	Can freeze

Nell Tabor Hartley

BRAIDED HERB BREAD
"A really different taste"

2 pkgs. active dry yeast
2½ cups warm water
6 tbsp. sugar
2 tsp. salt
⅓ cup salad oil
4 eggs
2 tbsp. parsley, chopped
2 tbsp. chives, minced
1 tbsp. lemon peel, grated
2 tbsp. dried tarragon
8⅔ cups all-purpose flour
1 egg yolk mixed with cold
water
5 tsp. poppy seeds

Dissolve yeast in warm water and proof. Add sugar, salt, oil, eggs, parsley, chives, lemon peel, tarragon and 6 cups flour. Beat with a spoon. Add more flour until the dough is too stiff to beat with a spoon. Knead remaining flour into dough until smooth. Place dough in large covered bowl and let rise in warm place for 1½ hours or until tripled in size. Punch down, divide into 12 portions. Shape each portion into a rope 1" in diameter. Braid 3 ropes together. Repeat with remaining ropes. Place each braid in well-greased 4½ x 8" loaf pan. Let rise ¾ hour until tripled in bulk. Brush tops of dough with egg wash and sprinkle with poppy seeds. Bake at 375° for 25-30 minutes.

Preparation: 2½ hours	Moderately difficult	Yield: 4 loaves
Cooking: 25-30 min.	Can do ahead	Can freeze

Phyllis Lynch

DINNER ROLLS
"Start these the night before"

1 cake yeast
½ cup sugar
1 cup milk
2 eggs, well-beaten
1 tsp. salt
4 cups flour
½ cup butter, melted

Crumble yeast in the milk, then mix with the sugar and let stand ½ hour. Add eggs, salt, flour and butter. Knead. Cover and let stand overnight without refrigeration. Next morning, punch down the dough. Take about ¼ of the dough at a time and roll each hunk out on a floured surface to pie-pan size, about ½" thick. Cut each of these round shapes into 8 wedges and roll up the wedges from the wide end. Place on a well-oiled cookie sheet and let rise 3 to 4 hours. Bake at 400° for 10 minutes.

Preparation:	30 min.	Easy	Yield: 32 rolls
Cooking:	10 min.	Must do ahead	Can freeze

Don Riggs
WPXI-TV

GOLDEN WHEAT BREAD
"Smells so good in the kitchen"

3 cups lukewarm water
½ cup honey
2 tbsp. molasses
3 pkgs. active dry yeast
1 tbsp. salt
¼ cup oil
5 cups stoneground wholewheat flour
3 cups unbleached white flour (approx.)
1 cup cracked wheat

Mix warm water, honey, molasses and yeast together. Let stand 5 minutes. Stir in the salt, oil, wholewheat flour, 2 cups unbleached white flour and the cracked wheat. Mix well. Turn the dough onto a floured board and gradually add enough remaining flour to make dough that is not sticky. Knead until smooth and satiny, about 10 minutes.

Place in an oiled bowl; turn to oil top of dough. Cover and let rise in a warm place until doubled in bulk, about 1½ hours. Punch down, fold and turn so that smooth side is up. Cover and let rise again, about 45 minutes. Divide the dough into 2. Shape each portion into a round loaf and place on a cookie sheet. Cover and let rise until doubled in bulk, about 45 minutes. Preheat oven to 350°. Bake about 50 minutes or until loaf sounds hollow when tapped on the bottom.

Preparation:	30 min.	Easy	Yield: 2 loaves
Baking:	50 min.	Can do ahead	Can freeze

Marlene Parrish

SWEDISH RYE BREAD

"Tuck a few loaves in your freezer"

1 env. dry yeast
1 tbsp. sugar
¼ cup lukewarm water
1 qt. lukewarm water
½ cup margarine, melted
¾ cup molasses
1 cup brown sugar, packed
4 cups rye flour, unsifted
8½ cups white flour, unsifted

Dissolve yeast and sugar in ¼ cup water. Add 1 quart water, margarine, molasses and brown sugar; mix well. Stir in rye flour, then white flour, up to 8½ cups. Knead on well-floured surface until smooth and elastic, 8-10 minutes. Dough should be slightly sticky. Place in greased bowl, turn to grease top. Cover. Let rise until doubled. Punch down. Cut into 4 equal parts. Shape into loaves. Put in greased pans. Grease tops. Cover. Let rise again. Bake at 350° for 45 minutes or at 325° for 1 hour. Recipe works well halved and prepared using dough hook and mixer.

Preparation: 35-45 min.   Moderately difficult   Yield: 4 loaves
Cooking: 1 hour   Can freeze

Mrs. Lee M. Huizenga

TOASTED WALNUT HERB BREAD

"This is especially delicious - with or without nuts"

1 cup milk
2 tbsp. sugar
1 tbsp. salt
2 pkgs. active dry yeast
1 cup lukewarm water
1 tsp. thyme
3 tbsps. fresh parsley, chopped
1½ tsp. dried basil
1½ tsp. dried tarragon
1 small clove garlic, minced
4½ cups flour, sifted
¾ cup toasted walnuts,
   chopped

Scald milk. Add sugar and salt and cool the mixture. Sprinkle yeast over the warm water; add a pinch of sugar and let stand 5 minutes. Blend milk mixture into yeast mixture. Add thyme, parsley, basil, tarragon, garlic and 3½ cups flour to yeast mixture and beat at medium speed on electric mixer for 2 minutes. Add remaining flour and beat until batter is smooth: it will be sticky. Let rise in warm place until doubled in bulk, about 45 minutes. Add toasted nuts and stir. Turn into 1½-quart casserole and let rise until doubled. Bake at 375° for 1 hour.

Preparation: 30 min.   Easy   Yield: 1 loaf
Cooking: 1 hour   Can do ahead   Can freeze

Yard Birds Garden Club

OVERNIGHT ROLLS

¼ cup warm water
1 tbsp. sugar
1 pkg. dry yeast
½ cup sugar
2 cups lukewarm water
½ cup oil
3 tsp. salt
1 egg
7 cups flour, approx.

Mix first 3 ingredients and let stand 10 minutes. Blend remaining ingredients and mix with the liquid mixture. Let rise until doubled in bulk, knead down and let rise a second time. Shape into rolls, cover with a cloth and let stand overnight. Do not refrigerate! Bake next morning at 350° until brown, about 15 minutes.

Preparation: 20 min.	Easy	Yield: 36 rolls
Cooking: 15-20 min.	Must do ahead	Can freeze

Carol Regan Dickson

BREAD PRETZEL
"You will find this a remembered delight"

2 cups water
1 pkg. yeast
½ tsp. sugar
4½-5 cups flour*
1 egg, beaten
coarse salt

*a good variation is half whole-wheat & half white flour

Combine the water, yeast and sugar and let stand 1 hour. Mix in the flour and knead 10 minutes. Let rise until doubled in bulk in a greased bowl. Punch down and form into pretzel. Brush with egg wash and sprinkle with salt. Let rise again until doubled. Bake at 425° for 15-20 minutes. Serve warm with butter.

Preparation: 20 min.	Easy	Yield: 1 very large pretzel
Baking: 15-20 min.	Can do ahead	Can freeze

Susan Gaca

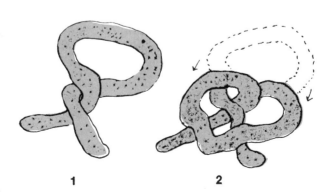

1   2

ENTRÉES

THE GRAND CONCOURSE RESTAURANT

The Grand Concourse Restaurant serves as an elegant centerpiece for a 40-acre shopping, working and entertainment complex on the site of the former Pittsburgh & Lake Erie Railroad transportation center. In its heyday, the P.&L.E.R.R. played a vital part in the industrial development of Pittsburgh. After months of preparation, which included washing the stained glass dome—a task not undertaken since its installation in 1900—the main waiting room with its Edwardian interior of marble, gilt, mosaic and stained glass opened in November, 1976 and quickly became one of Pittsburgh's finest restaurants.

Additional illustrations in this section:

A mini-regatta at Point State Park reflecting pool.

Bakewell Glass: "Argus," "Tulip," "Pear," "Excelsior," "Loop," and "Bell Flower." Established in 1808 by Benjamin Bakewell, father of American Flint Glass work, the company was the first to make cut glass wares, and counted the White House among its customers.*

Bakewell Pitcher and 1840 Apothecary Jar.

Meat rack from A. W. Gums Market at Avery and Nash Avenue on the North Side of Pittsburgh.

Early scale from A. W. Gums Market.

Atterbury's patent melon ware, 1878, in opal or flint glass.

Pittsburgh's Convention-Exposition Center.

Palm Court Room - William Penn Hotel.

Free blown covered urns, circa 1860.

Pipe Dreams - Gateway Center Sculpture.

"We Are Family" baseball banner — reflecting a refrain heard often during baseball season at Three Rivers Stadium.

Three-dimensional art in City Park.

Early meat scale from Northside market, courtesy of Pittsburgh History and Landmarks Foundation, Old Post Office Museum Collection.

City of Pittsburgh from Three Rivers Stadium.

Pit Panther in Schenley Park.

Newel post from a Manchester house.

Gateway Center tulips.

Bas-relief gargoyles at Heinz Hall.

Opal glass novelties from farmyard assortment. Challinor, Taylor & Co. Glassware.

"Lady Grace," built by Capt. Frederick Way, Jr. of Sewickley, sailing on the Allegheny River. Capt. Way, a life-long Sewickley resident, was born in 1901 and is a respected authority on the inland rivers, having written widely on the subject.

Banner for the Three Rivers Regatta which started in 1977 to dramatize Pittsburgh's position as the largest inland port in the country. Pittsburgh and the county surrounding it Allegheny, have more registered motor boats than Miami, Florida! The Regatta covers three days and provides entertainment on the water, land and in the air.

Opal glassware - opal-eyed fish.

The Sewickley Bridge, 1910-1980. Rebuilt in 1981. Construction on the Sewickley Bridge began in 1909 by the Ft. Pitt Bridge Works, and the official opening was September 9 1911. At that time the only bridge over the Ohio River between Pittsburgh and Wheeling W. Va. (a distance of 100 miles), was the recently completed Rochester Monaca Bridge. The free Sewickley Bridge opened trade between Sewickley and Coraopolis, and its spires served as a landmark to traffic going up and down the Ohio River

Natural stone entrance to Frick Park.

Early Heinz Pickle Bucket, courtesy of the Pittsburgh History and Landmarks Foundation Old Post Office Museum Collection.

*All glassware is early Pittsburgh unless otherwise indicated.

BUCKINGHAM EGGS

"Call out the guard, they'll be eternally grateful"

6 slices bread
2 tbsp. butter
2 tbsp. anchovy paste
1 tsp. English mustard
8 eggs
3 tbsp. cream
¼ tsp. salt
⅛ tsp. pepper
1 tbsp. onion, minced
Cheddar cheese, grated
Butter, melted
Worcestershire sauce, optional

Trim bread crusts and toast bread lightly. Cream the butter, anchovy paste and mustard together. Spread butter mixture on toast and keep warm. Beat the eggs with the cream, salt and pepper. Add onion, if desired. Melt butter in skillet over low heat; pour in egg mixture. When eggs begin to thicken, stir with a wooden spoon. Remove from skillet while still moist and undercooked. Mound on anchovy toast. Sprinkle each with a tablespoon of grated cheese, dot with melted butter. Sprinkle with a few drops of Worcestershire, if desired. Place under a hot broiler until cheese melts.

Preparation: 10-15 min.   Easy   Serves: 6
Cooking: 15 min.   Serve immediately

Mrs. Donald Brewster

FRIANDISIS

"If you can pronounce it, you can make it"

8-10 eggs
½ cup cream
salt & pepper
butter
12 thin slices ham
¼ - ½ lb. Swiss cheese or white
    Kraft American, grated
1 cup heavy cream

Beat eggs with ½ cup cream, salt and pepper. Heat butter in a small pan; when butter is hot, fill a large kitchen spoon with the egg mixture and pour into the pan—just enough for a thin omelette. Cook on each side, then flip onto a plate, cover with a slice of ham and roll up. Continue until 12 are completed. Pack rolls together tightly in an ovenproof dish. Cover completely with lots of grated cheese and dot with butter. At this point, can be refrigerated to serve the next day. One half hour before serving, pour heavy cream over the friandisis and bake at 300° until cream starts to bubble. Brown the cheese under the broiler.

Preparation: 30 min.   Easy   Serves: 6-8
Cooking: 15-20 min.   Can do ahead

Joyce Lester

CHILIES RELENOS CASSEROLE

"Hot or cold, this is a winner"

2-3 4-oz. cans green chilies
1 lb. Cheddar cheese, grated
1 lb. Monterey Jack cheese,
    grated
4 eggs, separated
1 13-oz. can evaporated milk
3 tbsp. flour
salt & pepper, to taste

Remove seeds, rinse and flatten chilies. Put half on bottom of a 9 x 13″ baking dish. Cover with Cheddar cheese, then remaining chilies and Monterey Jack cheese. Beat egg yolks with milk, flour, salt and pepper. Beat egg whites until stiff and fold into yolk mixture. Pour egg mixture over casserole. Bake at 325° for 45 minutes to 1 hour, until lightly browned.

Preparation: 30 min.   Easy   Serves: 6
Baking: 45-60 min.   Can freeze

Clara Obern

EGG AND SAUSAGE BAKE

"So wholesome and hearty - makes you feel good to make it"

1 lb. bulk sausage
9 eggs
3 cups milk
1½ tsp. dry mustard
1½ tsp. salt, or to taste
dash pepper
12 slices white bread, crust
  removed & cubed
1½ cups sharp Cheddar
  cheese, grated

Brown and drain sausage. Cool. Beat eggs and milk; add seasonings and bread cubes. Fold in sausage and cheese. Put in a 9 x 13" pan and refrigerate overnight. Remove from refrigerator 1 hour before baking. Bake at 350° for 1 hour. Cool slightly before cutting.

Preparation: 20 min.	Easy	Serves: 8-10
Baking: 1 hour	Must do ahead	

Mrs. P. M. Snyder, Jr.

CHEESE PUDDING WITH CREOLE SAUCE

2 tbsp. butter or margarine
2 tbsp. flour
½ tsp. dry mustard
⅓ tsp. white pepper
scant tsp. salt
¼ tsp. Tabasco sauce
8 eggs
1 13-oz. can evaporated milk
4 cups milk
6 cups tiny soft bread cubes
8 oz. sharp Cheddar cheese,
  grated
4 oz. American cheese, grated

Creole Sauce:
½ cup water
1 med. onion, diced
½ green pepper, diced
1 16-oz. can crushed tomatoes
1 15½-oz. jar Ragu spaghetti
  sauce
1 tbsp. sugar
dash Tabasco sauce
½ tsp. chili powder
salt & pepper, to taste

Pudding: Melt butter; add flour, mustard, pepper, salt and Tabasco and mix to a well blended roux. Transfer roux to a large bowl and cool. Add eggs and beat thoroughly. Add both milks. Mix bread cubes and cheeses together in separate bowl.

Butter a 9x13x2" casserole, arrange a layer of bread cube mixture on bottom and pour in ⅓ of milk mixture. Repeat layers 2 more times. Bake at 375° for 45-50 minutes or until puffed and a knife inserted in middle comes out clean. Serve with Creole Sauce.

Creole Sauce: Cook onions and pepper in water until soft. Add remaining ingredients and bring to a boil. Stir to blend.

Preparation: 40 min.	Easy	Serves: 8-10
Cooking: 1 hour	Can do ahead	Can freeze

Christina Bradley

ARTICHOKE AND HAM CASSEROLE

"Consider this casserole for a party lunch or brunch"

2 10½-oz. cans condensed
  cream of mushroom soup
1½ lbs. cooked ham, diced
1 14-oz. can artichoke hearts,
  drained
6 hard-cooked eggs, quartered
1 tbsp. onion, minced
¼ cup medium Sherry
¼ tsp. garlic salt
⅛ tsp. pepper
4 slices Cheddar cheese, grated

Combine all ingredients, except cheese, in a 3 quart casserole. Top with grated cheese. Bake, uncovered, at 350° for 40 minutes.

Preparation: 30 min.   Easy   Serves: 8
Baking: 40 min.   Can do ahead

Kathy Leighton

CHEESE-HAM STRATA

"Perfect before the football game"

12 slices Pepperidge Farm
   white bread
¾ lb. sharp American cheese,
   sliced
1 10-oz. pkg. chopped frozen
  broccoli, cooked & drained
2 cups cooked ham, diced
3½ cups milk
2 tbsp. instant minced onion
½ tsp. salt
¼ tsp. dry mustard
6 eggs, lightly beaten
cheese, shredded

Cut 12 donut shapes and holes from bread and set aside. Remove crusts from bread scraps and place in bottom of 13 x 9" baking dish. Place a layer of cheese over bread; add a layer of broccoli and a layer of ham. Arrange bread shapes on top. Combine remaining ingredients, except cheese. Pour over strata and cover. Refrigerate at least 6 hours or overnight. Bake, uncovered, for 50 minutes at 350°; sprinkle with shredded cheese last 5 minutes of baking. Let stand 10 minutes before cutting into squares.

Preparation: 30 min.   Easy   Serves: 6
Baking: 50 min.   Can do ahead

Mrs. Gary R. Bauer

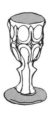

MUSHROOM CREPE WITH HAM

"Don't give up - this is a really special recipe"

Crepe batter:
¾ cup flour
1¼ cups milk, divided
pinch salt
1 egg yolk
1 egg
1 tbsp. butter, melted or light oil

Filling:
3 tbsp. butter
3 shallots or ½ onion, finely
  chopped
1½ cups mushrooms, thinly
  sliced
2 tbsp. lemon juice
½ cup chicken broth
salt & pepper
½ cup Swiss or Gruyere
  cheese, grated
¼ cup whipping cream
1 tbsp. cornstarch dissolved in
  2 tbsp. cold water
8 thin slices boiled ham
butter

Sift the flour into a mixing bowl. Add salt, egg yolk and whole egg and ½ of the milk. Stir with a wire whisk until smooth. Add remaining milk and butter or oil. All ingredients can be put in the blender for 10 seconds. If it is mixed in the blender, it may be used immediately. If it is prepared by hand, allow it to rest for 1 hour so that the milk and flour will be well combined. The batter may be prepared for later use and will keep in the refrigerator all day. If it is left for the next day, it may need to be thinned with 2 tablespoons milk.

If using a crepe maker, follow manufacturer's directions. If using skillet, melt butter, and add batter to just barely cover bottom of skillet. Tilt to spread to edges. Cook until lightly browned and turn. Store cooked crepes between layers of waxed paper to prevent sticking.

Filling: Sauté the onions in butter until soft. Add the mushrooms with lemon juice to prevent discoloration; cook for 1 minute. Add the broth and cook over high heat, uncovered, for 1 more minute. Lower heat; add cheese and cream. Do not heat the cheese too quickly or it will spin into threads. Add cornstarch and stir; the mixture will thicken immediately. It should be thick enough to hold its shape in the rolled crepe. Adjust the seasoning, adding salt and pepper to taste.

Lay a piece of boiled ham on each crepe. Put about 3 tablespoons of the mushroom mixture over the ham and roll the crepes. Place in a buttered oven-proof dish and dot with butter. Bake in a preheated 400° oven for 15 minutes. Can assemble ahead up to baking.

Preparation: 40 min.   **Moderately difficult**   Yield: 12 crepes
Cooking: 35 min.   **Serve immediately**

Mrs. Roger E. Wright

EGGS ARGOSY

"A very sophisticated lovely flavor"

1 tbsp. oil
1 tbsp. butter
3 tbsp. onion, finely chopped
¼ lb. mushrooms, finely
  chopped
1 tbsp. tomato purée
1 tbsp. parsley
salt & pepper, to taste
6 hard-boiled eggs
1 cup Mornay sauce
Gruyere or Parmesan cheese,
  grated

Mornay Sauce:
1 cup milk
mace
bay leaf
shallot
peppercorns
1 tbsp. butter
1 tbsp. flour
salt & pepper, to taste
1 tsp. French mustard
cream, if desired
1½ oz. cheese, grated

Heat oil and butter together and sauté onion until translucent. Add mushrooms and cook lightly. Mix in purée, parsley and seasonings. Cut the eggs lengthwise, remove yolks, and combine yolks with mushroom mixture. Fill whites with mushroom mixture, arrange in baking dish and cover with Mornay sauce. Sprinkle with grated cheese and bake at 325° for 15-20 minutes.

Mornay Sauce: Heat spices with milk for 7 minutes. In separate pan, melt butter, add flour and stir until smooth. Add milk and bring to a boil over moderate heat; simmer 2-3 minutes. Remove from heat and beat in cheese.

Preparation: 1 hour   Easy   Serves: 6
Baking: 15-20 min.   Can do ahead

Audrie Borchardt

ZUCCHINI CRESCENT PIE

4 cups zucchini, thinly sliced
1 cup onion, chopped
½ cup margarine
½ cup parsley, chopped, or 2
  tbsp. flakes
½ tsp. salt
½ tsp. pepper
¼ tsp. oregano
2 eggs, beaten
8 oz. Mozzarella cheese,
  shredded
8-oz. can refrigerator crescent
  rolls

Preheat oven to 375°. In skillet, sauté zucchini and onion in margarine for 10 minutes. Stir in seasonings. Blend eggs and cheese and stir into vegetable mixture. Separate dough into 8 triangles. Place in an ungreased 11" quiche pan or 8 x 12" baking pan; press over bottom and up sides to form crust. Pour vegetable mixture evenly into crust. Bake at 375° for 18-20 minutes. Let stand 10 minutes; cut into wedges to serve.

Preparation: 30 min.   Easy   Serves: 8
Baking: 18-20 min.   Can do ahead

Chappy's Choice

REUBEN QUICHE
"How about this for Sunday night supper?"

9" pastry shell
1 tbsp. caraway seeds
8-oz. corned beef, shredded
1 tbsp. Dijon mustard
¾ cup sauerkraut, squeezed & drained
2 cups Swiss cheese, grated
2 eggs, beaten
1 cup light cream
1 tsp. onion, grated
½ tsp. dry mustard

Preheat oven to 375°. Sprinkle caraway seeds over pie crust; Prick crust and bake for 7 minutes. Fill pie shell with corned beef. Spread mustard over meat, top with sauerkraut and cheese. Mix eggs, cream, onion and dry mustard together. Pour into pie shell and bake for 40 minutes. Let stand 5 minutes before cutting. *Note:* unwashed sauerkraut is more flavorful in this recipe.

Preparation: 20 min.	Easy	Serves: 4
Baking: 40 min.		

Betty Mae Van der Veer

EGGS FLORENTINE
"Who doesn't love creamy spinach and eggs"

Sauce:
1 small onion, minced
3 tbsp. butter
3 tbsp. flour
2 cups milk
3 drops Tabasco
1 tsp. Worcestershire sauce
½ lb. Swiss cheese, grated
salt & pepper, to taste
2 10-oz. pkgs. frozen chopped spinach, or 2 pkgs. fresh spinach, chopped
8 eggs
1 small can artichoke hearts, drained & rinsed
½ cup Parmesan cheese, grated

Sauce: Sauté onion in butter; add flour and cook, stirring, for 2-3 minutes without browning. Add milk, continue cooking and stirring with a whisk until smooth. Add salt, pepper, Tabasco and Worcestershire sauce. Add cheese in small handsful; cook and stir until melted.

Cook spinach until wilted; squeeze and drain. Poach eggs lightly; transfer to cold water to stop cooking and drain on paper towels.

Assemble by adding ⅓ of sauce to spinach; layer spinach mixture on bottom of well-greased individual baking dishes or 1 large shallow baking dish. Quarter artichoke hearts and distribute over spinach. Place poached eggs on top. Spread sauce evenly over top, sprinkle with Parmesan cheese and dot with butter. Can be covered tightly and refrigerated up to 24 hours at this point. Return to room temperature before baking. Bake in preheated oven at 350° for 10 minutes or until bubbly; then brown 2 minutes under the broiler.

Preparation: 45 min.	Moderately difficult	Serves: 4
Cooking: 12 min.	Can do ahead	

Mrs. Edward A. Montgomery, Jr.

EGGPLANT-TOMATO QUICHE

"Marvelous with or without fresh eggplant and tomatoes from your garden"

2 8" pastry shells
1 med. eggplant
1 tbsp. salt
2 tbsp. olive oil
1 med. onion, chopped
4 med. tomatoes, peeled,
  seeded & chopped
½ tsp. salt
pepper
dash Tabasco
¼ - ½ tsp. each: thyme, basil,
  oregano
4 eggs
parsley, garnish

Bake shells at 425° for 10 minutes. Cut eggplant into ½" slices, sprinkle with salt and let drain on paper towels for 20 minutes. Dry slices and cut into ½" pieces. Heat oil in skillet and sauté onion until softened. Add eggplant and cook until soft. Add tomatoes and simmer a few minutes. Stir in seasonings. Remove from heat and let cool slightly. Beat eggs and stir into eggplant mixture. Pour into pastry shells and bake in preheated oven at 325° for 30 minutes, or until set. Serve hot or cold.

Preparation: 45 min.   Easy   Serves: 8
Baking: 30 min.

Mrs. Charles Dithrich

RICOTTA AND SPINACH QUICHE

"A quiche most everyone loves - this makes a large one"

pastry
1 bunch fresh spinach or 1
  10-oz. pkg. frozen spinach
1 cup Ricotta cheese
nutmeg, grated
1 cup Parmesan cheese, grated
1 cup cream & 1 cup milk, or 2
  cups half & half
4 eggs, lightly beaten
salt & pepper

Line a deep 10" quiche pan with your favorite tart pastry, prick and bake 15 minutes at 425°. Meanwhile, wash spinach and cook for a few minutes. Squeeze out all liquid and chop: should be about ¾ cup. Combine spinach with Ricotta, a little nutmeg and ½ cup of Parmesan cheese. Spread over the bottom of pie shell. Combine eggs with cream, milk, salt and pepper. Pour over Ricotta-spinach mixture. Sprinkle with remaining Parmesan and bake at 375° for 30 minutes, or until puffed and a knife inserted in the center comes out clean. Let quiche sit 10 minutes before serving.

Preparation: 10 min.   Easy   Serves: 8
Baking: 30 min.

Marlene Parrish

"EVENING MAGAZINE" ARTICHOKE PIE

"Now don't nibble on the artichokes or you'll need 5 jars"

Crust:
1 cup wholewheat flour
⅛ tsp. salt
⅓ cup butter
¼ cup ice water

Filling:
2 jars marinated artichoke
   hearts
5 eggs
½-1 cup Parmesan cheese,
   freshly grated
garlic powder
parsley
bread crumbs

Cut butter into flour until pieces are pea size. Add salt and sprinkle with water. Mix with a fork. Knead several times. Chill 30 minutes. Roll out for a 9″ shell. Bake at 450° for 5 minutes. Cool.

Drain artichokes and cut in half. Beat eggs lightly; add cheese and garlic. Arrange artichokes in shell and pour egg mixture over artichokes. Sprinkle with bread crumbs and parsley. Bake at 350° for 45-60 minutes or until a knife inserted in the center comes out clean.

Preparation: 30 min.   Easy   Serves: 6
Baking: 45-60 min.   Can do ahead

Liz Miles and Dave Durian

JILL'S BEST QUICHE

"Jack just loved this"

Crust:
2 oz. Velveeta cheese
½ stick butter, softened
¾ cup flour

Filling:
1 lb. spinach, blanched &
   chopped
1 bunch scallions, chopped
¼ lb. mushrooms, chopped
6 slices bacon, cooked &
   crumbled
salt & pepper
nutmeg
3 eggs, beaten
1½-2 cups Swiss cheese,
   shredded
¾ cup sour cream or heavy
   cream
Parmesan cheese, grated

Mix crust ingredients thoroughly with hands and press into a quiche pan or deep dish pie pan. Layer the spinach, onions, mushrooms and bacon over crust. Season to taste. Mix eggs with the cheese and cream. Pour into shell. Top with lots of Parmesan cheese and bake at 375° for 30-45 minutes until set.

Preparation: 45 min.   Easy   Serves: 6-8
Baking: 40 min.   Can do ahead

Dorothy Hartley

A. W. GUMS

BEEF

ROAST BEEF WITH SEASONED SALT
"Try this at Christmas"

4-8 lb. rib roast
oil

Seasoned salt:
¼ cup salt, or to taste
¼ tsp. thyme
¼ tsp. oregano
¼ tsp. garlic powder
½ tsp. paprika
½ tsp. dry mustard
¼ tsp. curry powder
⅛ tsp. onion powder
⅛ tsp. dillweed

Horseradish mousse:
½ cup whipping cream
3 tbsp. prepared horseradish,
    well drained
¼ tsp. salt
2 tsp. onion, grated
1 tsp. lemon juice

Mix the salt and seasonings together. Store in a tightly capped jar.

Preheat oven to 450°. Rub roast with oil, then a small amount of seasoned salt. Place meat thermometer in the center of the roast. Place fat side up on a rack in an open pan. Roast at 450° for 5 minutes, then reduce temperature to 325°. Continue roasting until thermometer registers 130-135° for rare, 140-145° for medium rare, 150° medium, or 160° for well done. Remove from oven and allow to absorb juices for ½ hour before carving. Serve with horseradish mousse.

Horseradish mousse: Whip cream and gently fold in horseradish, salt, onion, and lemon juice. Chill. Must do ahead for flavors to develop.

Preparation: 5-10 min.   Easy
Cooking: 20 min. per lb.

Serves: ⅓ to ½ lb. per serving

Mrs. Benjamin V. Smith, Jr.

72

FABULOUS FILET OF BEEF
"A dinner party 10!"

2 or more lbs. beef filet
salt
Dijon mustard
fine bread crumbs
⅓ cups Brandy, heated

Béarnaise sauce:
6 green onions
¼ cup tarragon vinegar
4 egg yolks
2 tsp. dry tarragon
¼ tsp. salt
¼ tsp. dry mustard
dash Tabasco
1 cup butter, melted

Cut 1" deep gash down length of filet. Rub with salt. Coat with mustard and roll in fine bread crumbs. Roast at 400° until meat thermometer registers rare. Slice, reassemble, and fill gash with Béarnaise sauce. Pour ⅓ cup heated Brandy over meat, ignite it and shake platter until the flames die.
Béarnaise Sauce: Combine vinegar and onions in skillet; reduce almost completely. Place in blender with egg yolks, tarragon, salt, mustard and Tabasco. Slowly add **hot** melted butter and whirl until smooth.

Preparation: 30 min.
Cooking: 30-45 min.

Serves: 4-6

Mrs. Jon E. McCarthy

STEAK AU POIVRE
"Piquant flavor"

2 2" N.Y. strip steaks
black pepper, coarsely ground*
coarse salt
¼ cup butter
¼ cup olive oil
⅓ cup dry white wine
¼ cup Cognac
*or fresh peppercorns, crushed

Press coarsely ground pepper or crushed peppercorns into both sides of steaks; sprinkle lightly with coarse salt. Heat butter and olive oil in heavy skillet. Sear steaks on both sides, then cook for 5-7 minutes on each side, depending on degree of rareness desired. Transfer steaks to warm platter. Heat
wine with pan juices, add Cognac and swirl pan over heat for 1 minute. Pour pan juices over steaks and serve.

Preparation: 10 min.   Easy   Serves: 2
Cooking: 15-20 min.   Serve immediately

Mrs. Ronald E. Long

LENA'S GINGERBEEF
"A nice change from Béarnaise Sauce"

½ whole tenderloin
6 thin slices of fresh ginger root
2 cups Brandy
1 tbsp. Worcestershire sauce
1 tsp. curry powder
3 tbsp. A-1 sauce

Sliver meat every inch and insert thin slices of ginger. Mix Brandy, Worcestershire sauce and curry and pour over meat. Marinate overnight. Pour A-1 sauce over top of beef. Brown for 10 minutes in 400° oven; reduce heat to 350° and cook for 25 minutes. Remove ginger slices before serving. Surround with watercress or parsley. *Note:* This filet is to be cooked without larding.

Preparation: 10 min.   Easy   Serves: 4-6
Cooking: 35 min.   Must do ahead

Mrs. William Penn Snyder, IV

CARBONNADE OF BEEF
"Delicious served over noodles"

2½ lbs. boneless chuck or
　　round steak, cubed
½ cup flour
salt
pepper
4 tbsp. butter
2 tbsp. oil
1 cup beer
¼ cup brown sugar
2 lbs. med. onion, peeled
2-3 slices rye bread
mustard

Shake the meat in flour, salt and pepper. Heat butter and oil in dutch oven and brown the meat, a little at a time. Add the beer, then the brown sugar. Mix well. Add the whole onions. Spread the slices of rye bread with mustard and invert them over the onions. Cover. Let simmer until meat is tender, about 1½ hours. Stir occasionally, being careful not to disturb the bread. Before serving, remove the bread and discard. Thicken sauce, if necessary.

Preparation: 30 min.   Easy   Serves: 6-8
Cooking: 1½ hours   Can do ahead

Mrs. John G. Zimmerman, Jr.

BEEF STROGANOFF

"A delicious version of an old favorite"

1½-2 lbs. tenderloin tips, sliced
2" thick
¼ cup butter
¼ lb. fresh mushrooms or 1
small can mushrooms, sliced
3 tbsp. flour
2 10-oz. cans beef stock
½ cup white wine
2 tbsp. vinegar
½ cup sour cream

Sauté tips of beef, then mushrooms, in butter until brown. Add flour and cook until browned. Add hot beef stock, bring to a boil and remove from heat. Reduce wine and vinegar to half original amount and add to above. Place sour cream into large bowl and slowly add half of beef sauce to sour cream, stirring constantly to prevent curdling. Then pour back into meat mixture. Reheat all to simmer for 10 minutes. Serve with noodles, rice or spatzle.

Preparation:	20 min.	Easy	Serves: 4
Cooking:	35-45 min.	Can do ahead	

Joseph D. Parrotto, Jr.
University Club

IRISH STEAK AND POTATO PIE

"A mashed potato crust, a mashed potato topping"

2 lbs. potatoes, sliced
8 tbsp. butter
1 tbsp. onion, finely minced
1½ tsp. salt
¼ tsp. pepper
2 lbs. round steak, cut into 1"
strips
1¼ cups beef stock or rich
consommé
Cheddar cheese, grated

Place potatoes in cold salted water, bring to a boil and cook until tender. Drain, add 5 tablespoons butter, onion, salt and pepper; then mash. Line a buttered, deep 3 quart baking dish with mashed potatoes; reserve some for topping. In a skillet, sauté steak strips in remaining butter for 2 minutes on each side. Remove and place meat in center of potato-lined dish; reserve butter in which meat was cooked. Cover pie with remaining potatoes. Simmer beef stock in reserved butter. Preheat oven to 350°. Dot top of pie with butter and sprinkle with grated cheese. Bake 30 minutes. While pie is baking, simmer sauce. Remove pie from oven when done, make a hole in the top and pour in sauce. Serve immediately.

Preparation:	30 min.	Easy	Serves: 6
Cooking:	40 min.		

Mrs. Benjamin V. Smith, Jr.

CURRY HOT POT

"Almost everyone likes curry for a change"

1½ lbs. boned chuck
2 tbsp. oil
2 med. onions, sliced
1 apple, peeled & cubed
1 tbsp. curry powder
2 tomatoes, chopped
¼ cup raisins
1 tbsp. flour
1 can beef broth
2 tsp. salt
¼ tsp. pepper
1 tbsp. brown sugar
fresh parsley, garnish
rice, cooked

Cut chuck lengthwise into 1½" strips and crosswise into thin slices. Brown in hot oil. Add onions, apple and curry and sauté. Stir in the tomatoes, raisins, flour, beef broth, salt, pepper and brown sugar. Bring to a boil. Simmer, covered, for 40 minutes or until the meat is tender. Serve over rice. Garnish with parsley.

Preparation: 45 min.
Cooking: 40 min.

Easy
Can do ahead

Serves: 4

Barbara Johns

STEAK BAKE CASSEROLE

1½ lbs. round steak or chuck,
   cut into strips
⅓ cup flour
1 tsp. salt
¼ tsp. pepper
1 onion, sliced
1 green pepper, sliced
1 lb. can tomatoes
1 4-oz. can mushrooms, drained
3 tbsp. soy sauce
3 tbsp. molasses
1 10-oz. pkg. frozen French
   green beans
1 tbsp. sesame seed

Tangy Muffins:
1¼ cups flour
1½ tsp. baking powder
1 tsp. dry mustard, or 2-3 tsp.
   prepared
½ tsp. salt
½ cup milk
2 tbsp. oil
1 egg

Place meat in 2½ quart casserole. Sprinkle with flour, salt and pepper; toss to coat meat. Bake, uncovered, at 400° for 20 minutes. Add onion, green pepper, tomatoes, mushrooms, molasses and soy sauce and mix well. Cover and bake at 400° for 30 minutes. Stir in beans. Prepare muffin batter and drop by tablespoons onto hot meat mixture. Sprinkle with sesame seeds. Bake, uncovered, at 400° for 15-18 minutes.

Tangy muffins: Combine dry ingredients in 1 bowl. Mix milk, egg and oil together. Add egg mixture to dry ingredients, stirring just until moistened.

Preparation: 20 min.
Cooking: 65 min.

Easy

Serves: 6-8

Martha Wren Gregg

ROUND STEAK SAUERBRATEN

"With old world flavor"

1½ lbs. round steak, ½" thick
1 tbsp. oil
1 env. brown gravy mix
2 cups water
1 tbsp. onion, minced
2 tbsp. white wine vinegar
2 tbsp. brown sugar
½ tsp. salt
½ tsp. ginger
½ tsp. pepper
1 tsp. Worcestershire sauce
1 bay leaf

Cut meat into 1" strips. In large skillet, brown meat on all sides in hot oil. Remove meat from skillet; add gravy mix and water. Bring to boiling, stirring constantly. Stir in remaining ingredients. Return meat to skillet, cover and simmer for 1½ hours, stirring occasionally. Remove bay leaf. Serve over hot buttered noodles.

Preparation: 30 min.   Easy   Serves: 6
Cooking: 1½ hours

Mrs. Robert S. Grigsby

SHORT RIBS ROYALE

"Lovely marriage of herbs and flavors"

10 or 12 large meaty short ribs
   of beef
4 cloves
4 peppercorns
dash salt
2 bay leaves
1 med. onion, minced
1 clove garlic, crushed
1½ sticks butter
1 tbsp. oil
2 cups dry red wine
4 tsp. instant beef bouillon,
   divided
salt & pepper
½ cup Brandy or Bourbon
12-14 small onions, peeled
12-14 small red potatoes
½ cup water
parsley

Put ribs in a large kettle and cover with water. Add cloves, peppercorns, salt and 1 bay leaf. Simmer 1 hour. Reserve stock for soup. Remove ribs to paper towels to drain. In a large round casserole, brown onion and garlic in ¼ cup butter and oil. Add the red wine, 2 teaspoons beef bouillon, salt and pepper and 1 bay leaf. Simmer 5 minutes. Add short ribs. Heat the Brandy, flame and pour over ribs. Cover. Bake at 350° for 1 hour. Scrub potatoes: do not peel. Sauté potatoes and onions in ¼ cup butter and add ½ cup water with 2 teaspoons beef bouillon. Continue cooking until onions and potatoes are coated with thick brown residue. After ribs have cooked 1 hour, add onions and potatoes and continue cooking until potatoes are done. In a skillet, melt ¼ cup butter, add 2 tablespoons flour; stir to blend. Add juices from meat. Simmer, stirring, until thickened. Pour over the finished dish and sprinkle with parsley. Serve with a green salad, crusty French bread and red wine.

Preparation: 2½-3 hours   Easy   Serves: 4-6
Cooking: 2½ hours   Can do ahead   Can freeze

Sandy Hamilton

OVEN BEEF BOURGUIGNON
"Wonderful family fare for a cold winter's night"

2 lbs. stewing beef
1 tbsp. Kitchen Bouquet
3 tbsp. minute tapioca
4 carrots, peeled & chopped
2 cups onions, sliced
1 cup celery, sliced
1 clove garlic, minced
2 tsp. salt
½ tsp. pepper
½ tsp. crushed marjoram
½ tsp. thyme
1 cup red wine
1 6-oz. can sliced mushrooms

Cut meat into 1" cubes. Place in a 2½ quart casserole and toss with Kitchen Bouquet, coating meat on all sides. Mix in tapioca. Add remaining ingredients and mix gently. Cover and bake at 350° for 2½ hours, stirring every 30 minutes. Fresh mushrooms, sautéed, can be substituted for canned.

Preparation: 20 min. Easy Serves: 6-8
Cooking: 2½ hours Can do ahead Can freeze

Mrs. Richard Greene

WONDERFUL CHILI
"Try this chili at your next roundup"

½ lb. pinto beans
5 cups canned tomatoes
1 lb. green peppers, chopped
1½ lbs. onions, chopped
2 cloves garlic, crushed
1½ tbsp. salad oil
½ cup parsley, chopped
½ cup butter, melted
2½ lbs. lean ground chuck
1 lb. lean ground pork
⅓ cup chili powder
2 tbsp. salt
1½ tsp. pepper
1½ tsp. cumin seed

Soak beans overnight in water 2" above the beans. Simmer beans in same water until tender, 1 hour. Add tomatoes and simmer 5 minutes. Sauté pepper, onion, and garlic in oil until tender, but not browned. Remove vegetables and set aside. Add the parsley. In same skillet, sauté the meats for 15 minutes in butter. Add onion mixture and chili powder and cook 10 minutes. Combine remaining ingredients and mix thoroughly. Simmer, covered, for 1 hour. Uncover and simmer another hour. Skim fat.

Preparation: 2 hours Easy Serves: 8
Cooking: 2 hours Must do ahead Can freeze

Catharine M. Boyd

WEST VIRGINIA POT ROAST

"Add vegetables to make an easy meal"

3-4 lbs. chuck roast
salt & pepper
½ cup water
1 8-oz. can tomato sauce
1 large onion
½ tsp. paprika
2 tbsp. brown sugar
½ tsp. dry mustard
¼ cup ketchup
¼ cup lemon juice
¼ cup vinegar
1 tbsp. Worcestershire sauce

Brown meat; salt and pepper lightly. Add remaining ingredients. Cover tightly and bake at 275-300° until done, approximately 3 hours.

Preparation: 30 min.   Easy   Serves: 8
Cooking: 3 hours   Can do ahead

Anne Scott Sawhill

PARTY BEEF

"A good excuse to have a party"

2 lbs. ground round or chuck
½ cup onion, finely chopped
4 tbsp. butter
garlic
½ cup soft bread crumbs
2 eggs
salt & pepper
½ tsp. oregano
10 slices bacon
1 lb. mushrooms, sliced
1 cup Burgundy or other dry red wine
2 10½-oz. cans mushroom soup

Put beef in large mixing bowl. Cook onions in 2 tablespoons butter until soft. Remove with slotted spoon and add to beef. Brown garlic and bread crumbs lightly and add to beef. Add eggs, salt, pepper and oregano and mix thoroughly. Form into small balls. In a second skillet, cook bacon; remove and drain. Brown meatballs in bacon fat and put in a 2½ quart casserole. Using first skillet, sauté the mushrooms in 2 tablespoons butter. Add to casserole. Blend red wine and mushroom soup. Pour over meatballs. Crumble bacon and sprinkle over the top. May be done in advance and refrigerated. Bake, covered, at 350° for 45 minutes. Serve in casserole. If the casserole has been refrigerated, the bacon will be crisp if the cover is removed for the last 10 minutes.

Preparation: 45 min.   Easy   Serves: 6-8
Cooking: 45 min.   Can do ahead   Can freeze

Mrs. George D. Fry

HAMBURGER-CORN CASSEROLE

"A very easy but tasty sauce"

1½ lbs. ground beef
1 cup onion, chopped
1 12-oz. can whole kernel corn, drained
1 can cream of mushroom soup
1 can cream of chicken soup
1 cup sour cream
¾ tsp. salt
½ tsp. Accent
¼ tsp. pepper
3 cups med. noodles, cooked & drained
1 cup soft bread crumbs
3 tbsp. butter, melted

Lightly brown ground beef. Add onion; cook until tender, but not brown. Add the corn, the soups, sour cream, salt, Accent and pepper. Mix well. Stir in noodles. Pour into a 2 quart casserole. Make topping by combining bread crumbs and butter; sprinkle on top of casserole. Bake at 350° for 30 minutes or until hot.

Preparation: 30 min.   Easy   Serves: 8
Cooking: 30 min.   Can do ahead

Mrs. Larry A. Pryor

MEATBALLS A LA NANCY

"Rye bread gives the meatballs a unique taste"

4 slices rye bread, toasted
1 cup milk
1½ lbs. ground beef
1 egg, lightly beaten
1 tsp. onion, grated
1 tsp. salt
¼ tsp. pepper
¼ tsp. nutmeg
4 tbsp. shortening
1 cup consommé or beef broth
1 cup sour cream
2 tbsp. flour
2 tbsp. parsley, garnish

Cut toast; soak in milk 10 minutes. Mash with fork until smooth. Mix with meat, egg, onion and seasonings. Form into small balls about 2″ in diameter. Sauté balls evenly until brown. Combine broth and sour cream and add to meatballs. Simmer for 15 minutes until cooked. Serve over noodles or rice. Add flour, mixed with a little water, if needed, to thicken gravy.

Preparation: 25 min.   Easy   Serves: 6
Cooking: 30 min.   Can do ahead   Can freeze

Mrs. Frederic Kaufman

SWEDISH MEATLOAF

1½ lbs. ground beef
1 egg, lightly beaten
½ cup Pepperidge Farm herb
   stuffing, finely crushed
¼ tsp. ground nutmeg
1 can cream of mushroom soup
½ cup sour cream
nutmeg
cucumber slices

Thoroughly mix beef, egg, stuffing, nutmeg and ⅓ cup soup. Shape firmly into a loaf. Place in shallow pan and bake at 350° for 1 hour. Blend remaining soup and sour cream; heat and serve over meatloaf. Sprinkle with nutmeg and garnish with cucumber slices.

Preparation: 15 min.   Easy   Serves: 4-6
Cooking: 1 hour   Can do ahead   Can freeze

Mrs. Roger E. Wright

"MORE"

2 med. onions, chopped
1 green pepper, chopped
2 tbsp. bacon grease
2 lbs. lean ground beef
1 lb. med. noodles
1 qt. or 2 med. cans tomatoes
1 med. can whole kernel corn,
   drained
1 lb. sharp cheese, grated
salt & pepper, to taste

Sauté onions and green pepper in bacon grease. Brown the meat in same skillet. Cook noodles and drain. Add all ingredients, except cheese, to the noodles and mix well. Put mixture in a large buttered casserole or deep cake pan. Bake at 350° for ½ hour. Sprinkle grated cheese over the top and bake for an additional ½ hour. Salt and pepper may be added to taste.

Preparation: 20 min.   Easy   Serves: 8-10
Cooking: 1 hour   Can do ahead

Roselyn M. Allison

SOPHISTICATED MEATBALLS

1 lb. ground beef
⅓ cup dry bread crumbs
⅓ cup milk
1 egg, beaten
2-3 tbsp. onion, chopped
½ tsp. salt
pepper, to taste
2 tbsp. oil
1 can mushroom soup
1 8-oz. pkg. cream cheese
½ cup water

Combine first 7 ingredients and shape into large balls. Brown in oil in skillet; cover and cook 15 minutes. Remove meatballs, pour off fat and stir in remaining ingredients. Heat and serve over noodles or rice. This may also be used as an appetizer by making smaller meatballs and serving from a chafing dish.

Preparation: 15 min.   Easy   Serves: 4-6
Cooking: 25 min.   Can do ahead

Mrs. Roger S. Brown, Jr.

81

HAMBURGER BARBECUES

"Super flavor for your after-paddle parties"

½ loaf stale Italian bread, unsliced
1 lb. ground chuck
salt & pepper
½ green pepper, chopped
2 eggs
flour
oil
1 14-oz. bottle Heinz ketchup
14 oz. water
½ green pepper, chopped

Moisten bread with water, squeeze out excess and crumble into bowl. Add meat, salt, pepper, green pepper and eggs. Mix. Make patties, dip into flour and brown in oil. Place in roasting pan. Add ketchup, water and green pepper. Bake, covered, at 350° for 45 minutes until sauce is thickened.

Preparation: 20 min. Easy Serves: 4-6
Cooking: 45 min. Can do ahead

Mrs. Walter E. Gregg, Jr.

SPINACH LASAGNE

"Hooray! Only three noodles"

1 lb. lean ground beef
⅔ cup onion, chopped
2 garlic cloves, crushed
1 15-oz. can tomato sauce
1 tsp. oregano
½ tsp. salt
3 lasagne noodles
2 10-oz. pkgs. chopped frozen spinach, thawed & squeezed dry
1½ cups low fat cottage cheese
1 egg, lightly beaten
⅓ cup Parmesan cheese, grated
⅛ tsp. nutmeg

Pre-heat oven to 350°. Brown ground beef, remove beef with slotted spoon and discard all drippings but 1 teaspoon. Add onion and sauté until soft. Add garlic and continue cooking for 1 minute. Return beef to skillet. Add tomato sauce, oregano and salt. Heat to boiling; reduce heat to low, cover, and simmer 15 minutes. Remove from heat and set aside. Cook noodles. Drain. Mix spinach, cottage cheese, egg, Parmesan cheese and nutmeg together. Spread spinach mixture evenly in a greased 13x9" baking pan. Top with noodles. Top with meat sauce. Cover with foil. Bake at 350°, 40-45 minutes. Remove foil last 5 minutes, then let stand 10 minutes before cutting.

Preparation: 30-35 min. Easy Serves: 6-8
Cooking: 40-45 min. Can do ahead Can freeze

Mrs. Frank Vizza

LASAGNE

"How about this for after the game - a Steeler special"

1 lb. ribbed lasagne noodles
1 lb. Ricotta cheese
2 eggs
salt & pepper
¾ to 1 lb. Mozzarella cheese,
  sliced
4 cups combined Parmesan &
  Romano cheeses, freshly
  grated
tomato sauce
meat mixture

Tomato Sauce:
2 35-oz. cans plum tomatoes,
  crushed
1 12-oz. can tomato paste
12 oz. water
1 tbsp. sugar
1 ½ oz. wine or wine vinegar
5 beef bouillon cubes
1-1 ½ tsp. oregano
1-1 ½ basil leaves
¼ tsp. celery salt
garlic salt
pepper
fresh parsley

Meat Mixture:
1 lb. hot Italian sausage
1 lb. ground beef
garlic salt
pepper
handful Parmesan cheese,
  grated
1 egg
1 cup seasoned dry bread
  crumbs
½ cup milk
fresh parsley, minced

Cook noodles in 4 quarts boiling water with salt and 2 tablespoons oil for 7 minutes, until "al dente"; drain. Combine Ricotta, eggs, salt and pepper. Layer lasagne in 13x9x2" pan in following order: tomato sauce, noodles, sauce, grated cheese, ½ meat mixture, noodles, sauce, grated cheese, Ricotta, egg, sliced Mozzarella, noodles, sauce, grated cheese, remaining meat mixture, noodles, sauce and grated cheese. Bake in 375° oven for 40 minutes. Allow to stand 10-15 minutes before cutting. If top has dried during baking, serve with additional sauce.

Tomato Sauce: Combine all ingredients in large heavy pot. Cook over low heat for 3-5 hours.

Meat Mixture: Cook sausage, drain and crumble; set aside. Combine beef and remaining ingredients in bowl, then heat in skillet. Cook until meat is no longer red. Drain; combine with cooked sausage. Lasagne can be prepared, assembled ahead and frozen. Allow to defrost before baking.

Preparation: 2 hours	Moderately difficult	Serves: 12-16
Baking: 40 min.	Can do ahead	Can freeze

Steve & Debby Furness

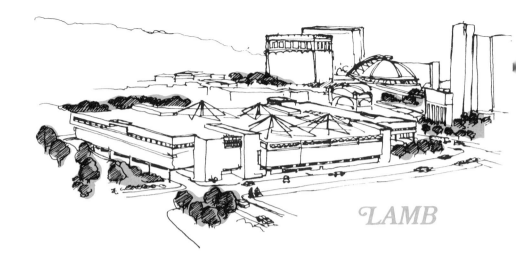

LAMB

ROAST LEG OF LAMB

5-6 lb. leg of lamb

Mint glaze:
1 onion, chopped
½ cup mint jelly
½ cup fresh parsley, chopped
1 cup beef bouillon

Honey-Mustard Glaze:
½ cup prepared mustard
½ cup honey
1 tsp. salt
½ tsp. pepper

Fresh Mint Sauce:
¼ cup mint leaves, finely
   chopped
2 tbsp. brown sugar
1 cup vinegar

Rub lamb with salt and pepper. Arrange fat side up on rack in roasting pan. Roast at 325° 28 minutes per pound for medium, or until meat thermometer registers 165°. Baste during last hour of cooking with either mint or honey-mustard glaze. Serve with mint sauce after roast has sat for 20 minutes to retain juices.

Mint glaze: Discard excess fat from roasting pan, add all ingredients and blend.

Mustard glaze: Blend mustard, honey, salt and pepper until smooth.

Prepare mint sauce at least 2 hours in advance of serving. Combine the mint leaves, sugar and vinegar and let stand for 2 hours, stirring occasionally to dissolve sugar. Serve cold with hot lamb.

Preparation: 10 min. **Easy** **Serves:** 8-10
Cooking: 2½ hours **Can do ahead**

Carmella Pennetti

84

ROAST RACK OF LAMB PERSILLÉ

Batter:
4 egg yolks
4 oz. dry white wine
3 oz. Dijon mustard

Breading:
2 oz. fresh parsley, chopped
1 oz. garlic, chopped
12 oz. fresh bread, grated
salt & pepper, to taste

Lamb Stock:
2 lbs. lamb bones & trimmings
1 onion
2 stalks celery
2 carrots
4 sprigs parsley
1 tomato
4 cloves garlic
2 bay leaves
12 peppercorns
2 qts. water

1 hotel rack of lamb, 7-8 lbs.
   split & chine bone removed
1 oz. rosemary leaves
salt & pepper, to taste

Dijon Mustard Sauce:
2 oz. flour
2 oz. butter
1 qt. lamb stock
2 oz. dry white wine
3 oz. Dijon mustard
white pepper, to taste
salt, to taste

Batter, breading and stock can be prepared the preceding day. Combine the egg yolks with wine and mustard, blend well: Cover and refrigerate the batter.

Breading: Chop parsley and garlic very finely and add to the grated bread. Salt and pepper to taste. Cover and refrigerate.

Lamb stock: Roast lamb bones at 400° until golden. Remove and place in stock pot. Pour a small amount of water into roasting pan and bring to a boil. Scrape bottom of pan to loosen any remaining bits of meat. Add to stock pot and cover with 2 quarts of water. Add remaining ingredients. Bring to a boil, reduce heat and simmer for 1½ hours. Discard bones and vegetables and strain stock.

Remove all external fat and deckel meat from the lamb, including the blade found on 1 side. Leave the eye of the rack with bones attached. With a sharp knife, cut down and up between each bone to remove the meat. Lay the meat on a baking sheet, sprinkle with rosemary; salt and pepper to taste. Roast at 400° for 25 minutes. Meat should be rare. Remove from oven, cool and cut down the center of each half: 4 bones per serving. Dip only the meat in the batter, then into bread crumbs. Line a baking sheet with foil to protect bottom of meat from burning. Transfer meat to sheet, wrap foil around bones to prevent excessive browning. Bake until desired degree of doneness: rare, 20 minutes; medium, 35 minutes; well, 45 minutes. Serve with Dijon mustard sauce.

Dijon Mustard Sauce: Melt butter, add flour and stir until a smooth roux. Gradually add the lamb stock, stirring until smooth and thickened. Add wine, stir; add mustard and season to taste. Serve warm.

Preparation: 1 hour   Difficult   Serves: 4
Cooking: 1 hour

Hyeholde Restaurant

JANE'S LAMB ROAST

"What an easy, interesting barbecue sauce"

5-6 lb. lamb roast
salt
pepper
1 jar black currant jelly or jam
1 cup ketchup

Place meat on rack in open baking pan. Salt and pepper lamb. Insert meat thermometer and roast at 325° until meat reaches a temperature of 175° for medium or 180° for well done. After one hour, baste with sauce. Combine jelly and ketchup over low heat until jelly melts. Baste every half hour. Potatoes and onions may be added after meat has cooked 1 hour.

Preparation: 10 min.   Easy   Serves: 6-8
Cooking: 3-3½ hours

Deborah Jealous

LAMB SHANKS

"A minty barbecue sauce is the topper"

flour
garlic salt
pepper
4 lamb shanks
oil
⅔ cup barbecue sauce
⅓ cup water
½ jar mint jelly

Combine flour, garlic salt and pepper. Dust shanks in flour mixture, then brown in oil. Combine the sauce, water and jelly and bring to a boil. Put lamb shanks in baking pan. Cover with sauce and bake at 350° for 2½ hours, turning occasionally.

Preparation: 15 min.   Easy   Serves: 4
Cooking: 2½ hours

Frances Merryman Rollman

BROILED LAMB STEAK

"Try these marinated steaks on your grill"

4 steaks from leg of lamb
1 clove garlic, crushed
1 tsp. salt
½ tsp. oregano
½ tsp. paprika
¼ tsp. pepper
¼ cup wine vinegar
¼ cup oil

Have steaks cut ¾" thick. Combine remaining ingredients in a shallow platter. Coat steaks on both sides; let stand at room temperature for 30 minutes to 1 hour, turning occasionally. Broil indoors or on outdoor grill, 6 minutes for rare, 7 minutes for medium per side.

Preparation: 5 min.   Easy   Serves: 4
Cooking: 12-15 min.   Must do ahead

Carmella Pennetti

LAMB RATATOUILLE

"An economical recipe using leftover lamb"

¾ lb. eggplant
olive oil
¾ lb. green peppers
butter
¾ lb. onions
¾ lb. zucchini
1 lb. cooked lamb
1 large can stewed tomatoes
2 tbsp. tomato paste
parsley leaves
garlic salt
1 tsp. basil
1 tsp. thyme
pepper
8 oz. sour cream
Parmesan cheese, grated

additional ingredients to taste:
black olives
mushrooms
whole green beans
corn

Peel eggplant and cut in 1″ cubes. Sauté in 2 tablespoons olive oil, 3-5 minutes, until lightly colored and completely cooked. Using a slotted spoon, transfer eggplant to a casserole. Cut green peppers into 1″ squares and sauté in 2 tablespoons butter for 5 minutes until tender. Transfer to casserole using slotted spoon. Slice onions thinly and sauté for 5 minutes. Add 1 tablespoon butter if needed. Transfer onions to casserole using slotted spoon. Slice zucchini and sauté for 3-5 minutes until lightly colored and tender. If more vegetables are desired, sauté lightly and continue to layer in casserole.

Sauté cooked lamb, cut into 1″ pieces, for 3 minutes. Use rosemary to season lamb first time it is cooked. Cut tomatoes into small pieces and add to lamb. Add parsley, garlic salt, tomato paste, dried basil, thyme, salt and pepper. Heat until the mixture is bubbly. Remove from heat and add sour cream. Mix thoroughly. Pour tomato and lamb mixture over the layered vegetables. Sprinkle with Parmesan cheese. Bake at 350° for 45 minutes until bubbly.

Preparation:	1 hour	Easy	Serves: 6
Cooking:	45 min.	Can do ahead	

Mrs. James H. Morgens

BROILED LAMB CHOPS

"A nice flavor change from the usual mint sauce"

8 lamb chops
salt & pepper
2 tsp. basil leaves
2 tsp. marjoram leaves
2 tsp. thyme leaves

Sprinkle chops lightly with salt and pepper. Mix herbs and rub into chops. Stack together, wrap and chill at least 1 hour. Broil 10 minutes for medium rare, 15 minutes for medium.

Preparation:	5 min.	Easy	Serves: 4
Cooking:	10-15 min.		

Chappy's Choice

LAMB CHOPS STUFFED WITH CHICKEN LIVERS

"Surely a gourmet recipe"

6 chicken livers, chopped
½ lb. mushrooms, chopped
5 tbsp. butter
salt & pepper
1 tbsp. parsley, finely chopped
6 double rib lamb chops

Sauté the livers and mushrooms in 2 tablespoons butter; do not let them brown. Season with salt and pepper. Add parsley. Trim fat from chops and slit them to make pockets. Stuff with liver mixture. Heat remaining butter in a heavy casserole, add chops and sear them over high heat on both sides. Cover casserole and bake at 350° for 25 minutes or until tender. Can skewer chops to close pockets and broil on both sides until cooked. Arrange chops on platter, pour pan juice over chops and serve.

Preparation: 20 min.   Easy   Serves: 4-6
Cooking: 25 min.   Can do ahead

Anna Rae Kitay

SHEPHERD'S PIE

"Be thrifty - use your leftover lamb"

3-4 tbsp. olive oil or drippings
1 large onion, chopped
1 clove garlic, minced
2 tomatoes, peeled & chopped
1½ lbs. minced beef or lamb,
   fresh or leftover
2 carrots, coarsely grated
salt & pepper
stock
water
parsley
bay leaf
thyme
1 tbsp. tomato puree
1 tbsp. flour
1 tbsp. butter
mashed potatoes

Heat oil or drippings in wide, shallow pan. Cook onion and garlic until brown. Add tomatoes. Cook rapidly, stirring, until all water has evaporated and sauce starts to brown. Add meat and carrots. Cook on high heat for 10 minutes or more. If using raw meat, turn often. Add half stock, half water to top of meat, but not covering. Add thyme, salt, pepper, bay leaf, tomato purée and a handful of chopped parsley. Leftover meat needs no more cooking at this point, but fresh meat should be simmered for 1½ hours. Add more stock as needed. Work flour into butter and drop into meat mixture, stirring to thicken. Cook 20 minutes longer. Put meat into a pie dish. Cover with mashed potatoes. Bake at 375° for 25 minutes until brown.

Preparation: 30 min.   Easy   Serves: 6
Cooking: 1-2½ hours   Can do ahead   Can freeze

Mrs. Simon Beloe

LAMB PIE WITH HERB CRUST
"Wonderful taste and aroma for a winter evening"

2 lbs. boneless lamb cubes
3 tbsp. flour, seasoned with salt
   & pepper
1 clove garlic, minced
3 tbsp. oil
2 cups bouillon, or ½ red wine
bouquet garni (bay leaf, thyme,
   parsley, rosemary)
18 small white onions, parboiled
18 very small new potatoes,
   scraped, or 3 large potatoes
   cut in cubes
1 cup ripe olives, pitted
2 cups peas

Herb Crust:
1 3-oz. pkg. cream cheese
½ cup butter
1¼ cups flour
½ tsp. salt
2 tsp. dill weed
2 tsp. chives, chopped

Glaze:
1 egg yolk
2 tbsp. milk or water

Dredge meat in seasoned flour. Using a deep oven dish, sauté garlic and meat in oil. When brown, add remaining ingredients, except peas, and olives. Simmer until thickened and meat is tender, about 1 hour, adding more broth if necessary. Remove bouquet garni. Cool. Add peas and olives.

Herb Crust: Mix ingredients together and chill before rolling out. Roll crust very thick into 1″ strips and arrange in lattice fashion over lamb. Glaze top of crust with egg yolk and milk; bake in preheated 400° oven until brown.

Preparation: 20 min.   **Easy**   Serves: 6
Cooking: 1½ hours

Mrs. K.B. Mellon

SPRINGTIME STEW

"Lima beans add a different touch"

1½ lbs. boneless lamb, cubed
¼ tsp. salt
generous dash pepper
2 tbsp. butter
1 cup water
2 10½-oz. cans mushroom
  gravy
½ tsp. mint flakes, crushed
4 carrots, cut into 2" pieces
12 small white onions
¼ cup white wine
1 10-oz. pkg. frozen lima beans

Season lamb with salt and pepper. Brown in butter in large heavy pan. Add gravy, water and mint. Cover. Cook over low heat 1 hour, stirring occasionally. Add carrots and onions. Cover and simmer 45 minutes longer, stirring occasionally, until vegetables are tender. Add wine and lima beans; cook 15 minutes longer.

Preparation: 15 min.   Easy   Serves: 6
Cooking: 1 hour, 45 min.   Can do ahead

Mrs. Donald Brewster

LAMB CURRY

"Curry lovers can use extra hot curry"

3 lbs. lamb shoulder, trimmed &
  cubed
2 cloves garlic, minced
4 onions, sliced
¾ cup butter or margarine
flour
3 tbsp. curry powder
3 apples, peeled, cored &
  chopped
2 lemons, sliced
4 tbsp. raisins
1 tbsp. salt
3 cups water

Sauté garlic and onions in butter until onions are golden. Roll lamb cubes in flour, sauté 10 minutes, stirring. Add curry powder and onions to lamb, simmer 5 minutes. Add remaining ingredients. Pour 3 cups water over all and bring to a boil. Reduce heat, cover and simmer mixture 1 hour. Serve with fluffy rice, rice pilaf and chutney or other curry condiments. Best if made 1 day ahead, chilled and reheated.

Preparation: 15 min.   Easy   Serves: 8
Cooking: 1½ hours   Can do ahead

Mrs. Dana M. Friedman

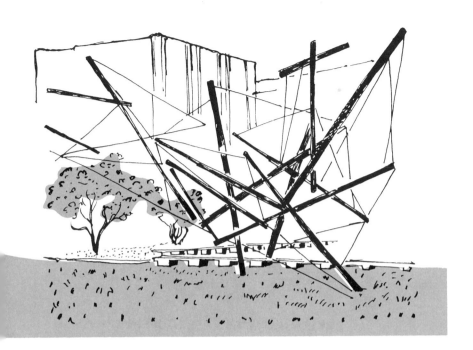

PORK & HAM

FRESH HAM

10-11 lb. fresh ham

Sauce:
½ cup soy sauce
¼ cup honey
¼ cup ketchup
2 cloves garlic, crushed,
   optional
2 tsp. ground ginger
¼ tsp. Tabasco or hot pepper
   sauce

Place a fresh ham on a rack in oven roasting pan. Bake at 325° for 35-40 minutes per pound. Bake until meat thermometer reaches185°, approximately 6 hours. About ½ hour before fully cooked, cut rind off ham and score fat. Remove rack from roaster pan and pour off grease. Place ham directly in pan and return to oven. Pour sauce over ham and bake additional ½ hour, basting frequently.

Preparation: 10 min.   Easy
Cooking: 6 hours   Can do ahead

Margaret Veland

HAM SLICE

"Very good and very easy - a winner."

½ " thick ham slice
¼ jar currant jelly
1 tbsp. prepared mustard
2 tbsp. onions, chopped

Heat ham in frying pan for 10 minutes. Remove from pan and make sauce. Heat jelly, mustard and onions together until the jelly has melted. Put ham in the sauce and heat slowly until ready to serve.

Preparation: 2 min.   Easy   Serves: 2-3
Cooking: 15 min.

Frances Merryman Rollman

BAKED HAM WITH PATÉ STUFFING

"Delicious, extravagant"

Paté Stuffing:
1 lb. mushrooms, finely chopped
½ cup onions, finely chopped
½ cup butter
1 tbsp. parsley
2 cups fine dry bread crumbs
2 4½-oz. cans liver paté
1 cup walnuts, chopped
¼ cup dry Sherry

½ ham, approximately 7 lbs.,
   fully cooked & boned
paté stuffing
⅓ cup honey
¾ cup walnuts, chopped
5-6 metal skewers (4 inch)

Stuffing: Sauté mushrooms and onion in butter until moisture has evaporated, 10 minutes. Add crumbs and parsley. Remove from heat. Work in paté, then add walnuts and Sherry. Add a tablespoon or two of Sherry if mixture seems dry.

Have ham boned. Pack as much stuffing as you can into the opening left by removal of bone. Save the rest of the stuffing and heat in a double boiler about an hour to serve along with the ham. Preheat oven to 325°. Insert skewers on open side of ham, to hold together. Bake ham approximately 2 hours. Remove ham from oven. Cut the fat in a diamond pattern and cover ham with half of the honey, sprinkle with the chopped nuts and cover with other half of the honey. Return ham to oven and bake until meat thermometer reaches 130°.

Preparation: 20-30 min.   Serves: 6
Baking: 3 hours

Mrs. K. B. Mellon

ROAST PORK FILLET IN WHITE WINE
"Wonderful on a chilly night"

4 lb. pork loin
1½ cups dry white wine
½ cup white wine vinegar
2 cloves garlic
10 peppercorns
1 bay leaf
salt & pepper
1 tsp. thyme leaves

Cut pork fillet from bones and tie with string; will weigh about 3 pounds. Combine wine, vinegar, garlic, peppercorns, bay leaf and thyme in a nonmetal baking dish just large enough to hold meat. Put pork in marinade and refrigerate overnight. Turn pork several times until ready to roast. Drain pork and sprinkle with salt and pepper. Pour ½ cup of marinade over meat and roast ½ hour per pound or until thermometer registers 170°. Let sit 15 minutes before carving.

Preparation: 10 min.   Easy   Serves: 6-8
Cooking: 1½ hours Must do ahead

Gerry Armstrong

? KEBABS
"The 64 dollar question - beef, lamb or pork"

1½ lbs. pork tenderloin, beef or lamb, cubed

Marinade:
1 oz. butter
2 onions, chopped
½ clove garlic, chopped
1 small can apricots, mashed
salt & cayenne
2 tbsp. curry powder
2 tbsp. vinegar
2 tbsp. brown sugar

Skewers:
cubes of: pineapple, green pepper, onion, nectarines

Sauté onions and garlic in butter until soft. Add other marinade ingredients and mix well. Marinate meat cubes 1 day, stirring occasionally. Drain meat, thread cubes on skewers with other ingredients. Barbecue on greased rack; baste with butter and marinade while cooking. Marinade can be heated and served with meat over Persian rice; see page 161. Cooking time: beef, 20-25 minutes; lamb, 15-20 minutes; pork, 25-30 minutes.

Preparation: 10 min.   Easy   Serves: 4
Cooking: 15-30 min. Must do ahead

Carolyn S. Hammer

SMOKY CHOPS OR CHICKEN

"Terrific leftovers - if you have any."

Sauce:
¾ cup maple syrup
¾ cup ketchup
3 tbsp. prepared mustard

Meat Dish:
4-6 thick cut pork chops
or
8-12 thin cut pork chops
or
3-5 lbs. chicken thighs or fryer
    parts
Spice Islands hickory smoke
    salt
2 large onions, sliced

Simmer sauce ingredients 10-15 minutes. Sprinkle all sides of meat liberally with smoke salt. Place in a roaster and cover with sauce. Cover the pan tightly and bake at 325° for a minimum of 2½ hours or a maximum of 4 hours. Place on gray coals for outdoor barbecue.

To prepare as a casserole, cover bottom of baking dish with onions. Place seasoned meat on top. Cover with the sauce and bake at 325° for 2½-4 hours, covered. Brown at 450° for 15 minutes, if needed.

Preparation: 10 min.	Easy	Serves: 4-6
Baking: 2½-4 hours	Can do ahead	

Patricia S. Casella

STUFFED PORK CHOPS WITH ORANGE SAUCE

"Plump raisins and crisp celery are in the stuffing."

½ cup dark raisins
2 tbsp. onion, chopped
½ cup celery, thinly sliced
2 tbsp. butter
⅓ cup hot water
1½ cups Pepperidge Farm
    seasoned stuffing mix
6 double pork chops with
    pocket for stuffing
1 6-oz. can frozen orange juice
    concentrate, thawed
2 tbsp. cornstarch
⅓ cup water, or more
¼ cup raisins

Sauté raisins, onion and celery in butter until soft. Add hot water and stuffing mix; blend. Brown chops. Fill with stuffing; secure with picks. Combine orange juice and an equal amount of water; add half to chops. Cover and cook over low heat 1 hour or until tender, adding remaining liquid as needed. Remove chops to warm platter. Add cornstarch mixed with water and remaining ¼ cup raisins to the liquid from the chops. Cook and stir until thickened. Serve over pork chops.

Preparation: 25-30 min.	Easy	Serves: 6
Cooking: 1½ hours		Can freeze

Mrs. William H. Riley

POLYNESIAN PORK

"Dark and juicy - looks lovely after four or five bastings."

4 lb. pork loin roast or 8 pork
   chops
salt
pepper
rosemary
½ cup soy sauce
½ cup ketchup
½ cup honey

Arrange chops in baking dish in single layer. Sprinkle with salt, pepper and rosemary. Combine other ingredients and pour over pork. Roast at 300° for 2-2½ hours, basting frequently. Chops can also be cooked in a crockpot - same amount of sauce - for 6 hours on high heat.

Preparation: 10 min.	Easy	Serves: 8
Baking: 2-2½ hours	Can do ahead	Can freeze

Sue Parker

PORK CHOPS ON RICE

1⅓ cups Uncle Ben's long grain
   rice, uncooked
1 10½-oz. can cream of
   chicken soup
1 10½-oz. can cream of celery
   soup
1 10½-oz. can water
6 pork chops
1 env. Lipton's dry onion soup

Sprinkle rice into 9 x 13″ pan. Heat soups and water and pour over rice. Arrange pork chops on rice. Sprinkle with dry onion soup. Cover pan with foil. Bake at 325° for 2 hours and 15 minutes without uncovering.

Preparation: 10 min.	Easy	Serves: 6
Baking: 2 hours, 15 min.		

Mrs. Allan W. Beatty

YAMS AND PORK CHOPS

"To have - 'When the frost is on the punkin.' "

3 large yams or sweet potatoes
2 large onions
4 large pork chops, 1-1¼″ thick
1 tbsp. shortening
2 tbsp. butter or margarine
3 tbsp. brown sugar
¼ tsp. maple flavoring
4 med. apples, cored &
   quartered
¼ cup pecans, walnuts or
   peanuts, coarsely chopped

Peel yams and onions. Slice into ½″ rounds. Trim all visible fat from chops. Melt shortening in skillet and brown chops on both sides. Remove from skillet, set aside. Melt butter in skillet with drippings. Mix brown sugar into drippings until smooth; stir in maple flavoring. Layer in 12 x 9 x 2″ baking dish: pork chops, onions, yams and then apples.

Pour brown sugar mixture over all and sprinkle with nuts. Cover with foil and bake at 350° 1 hour until vegetables and chops are tender. Remove foil and bake another 15 minutes.

Preparation: 20 min.	Easy	Serves: 4
Baking: 75 min.		

Cheryl W. Black

PORK AND SAUERKRAUT SUPPER

"Give this a try to bring you good luck in the New Year."

3 strips bacon, diced
6 pork chops
1 onion, diced
1 16-oz. can sauerkraut, drained
   & rinsed
1 tart apple, cut in 12 wedges
2 tsp. caraway seeds
salt & pepper
½ cup chicken broth

Brown bacon in heat-proof casserole; remove and reserve. Brown pork chops on both sides in bacon fat. Set aside. Cook onion in remaining fat until translucent. Add sauerkraut, apple wedges and seasonings; toss in fat. Add broth and reserved bacon. Arrange chops in sauerkraut, cover and bake at 350° for 1 hour or until chops are tender.

Preparation: 30 min.   Easy   Serves: 6
Baking: 1 hour   Can do ahead

Mary Ellen Reisdorf

HAM RING WITH APRICOT SAUCE

"So pretty with peas in the middle."

¾ cup Pepperidge Farm
   cornbread stuffing mix
1 cup evaporated milk
¾ lb. ground pork
¾ lb. ground ham
½ cup onion, finely chopped

Sauce:
½ cup apricot preserves,
   pressed through a strainer
1 tbsp. vinegar
¼ tsp. cloves
½ tsp. cinnamon
½ tsp. mustard

Soak cornbread stuffing in the evaporated milk. Add pork, ham and onion. Bake in a greased 5 cup ring mold for 1 hour at 375°. Drain excess fat. Unmold onto an ovenproof serving platter.

To make sauce, combine preserves, vinegar, cloves, cinnamon and mustard. Cover ham ring with this mixture. Bake 15 minutes longer at 375°. Fill center of ring with peas.

Preparation: 15 min.   Easy   Serves: 4-6
Baking: 75 min.   Can do ahead   Can freeze

Mrs. William H. Riley

SAUSAGE AND WILD RICE CASSEROLE

"Improves with age, so make a day ahead."

1 lb. link sausage
1 lb. regular sausage
2 onions, sliced
1 lb. mushrooms, sliced
1 pkg. Uncle Ben's long-grain &
 wild rice
¼ cup flour
½ cup cream
2 cups chicken stock
¼ tsp. thyme
¼ tsp. oregano

Cook sausage; sauté onions and mushrooms. Prepare rice as per package directions. Prepare thin velouté sauce by combining flour with cream. Add stock and seasonings. Blend with sausage, onions and mushrooms. Bake at 350° for ½ hour when freshly made. Adjust time if casserole has been made ahead and refrigerated or frozen.

Preparation: 30 min.	Easy	Serves: 10-12
Baking: 30 min.	Can do ahead	Can freeze

Deborah Jealous

SPINACH HAM ROLL

"Good for brunch"

Roll:
¼ cup butter or margarine
½ cup flour, unsifted
2 cups milk
½ tsp. salt
4 eggs, separated, room
 temperature

Filling:
2 tbsp. butter or margarine
½ cup onion, finely chopped
1 10-oz. pkg. frozen chopped
 spinach, cooked & well
 drained
6 oz. cooked ham, 1½ cups
 chopped
1 tsp. prepared mustard
½ tsp. salt
⅛ tsp. pepper
1 5-oz. pkg. spiced cheese with
 garlic and herbs

Preheat oven to 400°. Grease a 15½ x 10½" jellyroll pan and line the bottom with wax paper. Grease again and sprinkle with flour; remove excess. Melt butter in 2 quart saucepan. Add flour and cook, stirring constantly with a whisk, to make a smooth roux. Gradually stir in milk and salt and cook, stirring, until thickened. Remove from heat; stir in egg yolks, one at a time. Cool mixture to lukewarm. Beat egg whites until soft peaks form. Fold into egg yolk mixture and spread evenly in prepared pan. Bake 30 minutes until puffed and browned.

Filling: While roll bakes, melt butter in skillet; add onion and sauté until tender. Add spinach and cook 30 seconds. Stir in remaining ingredients and cook over low heat until cheese melts. Keep warm. When roll is done, immediately invert onto towel. Spread filling and roll up from 15" side, jellyroll fashion. Can keep warm at 200° for 30 minutes.

Preparation: 30 min.	Moderately difficult	Yield: 15 1" slices
Cooking: 30 min.	Can do ahead	

Mrs. Richard Greene

BARBECUE RIBS

"Think Big - great for a crowd."

30 lbs. ribs
1 46-oz. can pineapple juice
6-oz. soy sauce
2 bottles prepared barbecue
   sauce
Worcestershire sauce, to taste
Tabasco sauce, to taste
salt & pepper
8-oz. Rose's lime juice

The secret to these ribs is long, long slow cooking, having coals as low as possible, gray. While ribs cook, mix remaining ingredients for basting sauce. Do not baste until ribs are completely cooked and fat has cooked away, then ribs will act as a sponge.

Preparation: 5 min.   Easy   Serves: 15-20
Cooking: 4-6 hours

Mrs. Furman South, III

OREGON SPARERIBS

"Lemon adds zippity-do-da."

6 lbs. spareribs
1 lemon, thinly sliced
1 onion, finely chopped
1 tsp. salt
1 tsp. pepper

Sauce:
1 tsp. chili powder
1 tbsp. celery seed
¼ cup brown sugar
¼ cup vinegar
1 cup ketchup
¼ cup Worcestershire
dash Tabasco
2 cups water

Cut spareribs into individual serving pieces and place in a shallow baking pan in 1 layer. Cover with lemon slices, onion, salt and pepper. Bake at 450° for 45 minutes. Drain. Make sauce by combining all ingredients and heat to boiling. Pour hot sauce over ribs and bake at 350° for 1½ hours, turning once.

Preparation: 10 min.   Easy   Serves: 4
Baking: 2 hours, 15 min.

Catharine M. Boyd

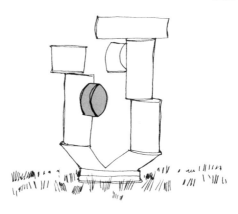

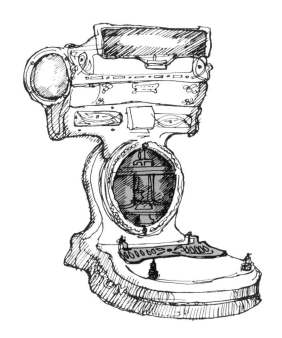

VEAL

VEAL WITH SOUR CREAM SAUCE

"Sesame seeds and Parmesan cheese - poetry"

¼ cup flour
1 tsp. salt
1 tsp. paprika
½ tsp. poultry seasoning
¼ tsp. pepper
1½ lbs. veal steak, cut in
  serving pieces
2 tbsp. oil
1 cup soft bread crumbs
2 tbsp. butter, melted
½ cup Parmesan cheese,
  grated
¼ cup sesame seeds, toasted
½ cup hot water
1 can cream of chicken soup
1 cup sour cream

Combine flour and seasonings; dredge meat in mixture. Brown meat in hot oil. Arrange in a 10 x 6 x 1½" baking dish and reserve drippings. Combine bread crumbs, butter, cheese and sesame seeds and spoon over meat. Add water to meat drippings; stir and pour around meat. Bake at 350° for 45-50 minutes, or until meat is tender. Mix soup and sour cream together, heat and serve with veal.

| Preparation: | 25-30 min. | Easy | Serves: 4 |
| Cooking: | 45-50 min. | Can do ahead | Can freeze |

Mrs. Furman South, III

PAUPIETTES DE VEAU
"Worth every minute"

Duxelles:
½ lb. mushrooms, trimmed & chopped
¼ cup onions, minced
2 shallots, minced
2 tbsp. butter
1 tbsp. oil
salt & pepper

Filling:
½ cup cooked ham, minced
3 tbsp. butter
¼ cup bread crumbs
1 egg, beaten
2 tbsp. parsley, chopped
thyme
salt & pepper

12 veal scallops, flattened
flour
2 tbsp. butter
2 tbsp. oil
½ cup white wine
1½ cups white veal or chicken stock

Bouquet Garni:
4 sprigs parsley
1 bay leaf
¼ tsp. thyme
1 clove garlic, bruised

1 tbsp. prepared mustard
1 tbsp. arrowroot, optional
1 tbsp. water
salt & pepper

Prepare duxelles by placing handsful of mushrooms in tea towel and squeezing hard to remove moisture. Place butter and oil in skillet, add mushrooms, onions and shallots; sauté until moisture has evaporated. Add salt and pepper; set aside. Sauté ham in butter; push mixture to one side of the pan. Add additional tablespoon butter and brown the crumbs in it. Transfer mixture to a bowl and add duxelles. Add just enough of the beaten egg to moisten the filling. Add seasonings and mix. Spread the filling on the scallops and roll them up, tucking in ends and tying with heavy thread. Dust paupiettes with flour.

In a skillet just large enough to hold them, brown paupiettes in butter and oil, a few at a time. Add more fat if necessary. Pour off any remaining fat. Add wine and deglaze pan, scraping well. Return meat to pan, add stock and bouquet garni and bring to a boil. Reduce heat, cover, and simmer for 15-20 minutes, or until tender. Discard bouquet garni, cut off thread, and remove to a serving platter. Reduce pan liquids over high heat to 1⅓ cups. Thin the mustard with 1 table-spoon of sauce and return to pan. If is thin, stir in mixed arrowroot and water. Add salt and pepper, return meat to pan, turning the paupiettes in the sauce until they are glazed and thoroughly heated. Pour sauce over paupiettes and serve.

Preparation: 75 min. Difficult Serves: 4-6
Cooking: 15-20 min. Can do ahead

Susan Gasparich

VEAL SCALLOPINE WITH PEPPERS

"Would you believe this is really easy - read the recipe"

Sauce:
1 onion, finely chopped
1 clove garlic, minced
2 tbsp. olive oil
1 tbsp. butter
1 2-lb. 3-oz. can Italian plum
  tomatoes
1 tsp. salt
½ tsp. pepper
1 tsp. sugar
1 tsp. oregano, pulverized
2 tbsp. Romano cheese, grated

1 lb. mushrooms, thinly sliced
½ tsp. salt
¼ tsp. pepper
1 tsp. olive oil

4-5 green bell peppers, cut into
  1" pieces
4 tbsp. olive oil
½ tsp. salt
dash pepper

2 lbs. Italian-style veal cutlets
2 tbsp. olive oil
2 tbsp. butter
½ cup flour
1½ tsp. salt
½ tsp. pepper
⅓ cup Sherry

Sauté the onion and garlic in olive oil and butter until translucent. Add the tomatoes, salt, pepper and sugar and bring to a boil. Partially cover and cook for 30 minutes over medium high heat. Add oregano and cheese and cook 5 minutes longer. Set aside. Sauté the mushrooms for 3-4 minutes over high heat with the butter, oil, salt, pepper and garlic. Remove from heat. Sauté the green peppers for 3 minutes until crisp-tender in 1 tablespoon oil with salt and pepper. Remove at once with a slotted spoon.

Pound the scallopine between wax paper prior to cutting into 1½ " squares. Flour veal pieces lightly in the flour blended with salt and pepper; transfer to a jellyroll pan in a single layer. Heat a heavy frying pan, add the olive oil and butter and fry the scallopine 2 minutes on each side. Remove as soon as they brown lightly. Combine the veal, mushrooms, peppers and sauce in a large casserole. Add the Sherry. Heat over low heat or bake at 325° for 30 minutes. Garnish with a ring of parsley.

To freeze: prepare sauce, mushrooms, peppers and veal as directed. Freeze each separately. Let ingredients come to room temperature, assemble casserole and heat as indicated above.

Preparation: 1 hour   Easy   Serves: 5
Cooking: 30 min.   Can do ahead   Can freeze

Mrs. William H. Riley

VEAL PAPRIKASH

"Serve with noodles and broccoli — even kids love it"

3 tbsp. oil
2 lb. veal, cubed
1 lb. lean pork, cubed
⅓ cup flour
1 cup Vermouth
1 cup hot water
1 4-oz. can mushrooms,
  undrained
3 tbsp. parsley, chopped
1 large onion, chopped
1½ tsp. paprika
1 6-oz. can tomato paste
salt & pepper
1 cup sour cream

Heat oil in heavy skillet. Dredge meat in flour and brown slowly on all sides; add any remaining flour. Add remaining ingredients except sour cream. Blend until smooth; cover and simmer 1½ hours or bake in 300° oven. Add sour cream and serve.

Preparation:	30 min.	Easy	Serves: 6-8
Cooking:	1½ hours	Can do ahead	

Mrs. Jon McCarthy

VEAL WITH MUSHROOMS A LA CREME

"This is sooo good - topped with melted cheese"

1½ lbs. veal, cut into 8 thin
  slices
3 tbsp. butter
1 tbsp. shallots, finely chopped
½ lb. mushrooms, thinly sliced
2 tbsp. dry white wine
1 cup heavy cream
8 thin slices prosciutto or boiled
  ham
8 thin slices Swiss cheese

Pound veal lightly with a mallet to flatten. Melt 2 tablespoons butter in a saucepan and add shallots. Cook briefly and add mushrooms; salt and pepper to taste. Sprinkle with wine and cook about 10 seconds. Add cream. Cook down over high heat until cream has a sauce-like consistency, 3-5 minutes. Set aside. Heat remaining butter in a heavy skillet. Add veal and brown lightly on one side, about 2 minutes, turn and cook, about 2 more minutes. Transfer veal to a platter. Cover each slice of veal with a slice of prosciutto, trimmed to fit the veal neatly or folded over. Spoon creamed mushrooms on ham. Top each serving with a slice of cheese and broil briefly until cheese melts.

Preparation:	20 min.	Moderately difficult	Serves: 4-6
Cooking:	10 min.	Serve immediately	

Jeanne Ahern

SCALLOPINE OF VEAL A LA MARSALA

"A special dish for a special occasion"

1½ lbs. veal scallops, sliced ⅜"
   thick, pounded to ¼"
salt
black pepper, freshly ground
flour
2 tbsp. butter
2 tbsp. olive oil
½ cup mushrooms, sliced; fresh
   or canned
½ cup dry Marsala wine
½ cup chicken or beef stock
¼ cup cream
2 tbsp. butter, softened

Season the veal with salt and pepper, dip in flour and shake off excess. In a heavy skillet, mix butter and olive oil over low heat. When foam subsides, add 3 or 4 scallops at a time and brown for 3 minutes on each side. Transfer veal to a plate. Pour off fat, leaving a thin film on the bottom; add mushrooms and brown lightly. Add the Marsala and ¼ cup stock; boil briskly for 1-2 minutes. Return veal to skillet, cover pan and simmer 10 minutes. Baste veal occasionally. To serve, transfer the scallops to plate. Add ¼ cup stock to the sauce remaining in skillet and boil briskly. When the sauce has reduced considerably, add cream and correct seasoning. Remove from heat, stir in butter and pour the sauce over the scallops. Serve with buttered vermicelli or noodles.

Preparation: 1 hour   Easy   Serves: 4
Cooking: 45 min.

Joseph D. Parrotto, Jr.
University Club

TARRAGON VEAL STEW

"A snap for a working girl"

2 lbs. veal stew meat
seasoned flour
3 tbsp. butter
2 shallots, chopped
2 cloves garlic, minced
1 cup dry white wine
1 cup beef broth or stock
1 tsp. dried tarragon
½ tsp. lemon peel, grated
2 tbsp. heavy cream
1 tsp. lemon juice
almonds, garnish

Flour meat and brown in 2 tablespoons of butter. Place meat in crockpot. Sauté shallots and garlic; add to veal. Deglaze pan with wine and broth, scraping pan well. Add tarragon and lemon peel. Pour over veal. Cover and cook 3 hours on high, or 8 hours on low. Before serving, ladle pan juices into a saucepan. Boil until reduced and slightly thickened. Add cream and lemon juice and remaining butter. Return to pot and heat thoroughly. Serve on pilaf or rice with toasted almonds.

Preparation: 15 minutes   Easy   Serves: 6
Cooking: 3-8 hours   Can do ahead

Mrs. Robinson F. Barker

EMINCÉ DE VEAU LAUSANNOISE

"A classic Swiss recipe — elegant and rich"

2 tbsp. shallots or scallions, chopped
¼ cup butter, not margarine
1 lb. veal, cut into 1 x ¼ x ¼ " strips
½ lb. fresh mushrooms, sliced
3 tbsp. flour
½ cup dry white wine
3 tbsp. fresh tarragon, chopped, or 1 tsp. dry
1 tsp. salt
freshly ground pepper
¼ -1 cup whipping cream
parsley, chopped

Sauté shallots in butter, 2-3 minutes. Add veal and mushrooms, raise heat and sauté until veal is barely cooked. Sprinkle with flour, stir to coat and brown flour slightly. Add wine and tarragon, stirring until thickened. Simmer 5 minutes; add salt and pepper. Reduce heat, thin sauce with cream; heat gently, do not let cream boil. Adjust seasonings to taste. Garnish with chopped parsley and serve over buttered noodles. Can be done ahead up to adding cream.

Preparation: 20 min.   Easy   Serves: 4
Cooking: 15 min.   Can do ahead

Dina Fulmer

STUFFED GREEN PEPPERS

"Moist and tender — much better than ordinary stuffed peppers"

8 green peppers
2 tbsp. butter
1 lb. veal & 1 lb. pork, ground together
1 cup seasoned bread crumbs
1 med. onion, grated
2 tbsp. oregano
3 eggs, beaten
1½ cups tomatoes, crushed
1 cup Parmesan cheese, grated
salt & pepper

Clean and hollow peppers. Brown meat in butter. Add remaining ingredients and mix together. Stuff peppers. Place in baking dish with 1" water. Cover and bake at 350° for 1½ hours.

Preparation: 20 min.   Easy   Serves: 6-8
Cooking: 1½ hours   Can do ahead

Mrs. Furman South, III

VEAL EXOTICA

"A super combination of flavors"

8 thin slices zucchini
1 cup chicken or veal stock
flour
8 veal scallops, flattened
4-6 tbsp. butter
2 tbsp. olive oil
1½ tbsp. shallots, minced
⅓ cup dry white wine
½ cup Italian plum tomatoes,
  seeded & chopped
½ cup mushrooms, finely
  chopped
1 tbsp. parsley, minced
¼ tsp. basil
¼ tsp. salt
pepper, freshly ground
8 thin slices Provolone cheese

Cook zucchini in chicken stock until slightly softened; remove and set aside. Reserve stock. Lightly flour veal; brown in 2 tablespoons butter and olive oil. Remove veal. In same pan, sauté shallots in 2 tablespoons of butter until translucent. Add ⅓ cup chicken stock, wine, tomatoes, mushrooms, and seasonings. Heat gently for 20 minutes; transfer to small saucepan and keep warm. Return veal to frying pan, cover with zucchini and cheese. Cook over low heat until cheese melts. Pour sauce over veal and serve.

Preparation:	30 min.	Easy	Serves: 4
Cooking:	30 min.	Can do ahead	

J.A. Raub

SWEETBREADS EUGENIE

"Incredibly tender and very mild"

4 pairs sweetbreads
2 tbsp. lemon juice
flour
salt & pepper
4 tbsp. butter
4 oz. Chablis, or more
8 mushrooms, sliced
½ pt. light cream
4 tbsp. butter
4 slices Virginia ham, cooked
whole mushroom caps, garnish

Soak sweetbreads in cold water for 2 hours, changing water at least once. Blanch in cold water to cover with 2 tablespoons lemon juice. Simmer 20 minutes; drain. Firm by immediately plunging into cold water. When cool, drain. Trim and remove covering membrane. Refrigerate for 2 hours. Roll sweetbreads in seasoned flour. Sauté in hot butter, 8-10 minutes, until lightly browned. Add wine and mushrooms; simmer 5 minutes. Add cream and butter; simmer 3 minutes. Warm ham slices. Place ham on warmed platter, top with sweetbreads and mushroom caps. Pour sauce over all.

Preparation:	4½ hours	Moderately difficult	Serves: 8
Cooking:	20 min.		

Mrs. M. G. Patton

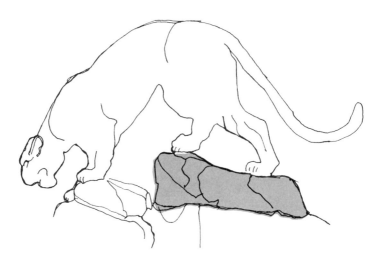

POULTRY & GAME

BREAST OF CHICKEN CASINO DE LA MONTE CARLO

"This is a truly different and delicious recipe"

4 14-16 oz. chicken breasts
almond paste
butter
pear halves
paprika
butter, melted

Sauce:
3 tbsp. butter
1 cup orange juice
½ cup maple syrup
1 tsp. sugar, optional
2 oz. Cognac
2-3 tbsp. cornstarch
water

Bone chicken breasts and spread out flat, skin side down. Combine almond paste and butter to a soft consistency. Spread approximately 2 teaspoons of mixture inside breasts. Place a pear half in the middle of each breast and wrap the breast tightly around it. Turn breast over, skin side up, sprinkle with paprika and brush with butter. Bake at 350° for 30-45 minutes or until cooked.

Sauce: During last 10 minutes of baking, make sauce by combining the butter, juice, syrup, sugar, if desired, and Cognac in saucepan; bring to a boil. Add cornstarch diluted with water and cook, stirring, until sauce is thickened and smooth. To serve, spread toast points with currant jelly and place them around breasts. Pour sauce over breasts.

Preparation: 25 min.
Cooking: 45 min.

Moderately easy Serves: 4
Can do ahead

Chef Decanini
Edgeworth Club

106

BAKED CHICKEN SUPREME

"Great flavor and so easy - good enough for company"

1 cup sour cream
2 tbsp. lemon juice
2 tsp. Worcestershire sauce
1 tsp. celery salt
1 tsp. paprika
2 cloves garlic, minced
2 tsp. salt
¼ tsp. pepper
4 chicken breasts, split & boned
1¾ cups corn flakes, crushed
¼ cup butter, melted

Mix sour cream, juice, Worcestershire sauce and seasonings together. Arrange chicken breasts in flat baking dish; spread marinade over pieces and marinate overnight in refrigerator. Preheat oven to 350°. Remove chicken, allowing as much marinade as possible to cling to all pieces and roll in crushed corn flakes. Bake, uncovered, for 45 minutes. Spoon butter over chicken and bake 10-15 minutes.

Preparation:	15 min.	Easy	Serves: 8
Cooking:	1 hour	Must do ahead	

Mrs. Frank C. McClellan

PEACH STUFFED CHICKEN BREASTS

6 whole chicken breasts,
  skinned & boned
1½ tsp. salt
⅛ tsp. pepper
3 fresh peaches, peeled & diced
½ cup onion, chopped
½ cup cashews, coarsely
  chopped
⅛ tsp. ground ginger
½ cup butter or margarine

Creamy Peach Sauce:
2 fresh peaches, peeled & sliced
8-oz. carton sour cream
½ cup brown sugar, firmly
  packed
2 tsp. Dijon mustard
1 tbsp. Brandy
¼ tsp. salt

Place each chicken breast on a sheet of waxed paper and flatten to ¼". Sprinkle salt and pepper over inside of each breast; set chicken aside. Combine peaches, onions, cashews and ginger, stirring well. Place ¼ cup filling in center of each breast; fold side of chicken over filling and secure with a toothpick. Melt butter in a 13 x 9 x 2" baking pan; place breasts top side down in butter. Bake, covered, at 375° for 25 minutes. Uncover, turn chicken and bake 20 minutes more. Serve with creamy peach sauce.
Sauce: In saucepan, combine ingredients and cook over low heat 8 minutes.

Preparation:	1 hour	Can do ahead	Serves: 6
Cooking:	45 min.		

Mrs. Robert Mitchell

ELEGANT CHICKEN HOLLANDAISE

"Cook this to celebrate something - it's special"

8 chicken breasts, boned
2 egg whites, lightly beaten with
  1 tbsp. water
1 cup seasoned bread crumbs
½ cup butter, melted
2 10-oz. pkgs. frozen spinach,
  cooked & drained
½ cup sour cream

Hollandaise Sauce:
3 tbsp. butter
3 tbsp. water
3 egg yolks
3 tbsp. lemon juice

Dip breasts in egg whites, then bread crumbs. Melt butter in baking pan and arrange breasts in pan—can be done a day ahead or frozen and then baked at 350° for 35 minutes. Shortly before serving, warm spinach with sour cream in double boiler. Make nests of spinach on a platter and arrange cooked breasts on top. Drizzle Hollandaise on top of each. To prepare sauce, melt butter, add remaining ingredients and whisk until thickened and smooth.

Preparation: 30 min.   Moderately difficult   Serves: 8
Cooking: 1 hour   Can do ahead

Laura Y. Theis

BREAST OF CHICKEN 'MONTE CARLO'

4 single breasts, boned &
  skinned
4 slices Virginia ham
4 whole apricots, fresh or
  canned
salt
white pepper
4 eggs
¼ cup milk
flour and bread crumbs
3 tbsp. olive oil
2 tbsp. butter

Sauce:
½ cup chicken stock, fresh or
  canned
¼ cup cream
2 tbsp. maple syrup

Split breast open and flatten. Place 1 slice of ham and 1 apricot in center and fold over. Press ends together with end of fork handle. Season breast with salt and pepper. Mix eggs with milk. Dip breast into flour, then dip into egg mixture. Shake off excess and dip into bread crumbs. In a 10 or 12" skillet, melt butter and olive oil. When foam subsides, add breasts and brown on 1 side, turn over and place in 350° oven for 25-30 minutes. Remove from oven and place on platter. Prepare sauce. Discard the grease, add chicken stock and cream and boil briskly. Add maple syrup and simmer 3-4 minutes. Strain sauce and pour over breasts.

Preparation: 45 min.   Easy   Serves: 4
Cooking: 25-30 min.   Can do ahead

Joseph D. Parrotto, Jr.
University Club

CHICKEN CELESTE

"Heavenly"

2 whole chicken breasts, skinned, boned & cut into strips
salt
lemon-pepper seasoning
1 tbsp. vegetable oil
1 tbsp. butter
1 8-oz. can pineapple chunks
1 13-oz. can chicken broth
1 cup carrots, sliced
4 oz. frozen snow peas
½ cup raisins
1 tbsp. soy sauce
1 tbsp. sugar
1 tbsp. vinegar
1 tbsp. cornstarch mixture with juice from pineapple

Season the chicken with salt and lemon-pepper. Heat vegetable oil and butter in skillet and stir-fry the chicken: chicken turns white when done in 4 minutes or so. Drain pineapple, reserving liquid, and add to chicken. Set aside. Heat the chicken broth and cook the carrots in it until crisp-tender. Remove from heat and add snow peas and raisins. Season with salt and pepper. Pour the broth mixture over the chicken and mix all together. Mix cornstarch with pineapple juice; add the soy sauce, sugar and vinegar. Cook and stir until thickened and smooth. Add some broth to this paste; stir, and then return to chicken mixture to thicken and season it. Heat thoroughly and serve over rice.

Preparation: 30 min.   Easy   Serves: 4

Mrs. David McCandless

CHICKEN ROYAL HUNGARIAN

½ lb. bacon, cut in ¼" wide julienne strips
½ onion, sliced
2 med. green peppers, cut in ¼" julienne strips
2 tbsp. paprika
½ gallon white chicken sauce
8 large chicken breasts, cooked & cut in large julienne strips
½ cup sour cream
salt

Cook the bacon until golden brown. Add onions and green peppers and sauté a few minutes. Blend in the paprika and chicken sauce. Add the chicken and cook 5 minutes more. Blend in sour cream, and correct seasoning.

Preparation: 20 min.   Easy   Serves: 15
Cooking: 15 min.   Can freeze

Joseph D. Parrotto, Jr.
University Club

CHICKEN BREAST SANTA MONICA

6 small whole chicken breasts, boned & skinned or 3 large breasts, split, boned & skinned
curry powder
Accent
1 large banana
¼ lb. smoked ham, thinly sliced
egg
bread crumbs
butter, melted

Flatten chicken breasts and season with a pinch of curry powder and Accent. Cut banana in ½ and divide each ½ into 3 pieces. Wrap each piece in a small slice of ham. Place in center of each breast. Brush rims with beaten egg. Fold meat around stuffing. Refrigerate 30 minutes. Dip in beaten egg, then crumbs. Bake at 350° for 20 minutes, occasionally sprinkling with butter. Serve with your favorite curry sauce.

Preparation: 15 min.   **Easy**   Serves: 6
Cooking: 20-30 min. **Must do ahead**

Mrs. P. J. Hannaway

CHICKEN BREASTS PIQUANT
"A low-calorie treat"

¾ cups chicken stock or bouillon
juice of 1 lemon
1 clove garlic, crushed, or equivalent in powder
½ tsp. salt
⅛ tsp. pepper
½ tsp. dried onion
1 tsp. paprika
2 chicken breasts split

Combine first 7 ingredients in skillet and bring to a boil. Add chicken, cover and simmer 15 minutes. Turn chicken and simmer 15 minutes longer or until tender. Sprinkle with parsley.

Preparation: 10 min.   **Easy**   Serves: 4
Cooking: 30 min.

Joanne Taylor

ORTEGA PEPPER CHICKEN

4 chicken breasts
1 can cream of mushroom soup
1 can cream of chicken soup
1 cup mushrooms
1 pkg. corn tortillas (10), torn in pieces
1½ cups Cheddar cheese, finely cut
1 cup milk or half & half
2 cans Ortega chili peppers, seeded & chopped

Bake chicken in foil until tender. Cut into pieces. Mix soups, mushrooms and milk. Layer tortillas, chicken, cheese and peppers in a baking dish. Pour soup mixture over all and top with tortillas and cheese. Bake at 350° for 1 hour until brown and bubbly. Let sit a day before baking.

Preparation: 30-40 min.   Easy   Serves: 6-8
Cooking: 1 hour   Must do ahead

Mrs. Nathan Pearson

STUFFED CHICKEN BREASTS
"Company fare you can be proud of"

4 whole chicken breasts, split & boned
1½ cups Gruyere or Swiss cheese, grated
¼ lb. salami, finely diced
½ cups scallions, chopped
1 egg, beaten
bread crumbs
¼ cup butter or margarine
¼ cup flour
2 cups milk
parsley

Preheat oven to 350°. Pound chicken with mallet until ¼" thick; set aside. Toss 1 cup of the cheese with salami and onion. Put ¼ cup of the cheese mixture in the center of each breast. Roll up and fasten with a toothpick. Dip chicken in egg, then roll in bread crumbs. Place in greased pan and bake for 40 minutes. Make sauce: Melt butter in saucepan, stir in flour, gradually stir in milk. Cook until thickened. Add remaining cheese and cook just until cheese melts. Pour over chicken, garnish with parsley.

Preparation: 45 min.   Moderately easy   Serves: 8
Baking: 40 min.

Mrs. Francis J. Sullivan

CHICKEN AND ARTICHOKES
"Artichoke lovers should sneak in an extra jar or two."

16 small chicken parts with bone in, or 8 whole breasts, split, boned & skinned
salt, pepper & paprika
6 tbsp. butter
1 lb. mushrooms, sliced
2 tbsp. flour
⅔ cups chicken bouillon
¼ cup Sherry
2-3 6-oz. jars marinated artichoke hearts, drained

Season chicken parts with salt, pepper and paprika. Brown 12-15 minutes in 4 tablespoons butter. Remove chicken from pan and place in casserole. Add 2 tablespoons butter to skillet and sauté mushrooms about 5 minutes. Stir in flour, bouillon and Sherry. Cook 5 minutes, stirring frequently. Arrange artichokes over chicken. Pour sauce over top. Bake, covered, for 1 hour at 375°.

Preparation: 20-30 min.   Easy   Serves: 8
Cooking: 1 hour   Can freeze

Mrs. Kenneth Jenkins

CHICKEN AND ASPARAGUS CASSEROLE

"Very much like Chicken Divan, only better"

2 chicken breasts, split, skinned
   & boned
¼ tsp. pepper
½ cup corn oil
2 pkgs. frozen asparagus
1 10½-oz. can condensed
   cream of chicken soup
½ tsp. curry powder
½ cup mayonnaise
1 tsp. lemon juice
1 cup sharp Cheddar cheese,
   grated

Sprinkle chicken with pepper. Sauté chicken in part of the oil over medium heat until white. Use more oil as needed. Remove and drain on paper towels. Cook asparagus according to directions; drain. In 1½ quart casserole, place asparagus, then chicken. Cover with sauce made of soup, mayonnaise, lemon juice and curry powder. Sprinkle with cheese and bake at 375° for 30 minutes.

Preparation:	30 min.	Easy	Serves: 4
Cooking:	30 min.		Can freeze

Clara Obern

CHICKEN CURRY MOUSSE

"A beauty for a warm summer evening"

2 envs. unflavored gelatin
½ cup water
4 chicken bouillon cubes
2 cups boiling water
⅓ cup lemon juice
1 tsp. dry mustard
1 tbsp. curry powder
1 tsp. salt
1½ cups mayonnaise
3 cups chicken, cooked & diced
1 cup celery, chopped
¼ cup green pepper, chopped
½ cup heavy cream, whipped
parsley sprigs

In large bowl, sprinkle gelatin over ½ cup cold water; let stand 5 minutes to soften. Dissolve bouillon cubes in boiling water. Add to gelatin, stirring to dissolve. Stir in lemon juice, mustard, curry powder, salt and mayonnaise. Refrigerate until consistency of unbeaten egg whites, about 1 hour, 15 minutes. Fold in chicken, celery, green pepper and whipped cream. Turn into 1½ quart mold; refrigerate 2 hours until firm. Unmold and garnish wtih parsley.

Preparation: 1 hour   Easy   Serves: 6-8
   Must do ahead

Mrs. Edwin H. Gott, Jr.

CHICKEN A LA ALMOND

1 15-oz. can pineapple chunks
  in natural juice
3 stalks celery, cut in 1″ pieces
1 onion, coarsely chopped
½ cup whole almonds, toasted
4 cups cooked chicken, diced
1 green pepper, cut in 1″ pieces

Sauce:
1 cup chicken bouillon
½ cup Sherry or white wine,
  optional
¼ cup soy sauce
¼ cup cornstarch
1 tsp. ground ginger
¼ tsp. garlic powder

Drain pineapple chunks and reserve juice. Combine pineapple chunks, chicken, celery, green pepper, onion and almonds. Place in casserole dish. Combine juice, bouillon, soy sauce, cornstarch and flavorings until dissolved. Heat on medium for 10 minutes until slightly thickened. Add to casserole. Bake at 375° for 45 minutes. Serve over rice.

Preparation:	1 hour	Easy	Serves: 6
Cooking:	45 min.	Can do ahead	

Mrs. George H. Craig, Jr.

CHICKEN CURRY

"Comments range from 'Delicious!' to 'Terrific!' "

2 chicken breasts, cooked
4 onions, chopped
6-7 tbsp. flour
1 qt. chicken stock
1 cup raisins
1 cup crushed pineapple, drained
juice of ½ lemon
1 cup coffee cream
1 tbsp. curry powder
salt, to taste
rice

Cook, drain and bone chicken breasts. Reserve stock. Sauté onions in butter until soft and brown. Stir flour into butter and blend. Cook over low heat, gradually adding chicken stock; stir until smooth. Add chicken and remaining ingredients. Simmer 1 hour or more.

Serve over rice with preferred condiments. Any of the following are suitable condiments: chopped nuts, pepper, onion, canned fried onion rings, candied ginger, olives, hard-boiled egg, crumbled bacon, chutney, coconut.

Preparation:	1 hour	Moderately easy	Serves: 4-6
Cooking:	1 hour		Can freeze

Mrs. Edwin H. Gott, Jr.

ARREZZO CHICKEN FENNEL

3-3½ lbs. chicken, cut up
salt & pepper, to taste
¼-⅓ cup Bertolli's olive oil
¼ cup fennel seed
onion slices

Rinse chicken and pat dry. Season with salt and pepper. Pour a small amount of olive oil in the bottom of a 9 x 13" baking pan. Place chicken in pan and cover with fennel seed and slices of onion. Place aluminum foil over the pan and seal edges. Bake at 350° for 1 hour. Remove foil and brown for 20-30 minutes. Baste occasionally. Delightful cold for a picnic.

Preparation:	15 min.	Easy	Serves: 4
Cooking:	1½ hours	Can do ahead	Can freeze

Mrs. Thomas Celli

CAROLINA CHICKEN
"Nothing could be finer"

2 2 lb. broilers or 12 fryer
   pieces
1 cup milk
1 tsp. salt
¼ tsp. pepper
½ cup flour
fat for deep frying
1 cup chicken stock
juice of 1 lemon

Cut chicken in half. Remove wing tips and neck to make stock. Combine salt, pepper and milk. Dip chicken in milk, dredge in flour and remove excess flour. Deep fry at 350° until golden brown, 10-15 minutes. Cover bottom of roasting pan with stock. Place chicken pieces in pan, sprinkle with lemon juice and bake, covered, at 350° for 45 minutes.

Preparation:	20-25 min.	Easy	Serves: 4
Baking:	45 min.	Can do ahead	

Mrs. Edward J. Klein

TOM'S FAVORITE CHICKEN

1 cup raw rice
2 cups chicken broth, or more
¼ cup butter
1 chicken, cut up or 4 breasts,
   split
1 4-oz. can mushrooms, drained
   or ½ lb. fresh, sliced
salt & pepper
2 tbsp. dry Vermouth
1 cup milk
Parmesan cheese
Hollandaise sauce

Cook rice in chicken broth. Brown chicken in butter and reserve drippings. Sprinkle with salt and pepper. Add mushrooms, Vermouth and milk. Cover loosely and cook until chicken is tender. Place rice in shallow, greased casserole and sprinkle liberally with Parmesan cheese. Pour reserved drippings over rice. Place chicken on rice and cover with Hollandaise sauce. Bake at 350° for 30 minutes.

Preparation:	1½ hours	Easy	Serves: 4
Baking:	30 min.		

Ann Selck

CHICKEN AND LOBSTER

"Have this on your anniversary, birthday, etc."

¼ cup butter
¼ cup onion, minced
¼ cup flour
1¼ cups milk
½ cup half & half
2 chicken bouillon cubes
1½ cups cooked chicken, cubed
¾ cup lobster, cubed, can use canned
1 4-oz. can mushrooms
½ cup Madeira
egg yolk, beaten
salt & pepper, to taste
almonds, optional

Sauté onion in butter. Blend in flour, milk, cream, bouillon and cook, stirring, until thickened. Add chicken, lobster and mushrooms; heat to serving temperature. Add wine, salt and pepper. Blend small amount of hot sauce with egg yolk; return to pan. Cook over low heat, stirring, until thickened. Serve over rice and top with toasted almonds.

Preparation: 20 min.   Can do ahead   Serves: 4

Mrs. Charles E. Hultman

CHICKEN SCALLOPS AMANDINE

6 chicken breasts, boned & skinned
1½ cups blanched almonds, sliced
1½ cups stale bread crumbs
⅓ cup parsley, minced
3 tbsp. lemon rind, grated
3 egg whites
¾ cup clarified butter
lemon slices

Flatten chicken breasts between waxed paper until they are ¼″ thick. Sprinkle with salt and pepper. Toast almonds lightly. In a shallow bowl, combine bread crumbs, almonds, parsley and lemon rind. In another shallow bowl, beat egg whites lightly. Dip the breasts in the egg whites and then crumb mixture, pressing the mixture into them. Chill the breasts on a baking sheet for 30 minutes. In a large skillet, sauté the chicken in ¾ cup clarified butter for 4-8 minutes on each side or until they are just cooked and golden. Transfer to a heated platter and garnish with slices of lemon.

Preparation: 15 min.   Easy   Serves: 6
Cooking: 10-20 min.   Can do ahead

Julie Pitcavage

CHICKEN CRAB VALENTINE

"Serve this to your sweetie - it's special"

6 tbsp. butter
6 tbsp. flour
1½ cups chicken broth
1½ tsp. salt
¾ tsp. paprika
1 clove garlic, crushed
⅛ tsp. nutmeg
5-6 drops pepper sauce
2½ cups sour cream
3 cups cooked chicken, cubed
2 7½-oz. cans crabmeat
8 slices bacon, cooked &
   crumbled
2 10-oz. pkgs. frozen peas,
   cooked

In double boiler, melt butter; add flour and stir until smooth. Gradually add broth and cook, stirring, until smooth and thickened. Add seasonings. Cover and cook 10-15 minutes. Add sour cream and continue heating over simmering water. Add chicken and crabmeat. Mix lightly. Heat 10-15 minutes. Add crumbled bacon, if desired. Serve in a chafing dish or arrange on platter surrounded by peas. Best served with walnut rice, page 160.

Preparation: 30 min.　　Easy　　　　　Serves: 8-10
Cooking:　　1 hour　　Can do ahead

Dorothy Hartley

TURKEY IN RICE PIE SHELL

"Remember this for your leftover turkey"

2½ cups cooked long grain rice
2 eggs, beaten
¼ cup butter, melted
¼ tsp. pepper, freshly ground
¼ cup butter
5 tbsp. flour
2 cups chicken broth
2 tbsp. dry Vermouth
½ tsp. pepper, freshly ground
4 tbsp. onion, chopped
½ cup fresh mushrooms, sliced
2 cups cooked turkey, diced
¼ cup Parmesan cheese,
   freshly grated
butter

Combine cooked rice with eggs, butter and pepper. Press into an ungreased 9" pie plate. Melt butter in a saucepan and blend in flour. Cook for 2 minutes: do not allow to brown. Add chicken broth, Vermouth and pepper. Cook, stirring, until mixture bubbles and thickens. Add onions and mushrooms which have been sautéed in butter for 5 minutes. Add turkey and mix well. Pour into prepared pie shell. Sprinkle cheese on top and dot with butter. Bake for 45 minutes at 350°. Let stand 5-10 minutes before cutting into wedges for serving.

Preparation: 20 min.　　Easy　　　　　Serves: 6
Baking:　　45 min.

Mrs. Edward A. Montgomery, Jr.

"SMOKED" TURKEY BREAST
"For those who love that smokey outdoor flavor"

1 turkey breast
1 stick margarine, melted
1 bottle liquid smoke
½ bottle barbecue sauce

Clean, rinse and pat turkey breast dry. Place in a "Brown-N-Bag" with other ingredients. Marinate for several hours. Add salt and pepper. Punch or cut several air holes in bag. Bake for 1 hour at 350°. Reduce to 250° and cook until thermometer registers done.

Preparation: 10 min.	Easy	Serves: 6-8
Cooking: 2-3 hours	Must do ahead	

Beth Smith

ROAST CHICKEN WITH ROSEMARY AND MARMALADE
"Makes beautiful gravy"

1 heaping tbsp. fresh, or 2 tsp. dry rosemary
3 tbsp. butter
3 tbsp. English marmalade
salt
3-3½ lb. chicken

Crush rosemary with mortar and pestle or whirl through blender. Put butter, marmalade and rosemary through processor or blender briefly. Without removing skin, gently separate skin from breast and legs. Pat chicken dry. Spread about half the butter mixture under breast and leg skin. Rub rest of butter mixture over outside of skin. Salt lightly. Roast in 400° oven for 5 minutes, lower temperature to 350° and roast for 1½ hours, basting occasionally with pan juices. Reserve juices for gravy.

Preparation: 30 min.	Moderately difficult	Serves: 4
Cooking: 1½ hours	Can do ahead	

Mrs. K. B. Mellon

SPECIAL POULTRY STUFFING

1 stick butter, melted
1 med. onion, chopped
1 green pepper, seeded & diced
1 heaping cup celery, diced
1 2-oz. jar pimentos, diced
1 cup pecans, split lengthwise
1 cup water
1 8-oz. bag Pepperidge Farm herb-seasoned stuffing

Melt butter. Add onion, green pepper, celery and pimento and sauté 1 minute. Add pecans and toss lightly. Add water. Cover and simmer 3 minutes. Add stuffing and mix well. Remove from heat and cool before stuffing poultry or pork chops.

Preparation: 25 min.	Easy	Yields: Stuffing for 8-10 lb.
Cooking: 10 min.	Can freeze	turkey or chicken

Mrs. Dennis L. Leonetti

SUPER DUCK

4-5 lb. duckling
1 tsp. salt & pepper
1 tsp. rosemary
½ apple, chopped
½ cup celery, chopped
1 small onion, minced
1 tbsp. lemon juice
bacon
⅛ tsp. paprika
1 tbsp. Burgundy or Claret
duck juice, degreased
1 cup currant jelly
1 cup Burgundy or Claret
juice of ½ lemon
½ tbsp. Worcestershire sauce
paprika, salt & pepper

Clean duck. Sprinkle rosemary, salt and pepper inside. Combine apple, celery, onion and lemon juice and stuff duck. Place bacon on breast and sprinkle with paprika. Just before placing in oven put 1 tablespoon wine in cavity. Bake 35-45 minutes at 550° depending on size of duck. Baste every 15 minutes, once with wine. Melt currant jelly in wine. Add lemon juice, Worcestershire sauce, several shakes of paprika and salt and pepper to taste. Simmer 10 minutes, add duck juices and simmer 5-10 minutes more.

Preparation: 15 min.   Easy
Cooking: 45 min.

Serves: 2

Mrs. Charles E. Hultman

FRUIT DRESSING FOR TURKEY

1 cup onion, chopped
1 cup celery, chopped
1 stick butter
2 cans sliced unseasoned pie
  apples
1 15-oz. pkg. white raisins, or
  less
1 bay leaf, crumbled
dash garlic powder
1 tsp. Worcestershire sauce
salt & pepper
thyme
¼ cup Sherry
1 16-oz. pkg. seasoned dressing
  cubes

Sauté celery and onion lightly in butter. Add apples and cook until onions and celery are not quite soft. Add remaining ingredients and mix well. Pour over bread cubes and mix thoroughly. Add more butter, poultry stock or water if more moisture is desired. Stuff bird or cook in a greased casserole at 350° for 30 minutes. Ingredients may be chopped ahead, but mix just before stuffing the bird. Can be done ahead if baked in a casserole.

Preparation: 45 min.   Easy
Cooking: 30 min.

Yield: Dressing for 16 lb.
       turkey

Mrs. Howard J. Morgens

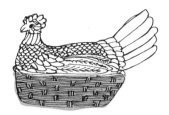

DUCKLING A L'ORANGE

¼ cup dark raisins
2 tbsp. Brandy
large apple, peeled & diced
½ 1-lb. can Food Club
  mandarin oranges, drained
  (save second half for sauce)
½ cup cooked long grain rice
1 tbsp. butter
sage
rosemary
4-5 lb. duckling
Burgundy
sweet orange marmalade

Sauce:
1½ tbsp. butter
duck liver
2 tbsp. Brandy
1½ tbsp. flour
1 tbsp. orange peel, grated
¼ tsp. garlic, minced
twist of pepper
¼ tsp. catsup
¼ cup Tang or orange juice
½ cup chicken bouillon
⅛ cup Burgundy
⅛ cup orange marmalade,
  sweet, not Seville
2nd half of mandarin oranges

Soak raisins in Brandy for 10 minutes. Drain and toss with apples and oranges. Add rice and butter and stir. Sprinkle with sage and pinch of rubbed rosemary. Toss. Rinse duckling and pat dry. Stuff loosely with dressing. Be aggressive and puncture the duck all over with a skewer to let the fat run out during cooking. Place on rack, sprayed with Pam to facilitate turning, in shallow roasting pan. Drip Burgundy over the duckling. Roast at 425° for 30 minutes, breast side up. Reduce heat to 375° and turn duckling; pour off fat from pan. Drizzle again with Burgundy. Roast about an hour, repeat turning and again drain fat. Do not add more wine. Roast 30 minutes more. Baste with orange marmalade, or liqueur, and roast 10-20 minutes. Let cool 10 minutes. Carve into halves and serve with sauce.

Sauce: Heat butter and sauté liver. Heat Brandy, ignite and pour over liver. Remove liver. Add peel and garlic and sauté 2-3 minutes. Stir in flour, pepper, catsup; add juice gradually with bouillon, Burgundy and marmalade. Bring to a boil; reduce heat and simmer 15 minutes, stirring. Chop liver very finely. Add liver and oranges and warm, stirring a few times.

Preparation: 20 min.
Cooking: 2 hours, 20 min.

Serves: 2

Carolyn S. Hammer

ROAST LEG OF VENISON WITH CUMBERLAND SAUCE

4-5 lb. leg of venison
salt water
buttermilk
½ lb. sliced bacon

Cumberland Sauce:
1 tsp. dry mustard
1 tbsp. brown sugar
¼ tsp. ground ginger
¼ tsp. ground cloves
¼ tsp. salt
1½ cups Ruby Port
½ cup seedless raisins
dash cayenne
2 tsp. cornstarch
2 tbsp. cold water
¼ cup currant jelly
¼ cup orange juice
2 tbsp. lemon juice
1 tbsp. orange rind, grated

Soak venison in salt water 1 day, refrigerated. Drain and rinse. Soak venison in buttermilk 2 days, refrigerated; turn several times. Remove meat and place on rack in shallow roasting pan. Cover with bacon slices. Roast at 350°, 20 minutes per pound. Can be turned halfway through roasting and again covered with bacon. Let stand 20 minutes before carving.

Cumberland Sauce: Combine first 8 ingredients and simmer, covered, in a small saucepan for 10 minutes. Dissolve cornstarch in water and add to sauce, stirring and cooking for 2-3 minutes. Add remaining ingredients and combine thoroughly. Serve hot. Will keep in refrigerator for 2 weeks.

| Preparation: 10 min. | Easy | Serves: 6-8 |
| Sauce: 15 min. | Must do ahead | Yield: 2 cups |

Carolyn S. Hammer

ROAST PHEASANT WITH BRANDY AND CREAM

8 shallots sliced
½ cup butter
3 pheasants
½ cup Brandy
2 cups chicken bouillon
salt
pepper
6 slices of bacon
¼ cup prepared horseradish
2 cups heavy cream

Preheat oven to 350°. Sauté shallots in roasting pan for 5 minutes. Add pheasants and sauté for 15 minutes over high heat, until brown on all sides. Pour Brandy into ladle, warm over match, light Brandy and flame pheasants. When flames die, add bouillon, salt and pepper. Place bacon strips over pheasant breasts and roast for 45 minutes at 375°; basting frequently. Stir horseradish and cream into pan juices and roast 15 minutes longer, and continue to baste. Serve pheasants and sauce with wild rice.

| Preparation: 25 min. | Moderately easy | Serves: 6 |
| Cooking 1 hour | | |

Mrs. Charles E. Hultman

WILD DUCK

1 tbsp. flour
½ cup orange juice
¼ cup dry white wine
1 wild duck
butter, melted
salt
½ apple

Preheat oven to 350°. Shake flour into oven cooking bag and put in shallow roasting pan. Pour wine and orange juice into bag, mixing well with flour. Brush duck with butter, sprinkle with salt, inside and out. Place apple in cavity and put duck in bag. Close bag with twist tie and make 6 ½" slits in top of bag. Cook 1½ hours or until tender. One duck, depending on size, will serve 1-2 people. Serve with your favorite game sauce.

Preparation: 5 min.   Easy   Serves: 1-2

Mrs. Edwin H. Gott, Jr.

VENISON FLAMBÉ

2 med. size venison round
   steaks, ¾" thick,
1½ tsp. salt
½ tsp. pepper
1 tsp. dry mustard
3 tbsp. butter
1 large onion, chopped
2 tbsp. tomato paste
1 cup dry white wine (Chablis)
⅓ cup Brandy

Rinse, trim and cut venison steaks into 6 individual pieces. Dry with paper towel. Combine salt, pepper and mustard; rub well into sides of meat. Melt 1 tablespoon butter in large skillet and brown steaks on both sides. Remove venison and set aside. Melt 2 tablespoons of butter and sauté the onion until golden. Stir in tomato paste and white wine. Return venison to pan, cover and simmer over low heat for 45 minutes or until tender. Arrange individual steaks on serving platter. Pour Brandy over them and ignite.

Preparation: 10 min.   Easy   Serves: 6
Cooking   1 hour

Carol B. Gamble

VENISON, MOOSE OR ELK ROAST

2 tbsp. flour
1 cup dry red wine
3-4 lb. roast
salt
bay leaf
6-8 whole cloves
1 onion, diced
1 tsp. thyme

Preheat oven to 325°. Spoon flour into oven cooking bag and shake until well covered. Place bag in shallow roasting pan and add wine, stirring to mix with flour. Rub roast with salt and put in bag. Add remaining ingredients, placing around roast. Close with twist tie and make six ½" cuts in the top of bag. Cook 2 hours or until a thermometer records an internal temperature of 180° or 20 minutes per pound. Use liquid as sauce. Plum sauce is also good with this.

Preparation: 10 min.   Easy   Serves: 6-8
Baking   2-2½ hours   Can do ahead

Mrs. Edwin H. Gott, Jr.

HENRIETTA'S CRABCAKES

"These can be small cocktail goodies or large dinner goodies."

1 med. onion, diced
1 cup celery, diced
¾ cup green or red pepper, diced
1 tsp. parsley, chopped
½ stick margarine
1 tbsp. cornstarch
½ cup milk
salt & pepper, to taste
juice of 1 lemon
1 lb. crabmeat, fresh or canned
2 eggs
12-14 Ritz crackers, crushed
crushed hot red pepper, to taste
seasoned bread crumbs
oil

Sauté onion, celery, peppers and parsley in margarine. Sprinkle mixture with cornstarch and stir. Add milk, salt and pepper. Mix. Let cool. Squeeze lemon over cleaned crabmeat. Add eggs to mixture and stir. Add crushed crackers and red pepper and mix well. Toss cooled vegetables with crab. Refrigerate several hours. Form chilled mixture into small cocktail patties or larger sized patties. Roll in crumbs and brown in oil. Serve with lemon wedges and tartar or cocktail sauce.

Preparation: 1 hour   Easy

Yield: 6 3" cakes
Can freeze

Eleanora Mitchell

122

STONE HARBOR CRAB BRUNCH

"You don't have to go to New Jersey to enjoy this."

2 eggs
2 cups milk
2 cups seasoned croutons
½ lb. Cheddar cheese, grated
1 tbsp. dry onion, minced
1 tbsp. parsley flakes, minced
salt & pepper, to taste
1 lb. lump crabmeat, picked
   over
Parmesan cheese, grated

Beat eggs. Mix in all other ingredients except Parmesan cheese. Pour into greased shallow casserole. Top with sprinkling of Parmesan cheese. Bake in 325° oven 1 hour, or until knife inserted in center comes out clean.

Preparation: 15 min.   Easy   Serves: 6
Cooking: 1 hour   Can do ahead

Mrs. Dana M. Friedman

MUSSELS IN HOT PEPPER SAUCE

"A nice change from mussels in broth"

2 qts. mussels
1-2 cups water
1 tbsp. oil
1 large clove garlic
½ cup onion, chopped
6 oz. tomato paste
2½ cups liquid from mussels
½ tsp. oregano
¼ tsp. red pepper flakes, crushed,
   or to taste

Rinse mussels in colander several times with cold water and scrub with a stiff brush to remove sand. Place mussels in pan with 1-2 cups water; steam until open. Reserve liquid, add enough water to make 2½ cups liquid and set aside. Heat oil. Sauté garlic and onion. Add remaining ingredients and simmer 30 minutes. Put mussels, in their shells, in a shallow baking dish. Cover with sauce. Bake at 425° for 15 minutes. Serve on the half-shell. *Note:* It might be necessary to strain reserved broth.

Preparation: 45 min.   Moderately difficult   Serves: 4
Cooking: 15 min.

Mrs. K. B. Mellon

PITTSBURGH
Three Rivers
REGATTA
AUGUST 4-10, 1980

SALMON EN CROUTE

"It's fun to work with frozen patty shells"

2 tbsp. butter, melted
1 onion, finely chopped
1 pkg. frozen chopped spinach
1 3-oz. pkg. cream cheese
salt & pepper
1 pkg. Pepperidge Farm frozen
   patty shells
16 oz. red salmon
1 lemon
½ cup Parmesan cheese,
   grated
egg whites, beaten

Sauté onions in butter until translucent. Add frozen spinach, cover and cook over low heat for 5 minutes. Add cream cheese, salt and pepper. Remove from heat. Let shells thaw slightly and roll on floured board into 6" or 8" squares. Place salmon in middle and squeeze lemon over it. Add equal portions of spinach. Place 1 tablespoon Parmesan on top. Bring outer edges into center and squeeze together. Brush with beaten egg whites. Bake at 450° for 10-15 minutes. Can be served with a white sauce combined with mushrooms, Cheddar cheese and paprika.

Preparation: 10 min.   Easy   Serves: 4-6
Cooking: 15 min.

Suzonne Smith -

SALMON NEWBURG SOUFFLÉ

"Asparagus adds color and flavor"

¼ cup onion, chopped
½ cup margarine
½ cup flour
1 tsp. salt
dash white pepper
2 cups milk
4 oz. Swiss cheese, shredded
½ tsp. dry mustard
½ cup milk
2 tbsp. dry Sherry
1 8-oz. can salmon
1 pkg. asparagus, cooked & cut
   in 1" pieces
4 egg whites
4 egg yolks

Cook onions in margarine until soft. Stir in flour, salt and pepper and cook until bubbly. Gradually add milk, stirring constantly until thickened. Boil 1 minute. Remove sauce from heat. Measure 1 cup sauce and set aside. Add cheese and mustard to sauce in pan and stir until cheese melts. Add milk and Sherry to reserved sauce. Fold in salmon and asparagus. Spoon into an 8 cup soufflé dish, pushing the salmon and asparagus against sides of the dish. Beat egg whites to soft peaks. Beat egg yolks at high speed, then beat in cheese mixture until smooth. Fold into egg whites. Pour over mixture in soufflé dish. Bake at 350° for 45 minutes.

Preparation: 50 min.   Easy   Serves: 4-6
Baking: 45 min.

Linda Manley

FILLETS OF VIRGINIA SPOTS AMANDINE VERONIQUE

"An elegant company dish"

6 fillets of Virginia spots,
    approximately 3-oz. each
¼ cup milk
seasoned flour
peanut oil
½ cup butter
¼ cup almonds, sliced
½ cup canned seedless grapes,
    drained
lemon juice
parsley, finely chopped

Add milk to barely cover fish and soak for 15 minutes. Pat fillets dry and dredge in seasoned flour. In skillet, add peanut oil to a depth of ¼". When hot, cook the fillets on both sides, 10 minutes, until golden brown. Transfer fillets to a hot platter and discard oil. Add butter to the skillet and when it starts to foam, add the sliced almonds and shake the skillet until almonds are a light golden color. Immediately add the seedless grapes, sauté for a few minutes and pour over the fillets. Sprinkle with lemon juice and garnish with lemon slices dipped in parsley.

Preparation: 10 min.	Easy	Serves: 2-3
Cooking: 20 min.		

Nick Coletti, Chef
Duquesne Club

SHRIMP AND SCALLOP QUICHE

"Hot, warm or cold - a super delicious quiche"

crust for 1 10" pie
½ to ¾ lb. med. shrimp,
    cleaned & cut into ½"
    pieces.
½ lb. scallops cut into ½"
    pieces
4 scallions, chopped
3 tbsp. butter or margarine
1 tbsp. Sherry
5 eggs
1 cup heavy cream
¾ cup milk
2 tbsp. flour
⅛ tsp. nutmeg
1 tsp. salt
½ lb. Swiss cheese, diced, 1½
    cups

Preheat oven to 425°. Sauté shrimp, scallops and scallions in 1 tablespoon butter and Sherry until cooked. Set aside to cool and drain thoroughly. Make filling by beating eggs with cream, milk, flour, salt and nutmeg. Melt remaining butter and whisk into filling. Spoon seafood into crust. Sprinkle with ¾ of Swiss cheese. Pour filling mixture over the cheese, sprinkle remaining cheese on top. Bake 15 minutes at 425°, then 40 minutes at 325° until knife inserted in center comes out clean.

Preparation: 35 min.	Easy	Serves: 8
Cooking: 55 min.	Can do ahead	

Michelle G. Smyser

LANGOSTINOS SUPREME

"Lobster lovers - this supreme is superb"

1 small stalk celery with leaves
3 carrots, sliced
2 large onions
juice of 1 lemon
¼ tsp. sugar
4 bay leaves
½ cup dry white wine
white pepper & salt
4 cups water with 2 tsp.
  seafood base
8 tbsp. butter
8 tbsp. flour
½ cup cream, or milk
2-4 tbsp. butter
¾-1½ lbs. fresh mushrooms,
  peeled & sliced
½ cup frozen peas
1 cup cheese, grated
24-oz. pkg. langostinos

Combine first 9 ingredients with the water in medium saucepan. Bring to a boil, reduce heat and simmer 20-30 minutes. Strain and set aside. Melt butter in pan over medium heat. Stir in flour. Remove from heat and gradually stir in 1½ cups reserved liquid. Return to heat and cook until thickened. Add cream or milk and season to taste with salt and pepper. Sauté mushrooms and peas in 2 tablespoons butter. Add cheese, mushrooms and peas to the sauce. When ready to serve, mix langostinos with the sauce and heat until the sauce bubbles and langostinos are completely heated. Serve over rice pilaf.

Preparation: 45 min.   Easy   Serves: 8
Cooking: 25 min.   Can do ahead

La Casa Domia

SHRIMP AND RICE CASSEROLE

"Marvelous for a buffet"

1 lb. raw shrimp
1 stalk celery
1 small onion, quartered
juice of 1 lemon
2 bay leaves
½ cup rice, uncooked
1 clove garlic, crushed
1 tsp. salt
juice of 1 lemon
dash pepper
2 cups mushroom soup,
  undiluted
2 tbsp. onion, grated
2 tbsp. butter
1 tbsp. parsley, chopped
Swiss cheese, thinly sliced
paprika
3 tbsp. butter, optional
parsley, garnish

Cook shrimp in water with celery stalk, onion, lemon juice and bay leaves. Cool. Cook rice in water with crushed garlic: cooked rice should equal 1½ cups. Add salt, lemon juice, pepper, soup, onion, butter and parsley to cooked rice. Mix. Add shrimp. Pour into a greased casserole. Cover with thin slices of Swiss cheese. Top with lumps of butter and paprika. Bake at 350° for 40 minutes. Garnish with parsley.

Preparation: 45 min.   Easy   Serves: 4
Cooking: 40 min.   Can do ahead

Mrs. William H. Geng

BARBECUE SALMON STEAKS
"Couldn't be easier"

salmon steaks
mayonnaise

Spread both sides of salmon steaks liberally with mayonnaise. Barbecue over medium flame or coals for 10 minutes. Turn, reduce flame to low and cook until fish flakes, about 15 minutes.

Preparation: 5 min.   **Easy**
Cooking: 25 min.

Nancy F. Lawton

FABULOUS SCAMPI
"You can't make shrimp any better than this."

3 lbs. jumbo shrimp, peeled &
   deveined
2 extra-large eggs, beaten with
   salt & pepper

Flour blend:
1 cup flour
2 tsp. salt
½ tsp. pepper

Sauce:
6 tbsp. butter
8 tbsp. olive oil
6 cloves garlic, minced
2 cups fresh bread crumbs
1 cup-plus fresh parsley,
   chopped & tightly packed
4 tbsp. lemon juice
1 tsp. salt
¼ tsp. pepper
⅓ cup water to add to crumb
   mixture for spreading
   consistency

Split each raw shrimp down the back. Pound a little to flatten. With scissor, make 1 cut on the outside of the tail to prevent curling. Drain shrimp. Place shrimp into egg mixture and dip each shrimp individually into the flour blend. Shake off excess flour and place the shrimp, loosely touching, on a teflon jellyroll pan which has been lightly greased with olive oil.

Sauce: Chop parsley in a processor or water-chop in blender and drain. In a large skillet, melt butter, add olive oil and sauté the garlic. Add bread crumbs, parsley, lemon juice, salt and pepper and enough water to make the consistency spreadable. Be generous with the parsley, as the parsley cuts the garlic. Spread this mixture over the scampi on the trays. This freezes well on the trays, wrapped in heavy duty foil, for up to six months. Defrost before serving. To serve: broil 8 minutes. Then bake at 325° for another 8 minutes.

Preparation: 3 hours   **Moderately difficult**   Serves: 8
Cooking: 16 min.   **Can do ahead**   Can freeze

Mrs. William H. Riley

DILLY FISH FILLETS

"Sour cream and dill - a happy combination"

1 stick butter or margarine
¼ tsp. thyme
1 bay leaf
1 tbsp. onion, minced
1 tbsp. fresh dill, chopped or ¾
  tsp. dill weed
¼ tsp. salt
⅓ tsp. pepper, freshly ground
1 tsp. sugar
1 cup sour cream
2 lbs. flounder, sole or haddock
  fillets

Prepare sauce: Melt butter, remove from heat, add thyme, bay leaf, onion, dill, salt, pepper, sugar and sour cream. Season fillets lightly with salt and pepper. Arrange on flat, buttered baking dish. Spread sauce over fillets. Bake at 375° for 15-20 minutes until fish can be flaked with a fork.

Preparation: 10 min.   Easy   Serves: 4
Cooking: 20 min.

Mrs. Frank C. McClellan

BAKED FISH FILLETS

"Neat servings of rolled fillets"

8 fillets of flounder or sole,
  skinned & boned
salt & freshly ground pepper, to
  taste
3 tbsp. butter
4 tsp. shallots, finely chopped
¼ cup dry white wine
¼ cup heavy cream
¼ cup fine fresh bread crumbs
1 tbsp. parsley, finely chopped

Preheat oven to 400°. Sprinkle fish fillets lightly with salt and pepper. Roll each of the fillets gently. With 1 tablespoon butter, grease a baking dish, large enough to hold the fish rolls in one layer. Sprinkle the dish with salt, pepper and 3 teaspoons of shallots. Arrange fish rolls on top, seam side down. Pour wine and cream over fish. Sprinkle

evenly with salt, pepper, bread crumbs, parsley and the remaining teaspoon of shallots. Melt the remaining butter and pour over all. Bak 20 minutes or until the fish rolls are cooked and the crumbs are lightl browned.

Preparation: 45 min.   Moderate   Serves: 4
Cooking: 20 min.

Jeanne Ahern

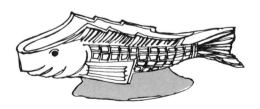

SOLE CALEDONIA
"So pretty with green asparagus and cherry tomatoes."

1 lb. sole fillets
½ cup dry white wine
1 cup frozen cut asparagus
½ cup cherry tomatoes, halved
½ cup mushrooms, sliced
2 tbsp. margarine
2 tbsp. flour
½ tsp. salt
dash pepper
1¼ cups milk
1 egg yolk, lightly beaten
1 cup soft bread crumbs
¼ cup Parmesan cheese,
   grated

Poach sole fillets in ¼ cup wine for 2-3 minutes in a covered saucepan. Drain and arrange in baking dish. Season with salt. Top with cooked asparagus, cherry tomatoes and mushrooms. Sauce: Heat margarine, add flour, salt and pepper and stir to blend. Gradually add milk, blending well. Mix 2 tablespoons of sauce into egg yolks, stir and add to sauce. Add remaining wine. Pour over fillets. Combine bread crumbs and cheese. Sprinkle over all. Bake, 30 minutes, uncovered, at 350°.

Preparation: 30 min.	Easy	Serves: 2-4
Cooking: 30 min.		

Terry Webb

DISHWASHER POACHED FISH
"Cook your whole catch"

trout or other fish
butter
lemon juice

Put each fish on a sheet of foil; add butter and lemon juice. Seal tightly. Place sealed packages in dishwasher, skip the detergent, and run through entire cycle. Open foil and serve.

Thomas Lawton

SOLE IN WINE SAUCE
"A divine divan"

1½ lbs. broccoli
1½ lbs. sole fillets
juice of 1 lemon
1 cup white table wine, heated
1 cup fresh mushrooms, sliced
2 tbsp. butter
2 tbsp. flour
½ cup light cream
½ tsp. salt
1 cup sharp Cheddar cheese,
   grated

Cook broccoli until tender. Sprinkle the sole with lemon juice and let stand for a few minutes. Drain and poach in the heated wine. Reserve wine. Place fish and broccoli in shallow baking dish. Sauté mushrooms lightly in butter. Blend in the flour; stir in cream and ½ cup of the reserved wine. Cook and stir until mixture boils and thickens. Blend in salt and cheese and stir over low heat until cheese is melted. Pour over fish. Bake at 350° for 20-30 minutes. Serve at once. Can prepare ahead up to baking.

Preparation: 20-30 min.	Easy	Serves: 6
Baking: 30 min.	Can do ahead	

Mrs. Douglas A. Jones

BROILED SOLE
"An old favorite - lovely and easy"

1 large or 4 small fillets of sole
¼ cup butter, melted
½ tsp. salt
½ tsp. garlic salt
½ tsp. paprika
dash pepper

Line shallow pan with foil and brush with melted butter. Lay fish on foil, meaty side up. Sprinkle with seasonings and dribble with rest of melted butter. Broil 12-15 minutes.

Sauce:
½ cup slivered almonds
⅓ cup butter
2 tbsp. lemon juice
2 tbsp. fresh parsley

Sauce: Sauté almonds in butter; add lemon and parsley. Pour over fish and serve.

Preparation: 10 min.   Easy   Serves: 4
Cooking: 12-15 min.

Mrs. Malcolm Hay, Jr.

BROILED ORIENTAL SWORDFISH STEAKS
"Fish lovers' delight"

1 or 2 swordfish steaks, 1"
    thick
¼ cup soy sauce
¼ cup olive oil
¼ cup Sherry
2 cloves garlic, finely chopped
1 tbsp. fresh ginger, finely
    chopped
1 tbsp. orange peel, grated

Combine the marinade ingredients and marinate fish 1 hour, turning several times. Place steaks on oiled rack in a broiling pan and broil 4" from heat for total of 10 minutes. Turn once during cooking and brush well with marinade. Allow 10 minutes cooking time per inch of maximum thickness.

Preparation: 5 min.   Serves: 4
Cooking: 10 min.

Marlene Parrish

FISH WITH VEGETABLE DRESSING

4 tbsp. butter
1 bunch scallions
1½-2 cups fresh parsley
1 cup celery, coarsely chopped
1-1½ cups tomatoes, coarsely
    chopped
¼ cup bread crumbs
white fish fillets: sole, flounder
salt & pepper
lemon butter:
1 or 2 tbsp. lemon juice
1 stick butter

Trim onions leaving as much green as possible. Melt butter and sauté onions and celery; add parsley, tomatoes and bread crumbs. Spread this mixture on bottom of baking dish. Top with fish fillets. Season fish and dot with butter or margarine. Bake in 350° oven for ½ hour. To serve, pour warm lemon butter over fish and filling. Pass extra lemon butter.

Preparation: 20 min.   Easy   Serves: 3-4
Cooking: 30 min.

Mrs. Charles Dithrich

WILD RICE SEAFOOD CASSEROLE

"Warm or cold - a casserole for a special occasion"

1¼ cups Uncle Ben's wild rice,
  cooked without seasoning
1 green pepper, diced
1 cup celery, diced
1 Bermuda onion, diced
1 lb. mushrooms, sliced
1 lb. lump crabmeat, cooked
1 lb. shrimp, cleaned
1 tsp. curry powder
1 tsp. Worcestershire sauce
1½ cups mayonnaise
salt & pepper, to taste
parsley, minced, optional
buttered bread crumbs, optional

Mix all ingredients and put in greased serving casserole. Bake 45 minutes at 350°. Garnish with minced parsley and buttered bread crumbs, if desired. Serve immediately.

Preparation: 30 min.	Easy	Serves: 8
Baking: 45 min.	Can do ahead	

Mrs. Dana M. Friedman

ZARZUELA

"A fantastic seafood feast"

¼ cup olive oil
1 cup onion, chopped
1 tbsp. garlic, chopped
2 small red peppers, chopped
6 tomatoes, skinned & chopped
1 bay leaf, crumbled
⅛ tsp. ground saffron
1 tsp. salt
pepper
3 cups water
½ cup white wine
1 tbsp. lemon juice
1½ lbs. lobster, cut in 1″ pieces
12 mussels in shells
12 clams in shells
12 large shrimp, peeled
½ lb. scallops, halved

In large casserole, sauté first 4 ingredients 5 minutes. Add tomatoes and seasonings and boil until pasty. Add water, wine and lemon juice and bring to a boil. Add lobster, mussels and clams and cook 10 minutes. Add shrimp and scallops; cook until shrimp turn pink and shells open. Be careful not to overcook the seafood.

Preparation: 1½ hours	Easy	Serves: 6
Cooking: 40 min.		

Betsy Von Dreele

SEAFOOD CONTINENTAL

½ cup light olive oil
1 clove garlic
1 lb. mushrooms, sliced
4 chicken breasts, skinned &
  boned
salt & pepper
flour
1 lb. can crabmeat
½ lb. can lobster meat,
  shredded
1 can langostino bisque
1 18-oz. can tomatoes
3 tsp. basil
2 tsp. salt
½ tsp. pepper
3 tbsp. fresh parsley, chopped

Sauté garlic in hot oil in a large skillet; discard garlic when it has turned golden. Sauté mushrooms and transfer to casserole. Cut chicken into chunks; dust with flour seasoned with salt and pepper. Sauté in oil until golden brown. Place chicken and all remaining ingredients, except parsley, in a chafing dish or casserole and mix lightly to blend. Bake at 300° for 45 minutes or on low flame of chafing dish. Serve over rice and garnish with parsley.

Preparation: 25-30 min.   Easy   Serves: 8
Cooking: 45 min.   Can do ahead

Nancy Toomey

SHRIMP SAUTÉ
"Gourmet shrimp in 5 minutes"

1 16-oz. pkg. frozen shrimp,
  cleaned & deveined
½ cup butter
¾ tsp. garlic salt
1 tbsp. flour
¼ - ½ cup dry white wine
1 tsp. parsley

Rinse shrimp in strainer under hot water to thaw. Drain. Stir garlic salt and flour into butter in large skillet until butter is melted. Add shrimp. Cook over medium heat until shrimp turn pink. Stir in remaining ingredients. Heat until hot and bubbly. Serve with hot rice.

Preparation: 5 min.   Easy   Serves: 3-4
Cooking: 10 min.

Mrs. John G. Zimmerman, Jr.

132

HALIBUT SALAD

"How about halibut instead of tunafish salad"

2 halibut steaks
2 carrots
4 celery stalks, with leaves
2 cloves garlic
3 tbsp. vinegar
6 eggs, hard-boiled
1 cup celery, finely chopped
juice of 1 onion
salt
Accent
lemon pepper
mayonnaise

Add first 5 ingredients to boiling water. Simmer 1 hour and cool. Remove dark meat from halibut. Flake white meat of halibut; add finely chopped egg whites, celery, onion juice, salt, Accent and plenty of lemon pepper. Moisten salad with mayonnaise. Serve on lettuce; garnish with paprika, lemon wedges and green pepper rings, or serve as an hors d'oeuvre with crackers.

Preparation: 2 hours   Easy   Can do ahead
Cooking: 1 hour

Guen Larson

EXOTIC SHRIMP SALAD IN AVOCADO SHELLS

"Crunchy and creamy"

2 lbs. shrimp, cooked & shelled
1 cup sliced water chestnuts, halved
¼ cup scallions, minced
¼ cup celery, finely minced
1 cup mayonnaise
2 tbsp. soy sauce
toasted slivered almonds
lettuce
avocados, halved

Cool cooked shrimp. Combine chestnuts, scallions, celery, mayonnaise and soy sauce. Mix with shrimp. Chill well. Serve in avocado cups placed on beds of lettuce and garnish with almonds.

Preparation: 1 hour   Easy   Serves: 6-8
                      Can do ahead

Mrs. K. B. Mellon

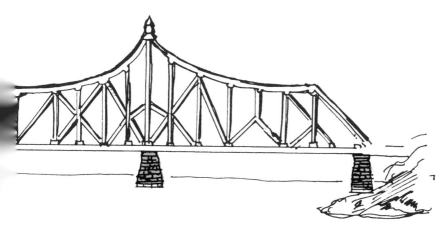

133

SANDWICHES

MEATBALL SANDWICHES
"A hearty meal in itself"

2 eggs, lightly beaten
3 tbsp. milk
½ cup Progresso breadcrumbs
¾ tsp. salt
⅛ tsp. pepper
1 lb. ground chuck

Sauce:
½ lb. Italian sausage
½ cup onion, chopped
½ cup green pepper, chopped
1 cup water
1 8-oz. can tomato sauce
1 6-oz. can tomato paste
2 tsp. sugar
1 tsp. garlic salt
½ tsp. oregano
¼ tsp. parsley flakes
8 French rolls

Combine eggs, milk, crumbs, salt and pepper. Add beef and mix well. Shape into 24 1½" meatballs. Brown. Remove from pan and add sausage, onion and green pepper; cook until sausage is browned. Drain fat; add water, tomato sauce, tomato paste, sugar, garlic salt, oregano and parsley. Return meatballs to skillet. Cover and simmer 15 minutes. Remove top crust from rolls and hollow out. Fill each roll with three meatballs and sauce.

Preparation: 30 min.	Easy	Serves: 8
Cooking: 35 min.	Can do ahead	Can freeze

Mrs. Herbert H. South

VEGIE-MELT

"Add a big slice of sweet onion"

1 cup fresh mushrooms, sliced
1 cup zucchini, sliced
1 tbsp. butter
4 pita or pocket breads
1 firm tomato, sliced
4 slices Monterey Jack cheese
alfalfa sprouts, optional

Sauté mushrooms and zucchini in butter for 5 minutes. Split pita bread and divide mushroom mixture evenly among 4 breads. Top each with a slice of tomato and cheese. Run under broiler just long enough to melt cheese. Can top with sprouts, if desired. Top with other half of pita bread. Can also add sliced, cooked chicken breast.

Preparation: 15 min.	Easy	Serves: 4
Cooking: 5 min.	Can do ahead	

Guen Larson

TEXAS POW-WOWS

"Call the tribe together and toss these around"

1 lb. bacon, cooked & crumbled
1 lb. chipped ham
1 bottle chili sauce
¾ cup sweet green pickle relish
12 hamburger buns
Velveeta cheese

Mix bacon with ham, chili sauce and relish. Put a tablespoon of ham mixture on a sliced hamburger bun. Top with a slice of cheese. Close bun and wrap in foil. Heat 20 minutes in 350° oven.

Preparation: 30 min.	Easy	Serves: 12
Cooking: 20 min.	Can do ahead	Can freeze

Mrs. Allan W. Beatty

HOT SHRIMP ROLLS

"Gourmet filling for hamburger buns"

2 cups fresh shrimp, cooked &
   chopped
1 cup Swiss cheese, grated &
   lightly packed
¼ cup scallions, sliced
½ tsp. dill weed
¼ cup mayonnaise
1½ tsp. white vinegar or
   tarragon vinegar
6 sesame seed hamburger rolls

Mix all ingredients, except rolls, together. Divide mixture evenly among rolls. Wrap individually in foil. Can be frozen at this point. Bake 30 minutes at 350°. Increase baking time to 40 minutes, if frozen.

Preparation: 10 min.	Easy	Yield: 6
Cooking: 30 min.		Can freeze

Catharine M. Boyd

GORDON'S FAMOUS BARBECUES

"Who knows, maybe you'll become famous too"

1 lb. chipped ham
1 tsp. red wine vinegar
¼ cup water
4 tbsp. brown sugar
1 cup ketchup
dash Worcestershire sauce
6 hamburger buns, toasted
butter

In a skillet, mix all ingredients, except the ham, buns and butter, and heat until mixture bubbles. Shred and add chipped ham. Stir until hot and pile on toasted and buttered hamburger buns. Ingredients can be measured roughly.

Preparation:	5 min.	Easy	Yield: 6 buns
Cooking:	5 min.	Can do ahead	

Mrs. F. Gordon Kraft

TANGY SUPPER SANDWICHES

"For something different, try this on pumpernickel"

½ lb. bacon, diced
2 tomatoes, peeled & chopped
½ lb. sharp cheese, grated
1 tsp. Worcestershire sauce
2 tbsp. mayonnaise
¼ tsp. garlic salt
8 hamburger buns, or English
  Muffins

Fry bacon until crisp: drain on paper towels. Mix with tomatoes, cheese, sauce, mayonnaise and garlic salt, blending well. Spread on hamburger buns, toasted if desired, and broil until bubbly.

Preparation:	15-30 min.	Easy	Yield: 8
Cooking:	5 min.	Can do ahead	

Mrs. James Lawler

BROILED HAM TOWERS

*"Open your mouth - close your eyes and you will have
a delicious surprise"*

2 cups cooked ham, diced
½ cup green pepper, finely
  chopped
½ cup mayonnaise
1¼ tsp. Italian herb seasoning
⅛ tsp. ground black pepper
dash ground nutmeg
6 hamburger rolls
2 tbsp. butter
2 large ripe tomatoes
½ tsp. Beau Monde seasoning
6 slices Swiss cheese

Combine ham, green pepper and mayonnaise in a small bowl. Blend in 1 teaspoon herb seasoning, black pepper and nutmeg. Split rolls; butter lightly. Place on cookie sheet, spoon ham mixture onto bottom half, heaping well. Top with slice of tomato, sprinkle lightly with Beau Monde and top with Swiss cheese. Sprinkle with ¼ teaspoon herb seasoning. Place 4" from broiler and broil 4-5

minutes until cheese is bubbly and top half of rolls are toasted. Can do ahead and refrigerate, then broil at last minute.

Preparation:	20 min.	Easy	Yield: 6 buns
Cooking:	5 min.	Can do ahead	

Mrs. Wesley E. Smith, Sr.

PIZZA PUFF
"Pizza with an elegant crust"

1 pkg. 6 puff pastry shells,
   thawed
¼ cup onion, chopped
2 tbsp. butter or margarine
⅓ cup Ragu Thick & Zesty
   sauce
6 oz. each of boiled ham,
   pepperoni & Mozzarella
   cheese
egg yolk, beaten

Sauté onion in butter until translucent, add sauce and cook 5 minutes. Arrange the thawed pastry shells into a rectangle, 3 shells long by 2 wide, overlapping slightly. Roll into a 15 x 9" rectangle. Divide into 2 pieces: the first 4 x 15", the second 5 x 15". Place smaller piece on greased cookie sheet with sides. Spread sauce on smaller half of pastry to within 1" of edges. Baste edge with beaten egg yolk. Pile ham, pepperoni and cheese in center. Top with larger piece of pastry, and crimp edges together. Bake at 400-425° for 20 minutes or until done.

Preparation: 20 min.   Easy   Serves: 4-5
Cooking: 20 min.   Can do ahead

Mrs. Robert G. Morrell

TOASTY TUNA SANDWICHES
"A smooth and creamy open face sandwich"

1 stick butter
3-5 tbsp. flour
salt & pepper, to taste
4-6 cups, milk
2 9¾-oz. cans tuna, drained
¼ cup ketchup
1 tbsp. Worcestershire sauce
bread
butter
green pepper rings, garnish

Prepare white sauce: melt butter, add flour and stir to blend. Season and then add milk gradually. Cook and stir until sauce is smooth and thickened to medium consistency. Stir tuna, ketchup and Worcestershire into white sauce. Simmer 10-15 minutes until tuna is warm. Toast lightly buttered bread. Pile tuna mixture on top and garnish with a pepper ring to serve as an open face sandwich or top with another slice of toasted bread.

Preparation: 20 min.   Easy   Serves: 4-6
Cooking: 15 min.   Can do ahead

Mrs. Louis D. Ruscitto

TEXAS BARBECUE

"Meanwhile, back at the ranch, they're having a hot time"

4-6 cups cooked beef or pork,
  sliced
1 med. onion, chopped
2 tbsp. butter
2 tbsp. vinegar
4 tbsp. brown sugar
1 cup ketchup
3 tbsp. Worcestershire sauce
½ tsp. prepared mustard
1 cup water
½ tsp. salt
½ tsp. pepper
1 tbsp. Tabasco, or to taste
12 buns

Combine all ingredients, except buns, and simmer, covered, for 1 hour. Serve on hot toasted buns.

Preparation: 10 min.	Easy	Yield: 12 buns
Cooking: 1 hour	Can do ahead	Can freeze

Barbara Olson

REUBEN ROLLUPS

"A superb variation on an old favorite"

1 pkg. crescent rolls
1 8-oz. can sauerkraut, drained
1 tbsp. Thousand Islands
  dressing
8 slices corned beef, thinly
  sliced
2 slices Swiss cheese, cut in
  ½" strips

Separate crescent rolls. Snip the sauerkraut; add the dressing and mix. Layer the corned beef, cheese and 2 tablespoons sauerkraut mixture on the wide end of the crescent triangle. Roll up, beginning at wide end. Bake on ungreased baking sheet at 375° for 10-15 minutes. Can be served as a sandwich or appetizer.

Preparation: 20 min.	Easy	Yield: 8
Cooking: 10-15 min.	Can do ahead	

Doris H. Paul

DILLED ONION RINGS

"Oh, how good and easy these are"

1 large sweet onion
½ cup sugar
2 tsp. salt
½ tsp. fresh dill weed
½ cup white vinegar
½ cup water

Separate onion into rings. Pack into jar. Combine remaining ingredients; heat to dissolve sugar, then pour over onion rings. Cool. Cover and store in refrigerator at least 12 hours. Will keep several days.

Preparation: 15 min.	Easy	Yield: 1 pt.
Cooking: 3-5 min.	Must do ahead	

Mrs. Frank Vizza

SAUCES & ACCOMPANIMENTS

MAMA'S SWEET BREAD AND BUTTER PICKLES

"One big sweet reason to grow some cucumbers this year"

35 small cucumbers	Rinse and slice cucumbers.
3 tbsp. kosher salt	Sprinkle with salt and let stand
4 cups vinegar	5 hours or overnight. Drain and
4½ cups sugar	rinse. Mix vinegar, sugar and
¼ cup mustard seed	spices; bring to a boil and let
1 tbsp. celery seed	boil 3 minutes. Heat cucumbers
1½ tsp. turmeric	in the liquid for a few minutes.
6 med. yellow onions, sliced	

In sterilized jars, place a slice of onion, fill halfway with cucumbers, add another slice of onion, fill with cucumbers and top with an onion slice. Fill jars with brine. Seal and store.

Preparation:	30 min.	Easy	Yield: 10 pints
Cooking:	10 min.	Must do ahead	

Dinah Strong

48 HOUR PICKLES

"Really one week pickles"

1¾ qts. water	Boil water, vinegar, salt and
1½ cups vinegar	sugar together. Cool. Quarter
⅓ cup salt	cucumbers lengthwise. Pour
½ cup sugar	cooled brine over cucumbers;
7-10 cucumbers, quartered	add garlic and dill to taste.
dill, to taste	Refrigerate for 1 week to
garlic, to taste	develop flavor.

Preparation:	10 min.	Must do ahead	Yield: 4-5 pts.
Cooking:	15-20 min.		

Phyllis Lynch

MANGO CHUTNEY
"Before you do anything, find the mangoes"

1 qt. mangoes, diced
2 green peppers, chopped
3 hot red peppers, chopped
1 onion, diced
1 clove garlic, minced
1 tbsp. salt
1 lb. white raisins, soaked in 1
   cup grapefruit juice
1 cup wine vinegar
1 lb. light brown sugar
1 tbsp. mustard seed
1 tsp. allspice
1 tsp. cinnamon
1 tbsp. preserved ginger or 1
   tsp. powdered ginger
½ cup pecans, chopped

Combine mangoes, peppers, onions and garlic with salt and let stand 15 minutes. At same time, soak raisins in juice. Combine the two mixtures and let stand 1 hour. Drain well. Bring to a full boil; let boil gently for 30 minutes. Add pecans if desired. Pour into sterilized jars and seal.

| Preparation: | 2 hours | Easy | Yield: 4 qts. |
| Cooking: | 40 min. | Must do ahead | |

Mrs. William S. Pampel, Jr.

MRS. FIFER'S SUPERIOR APPLE BUTTER
"Just like down on the farm"

3 qts. applesauce
6 cups sugar
1 tsp. each: cinnamon, ginger,
   ground cloves, allspice,
   nutmeg
juice of 1 lemon

In a large heavy saucepan, combine applesauce, sugar, spices and lemon juice. Mix well and cook slowly until very thick, stirring to prevent sticking. Pour in jars; seal or refrigerate.

| Preparation: 1 hour | Easy | Yield: 3 qts. |
| | Must do ahead | |

Susan Krauland

BRANDIED WHITE RAISIN SAUCE
"A heavenly sweet sauce"

½ lb. white raisins
2 cups water
3 oz. apricot brandy
¼ cup honey

Cook raisins in 2 cups water for ½ hour over low heat. Add apricot brandy and honey; simmer ½ hour more. Excellent with game.

| Preparation: | 5 min. | Easy | Yield: 2 cups |
| Cooking: | 1 hour | Can do ahead | |

K.C. Speer, Chef
Rae Lynn's Restaurant

HUNTLAND DOWNS MUSTARD SAUCE

"Something special to serve with salmon or swordfish steaks"

1 cup evaporated milk
¼ cup sugar
2 tbsp. Colman's dry mustard
1 tbsp. flour
¼ tsp. salt
1 egg yolk, beaten
¼ cup vinegar, heated

Heat ¾ cup of the milk in a double boiler. Add sugar. Mix mustard, flour and salt with the remaining milk. Add to first mixture and blend thoroughly. Pour small amount of hot sauce into egg yolk and stir; return to sauce. Cook, stirring, until mixture is thickened. Add heated vinegar. If refrigerated, can be thinned with a tablespoon or so of cream.

Preparation: 5 min.
Cooking: 20 min.

Easy
Can do ahead

Yield: 1½ cups

Mrs. K. B. Mellon

MUSTARD SAUCE

"Great with baked ham or on ham sandwiches"

1 egg yolk, lightly beaten
⅓ cup sugar
⅓ cup tomato soup, undiluted
⅓ cup butter
3 tbsp. vinegar
⅓ cup mustard, not spicy

Blend all ingredients together in a saucepan. Boil 1 minute, stirring constantly.

Preparation: 10 min.
Cooking: 3 min.

Easy
Can do ahead

Yield: 1¼ cups

Lucia Corduan Luce

SAUCE CHIEN

"French for spicy, tart, amusing, pungent and tempting"

⅓ cup lime juice
¼ cup vegetable or olive oil
½ clove garlic, minced
salt & pepper
3 tbsp. parsley, chopped
1 tbsp. scallion, finely chopped
1 tsp. hot green pepper, thinly
   sliced
cayenne pepper

Combine all ingredients, beating with a fork or whisk to blend. Will keep, refrigerated, for 4 months. Especially good with broiled fish or chicken.

Preparation: 15 min.

Easy
Can do ahead

Yield: 1 cup

Nancy Borger Wilkinson

BOURBON BARBECUE SAUCE

"Marvelous flavor - especially on chicken cooked on the grill"

1 cup ketchup
½ cup brown sugar
½ cup bourbon

Mix all ingredients and simmer for 45 minutes or until desired consistency for basting.

Preparation:	5 min.	Easy	Yield: 1½ cups
Cooking:	1 hour	Can do ahead	

Miriam A. Donnellon

MARYLAND BARBECUE SAUCE

"Spicy - sticks to the meat"

1 12-oz. can tomato paste
⅓ cup cider vinegar
¾ cup brown sugar
7-8 tbsp. Old Bay seasoning
1 tbsp. chili powder

Mix all ingredients in a small saucepan. Simmer until thickened and darkened, about 15-20 minutes. Will store indefinitely in refrigerator.

Preparation:	5 min.	Easy	Yield: 3 cups
Cooking:	15-20 min.	Can do ahead	

Susan R. Sour

SHISH-KEBAB MARINADE

"You will receive rave reviews for this marinade"

1 med. onion, minced
1 clove garlic, minced
1 tbsp. olive oil
1 tbsp. vinegar
1 tbsp. lemon juice
⅛ tsp. pepper
½ tsp. salt
1 tsp. oregano

Combine all ingredients and mix well. Pour over meat and marinate at least 2 hours. Enough marinade for 2 pounds of cubed meat, either beef or lamb.

Preparation:	5 min.	Easy	Serves: 6
		Must do ahead	

Carolyn K. Kastroll

BURGUNDY JELLY

"A delicious Christmas gift"

6 cups sugar
4 cups Burgundy
1 6-oz. bottle fruit pectin

Combine sugar and Burgundy and bring to a boil. Stir until sugar dissolves. Remove from heat and stir in pectin. Skim off any foam immediately. Pour into sterilized jars and seal.

Preparation:	5 min.	Easy	Yield: 8 cups
Cooking:	5-10 min.	Must do ahead	

Peggy Standish

HAM SAUCE
"A perfect reason to serve ham"

1 cup raisins
2 cups pineapple juice
⅓ cup liquid brown sugar
⅓ cup apricot brandy
¼ tsp. dry mustard
¼ tsp. crushed cloves
¼ tsp. cinnamon
¼ tsp. salt
1½ tbsp. cornstarch

Boil raisins in pineapple juice for 5 minutes. Mix and add all remaining ingredients; simmer for 5 minutes, stirring frequently.

Preparation: 10 min.	Easy	Yield: 3 cups
Cooking: 5 min.	Can do ahead	

Mrs. William C. Crampton, Jr.

ESCALLOPED APPLES
"A tradition at Sewickley Hunt breakfasts"

8 tart apples, McIntosh, Stayman or Winesap
⅓ cup water
1 cup brown sugar, firmly packed
⅓ cup white sugar
⅓ stick butter or margarine, cubed
½ tsp. cinnamon, optional

Preheat oven to 375°. Butter a shallow baking dish. Peel, core and quarter apples. Place in baking dish with water. Mix sugars and pat over the apples. Place butter bits on top. Bake for 20 minutes; lower heat to 350°, add cinnamon, if desired. Cover and bake for 15 minutes, or until apples are tender.

Preparation: 20 min.	Easy	Serves: 8
Baking: 35 min.	Can do ahead	

Christina Bradley

HILDA'S BREAKFAST APPLES
"Excellent accompaniment to sausages"

⅔ cup sugar
½ cup water
2 whole cloves
1 stick cinnamon
½ lemon peel, grated
6 med. cooking apples

Combine sugar, water, cloves, cinnamon and lemon peel. Pare apples, core and cut in eighths. Add to syrup and cook slowly 5-8 minutes, or until apples are almost tender. Remove cloves and cinnamon stick and serve warm.

Preparation: 20 min.	Easy	Serves: 6
Cooking: 5-8 min.	Can do ahead	Can freeze

Mrs. John B. McElderry

NO-COOK FROZEN STRAWBERRY JAM

1 qt. fresh strawberries
4 cups sugar
1 box Sure-Jell fruit pectin
¾ cup water

Rinse and hull berries. Crush fruit with fork or food processor. Stir in sugar and let stand 10 minutes. Mix water and pectin together in saucepan. Bring to a full boil and boil for 1 minute, stirring constantly. Add to berry mixture and stir for 3 minutes; do not cook.

Ladle into sterilized containers, cap tightly and let stand at room temperature for 24 hours. Freeze. Will keep, refrigerated, for 3 weeks, after thawing.

Preparation: 30 min.	Easy	Yield: 2½ pts.
Cooking: 5 min.	Must freeze	

Dinah Strong

STRAWBERRY-RHUBARB PRESERVES

"Fresh springtime rhubarb will make this super special"

4 cups rhubarb
4 cups sugar
1 3-oz. pkg. strawberry jello

Rinse and dry rhubarb; cut into ½" lengths. Place in bottom of heavy pot and cover with sugar. Begin heating very slowly until liquid begins to escape from rhubarb. Stir occasionally and raise heat slowly as mixture becomes more liquid. Do not scrape sides of pot or preserves will be sugary. Simmer until rhubarb falls apart. Remove from heat and stir in jello. No need to skim. Pour into jars and seal.

Preparation: 5-10 min.	Easy	Yield: 5 cups
Cooking: 45-60 min.	Must do ahead	

Diane Honatke

TOMATO MARMALADE

"Another delicious way to use your garden tomatoes"

2-3 cups tomatoes, skinned &
    coarsely chopped
1 lemon, seeded & ground
2 cups sugar
¼ cup sweet Sherry

2 tbsp. sweet Sherry

Combine all ingredients and let stand 2 hours. Bring to a boil; cook, stirring frequently, until syrup is thickened. Remove from heat and add another 2 tablespoons of Sherry. Pour into sterilized jars. Seal or refrigerate, according to own preference.

Preparation: 5-10 min.	Easy	Yield: 2-3 cups
Cooking: 1 hour	Must do ahead	

Mrs. Richard K. Foster

VEGETABLES

FIRST PRESBYTERIAN CHURCH

First Presbyterian Church, designed by Theophilus Parsons Chandler, Jr., was built between 1903-1905. It is a highly sophisticated example of Edwardian architecture - crisp and richly textured. The land around it provides a refreshing space among its surroundings.

Additional illustrations in this section:

Atterbury's patent melon ware.*

Double glass dolphin candlesticks, McKee Factory, circa 1886. Bakewell double glass goblet, circa 1875.

Pittsburgh's Strip District is the center of the wholesale produce yards, filled with bustling activity at Midnight, quiet at Noon.

Familiar scene in Market Square.

Soldiers & Sailors Memorial Hall in Oakland was designed by Palmer & Hornwastel. It was built in the Neo-Baroque style between 1907-1911 as a memorial to Civil War Veterans.

*All glassware is early Pittsburgh unless otherwise indicated.

BASIL BEANS

"On a scale of 1-5, this is a definite 5"

¼ cup cooking oil
¼ cup onion, chopped
1 cup green peppers, chopped
3 pkgs. frozen cut green beans
1 tsp. salt
2 tsp. dried basil

Sauté onion and peppers in oil until soft. Add uncooked beans, breaking them apart with a fork. Add salt and basil. Do not add water; cover and cook on low heat until tender, about 15 minutes.

| Preparation: | 10 min. | Easy | Serves: 6 |
| Cooking: | 15 min. | Can do ahead | |

Mrs. Charles Dithrich

GREEN BEANS A LA NICOISE

1 lb. fresh green beans
½ cup oil
1 onion, sliced
1 cup canned tomatoes
½ green pepper, chopped
½ cup celery, chopped
¼ cup water
1 tsp. salt
¼ tsp. pepper

Spice bag:
cheesecloth
2 cloves
1 bay leaf
6 sprigs parsley
½ tsp. chervil

Cook beans until tender; drain and set aside. Heat oil in separate skillet and sauté onion until golden. Add tomatoes, green pepper, celery, water, salt and pepper. Add beans. Make a small cheesecloth bag and fill with seasonings. Add to the green bean mixture. Simmer, uncovered, for 25 minutes. Remove spice bag and serve immediately.

| Preparation: | 40 min. | Easy | Serves: 4 |
| Cooking: | 25 min. | | |

Mrs. Louis Steup

PARTY BEETS WITH PINEAPPLE

2 tbsp. brown sugar
1 tbsp. cornstarch
¼ tsp. salt
1 8-oz. can pineapple tidbits
1 tbsp. butter or margarine
1 tbsp. lemon juice
1 16-oz. can sliced beets,
   drained

In saucepan, combine first 3 ingredients. Stir in pineapple with syrup. Cook, stirring constantly, until mixture thickens and bubbles. Add butter and lemon juice; stir. Add beets and heat thoroughly.

Preparation: 5 min.   Easy   Serves: 4-6
Cooking: 10 min.   Can do ahead

Mrs. Joseph W. Blackhurst

BROCCOLI AND CHEESE CASSEROLE

1 bunch broccoli
salt, to taste
3 tbsp. butter
2½ tbsp. flour
1 cup milk
salt, to taste
pepper, to taste
1 cup extra sharp cheese
4 tbsp. bread crumbs
1 tbsp. butter, melted

Parboil trimmed broccoli in salted water. Drain. In double boiler, melt butter, add flour and stir to blend. Gradually add milk, stirring until thickened. Season, remove from heat and mix with the cheese. Layer broccoli in a greased casserole with sauce, top with crumbs mixed with butter. Bake 30 minutes at 350°.

Preparation: 30 min.   Easy   Serves: 4
Cooking: 30 min.   Can do ahead

Mrs. Walter E. Gregg, Jr.

NUTTED BROCCOLI WITH POPPY SEEDS
"An elegant sauce for a favorite vegetable"

2 tbsp. butter
2 tbsp. onion, minced
1½ cups sour cream
1 tsp. vinegar
½ tsp. paprika
¼ tsp. salt
2 tsp. sugar
dash cayenne
½ tsp. poppy seeds
broccoli, 1 bunch or 2 pkgs.
   frozen spears, cooked
⅓ cup toasted cashews,
   chopped

Melt butter, add onion and cook until clear. Remove from heat and stir in sour cream, then remaining ingredients except nuts and broccoli. Keep sauce warm. Arrange cooked broccoli on heated platter. Pour sauce across the middle and sprinkle with nuts.

Preparation: 15 min.   Easy   Serves: 6
Cooking: 30 min

Dorothy Clark Schmidt

CARROT CASSEROLE
"A creamy cheesy delight"

2 lbs. carrots, thinly sliced
1 stick of margarine
¼ cup flour
1 tsp. salt
dash pepper
½ tsp. dry mustard
1 tsp. celery salt
1 small onion, diced
2 cups milk
½ lb. Velveeta cheese, sliced
bread crumbs

Cook carrots until tender and drain. In saucepan, melt the margarine, add the flour, salt, pepper, mustard, celery salt, onion and milk. Cook until thickened. Place half of the cooked carrots in a greased 3 quart casserole, add the cheese, then the second half of the carrots. Pour sauce over all. Top with bread crumbs. Bake at 350° for 15-20 minutes.

Preparation: 20-25 min. Easy Serves: 8
Cooking: 20 min. Can do ahead

Mrs. Dale E. Harry

HUNGARIAN SWEET-SOUR CARROTS
"A pretty dish with a tangy taste"

2 bunches fresh carrots
1 tsp. salt
hot water
2 tbsp. butter
½ cup vinegar
1 cup sugar
1 tbsp. parsley, chopped

Wash and scrape carrots. Cut into strips, 3 x ½ ". Place in saucepan with salted hot water to cover. Cook until tender. Drain and add butter, vinegar and sugar. Cook slowly until translucent. Serve hot, garnished with parsley. Can substitute 1 large bag of frozen baby carrots.

Preparation: 20 min. Easy Serves: 6-8
Cooking: 30 min.

Mrs. Stuart P. Moiles

CARROTS LYONNAISE

1 lb. carrots, sliced
¾ cup chicken stock or ¾ cup
    water & 1 chicken bouillon
    cube
¼ cup butter
3 med. onions, sliced
1 tbsp. flour
¼ tsp. salt
dash pepper
½ cup water
pinch sugar

Slice carrots in julienne strips. Cook in the stock, covered, for 15 minutes. Melt the butter, add onions and cook, covered, for 15 minutes. Stir the remaining ingredients into the onions and bring to a boil. Add the carrots and stock. Simmer, uncovered, 10 minutes.

Preparation: 45 min. Can do ahead Serves: 4
Cooking: 40 min.

Dinah Strong

CAPONATA

"So versatile-can be an appetizer, antipasto or vegetable"

2 med. eggplants, peeled & diced
¾ cup olive oil, divided
2 onions, chopped
1-2 cups celery, diced
4 med. tomatoes, chopped
¼ cup tomato sauce
¼ cup capers, drained
6 green olives, pitted & chopped
1 tbsp. pignoli (pine) nuts
¼ cup wine vinegar
2 tbsp. sugar
½ tsp. salt
¼ tsp. pepper

Fry eggplant in ½ cup oil until golden brown. Remove from skillet and reserve. Add remaining oil, onions and celery and cook until tender, stirring occasionally. Add tomatoes, sauce, olives, nuts, capers and eggplant. Heat vinegar and dissolve sugar in it. Add salt and pepper. Pour liquid over eggplant mixture and simmer, covered, for 20 minutes over very low heat, stirring frequently. Cool and serve. Will keep for weeks in refrigerator. May be used as a side dish with meat or poultry or as a sandwich filling or antipasto.

Preparation: 40 min. Easy Serves: 6-8
Cooking: 20 min. Can do ahead

Nancy Toomey

DEVONSHIRE CORN

2 pkgs. frozen corn, thawed
1 cup whipping cream
1 cup milk
1 tsp. salt
¼ tsp. Accent
pinch nutmeg
6 tsp. sugar
pinch cayenne
pinch white pepper

Beurre manié:*
2 tbsp. very soft butter
2 tbsp. flour

Combine the corn, cream, milk and seasonings in saucepan and bring to a boil; reduce heat and simmer 5-7 minutes, uncovered. Blend flour and butter together with fingers. Gradually drop small pieces into corn mixture, mixing well, and cook 2 more minutes to thicken.

*Can increase amount of beurre manié, if a thicker pudding is desired.

Preparation: 5 min. Easy Serves: 6
Cooking: 10 min.

Bonnie Wood

GREEN AND GOLD CASSEROLE

3-4 10-oz. pkgs. frozen chopped
    spinach, cooked & drained
1 5-oz. can water chestnuts,
    drained & thinly sliced
2 10-oz. pkgs. Stouffers frozen
    Welsh rarebit, thawed
8 slices bacon, crisp-cooked,
    drained & crumbled
2 oz. canned French-fried onion
    rings

Combine spinach, water chestnuts and one-third of the Welsh rarebit in a 10 x 6 x 1½ " baking dish. Top with crumbled bacon and spread remaining rarebit evenly over all. Top with onion rings. Bake, uncovered, at 350° for 15 minutes or until heated through.

Preparation: 30 min.   Easy   Serves: 6
Cooking: 15-20 min.   Can do ahead

Trudy Hetherington

STEWED EGGPLANT SUPREME
"Very colorful-resembles a ratatouille"

2 large eggplants
olive oil, to taste
salt, to taste
2 large onions, chopped
3 cloves garlic, minced
⅓ cup olive oil
3 large tomatoes, fresh or
    canned
1 cup spinach, chopped &
    cooked
¼ cup chives, chopped
½ cup celery leaves, chopped
1½ tsp. oregano
plenty of freshly ground pepper
2 tbsp. lemon juice
¼ cup sesame seeds

Peel and slice eggplants lengthwise, ⅓" thick. Cut each slice again in 2 or 3 lengthwise strips. Arrange on baking sheets, brush lightly with olive oil and salt lightly. Put in preheated medium broiler for 7-10 minutes until eggplant starts to turn golden brown. Turn and repeat on other side of eggplant. Meanwhile, peel and chop onions, mince garlic and sauté in olive oil until onions are translucent. Cut tomatoes in thin wedges, add to onions along with spinach, chives and celery leaves. Simmer for 10 minutes, then stir in oregano, salt, pepper and lemon juice. Place a few tablespoons of sauce in bottom of a large flameproof casserole and arrange ⅓ of broiled eggplant over it. Spoon over more sauce and continue layering until all eggplant is used; last layer should be sauce. Place lid or foil lightly over casserole and simmer over medium heat about 10 minutes. While casserole is simmering, toast sesame seeds in 350° oven. Stir occasionally until golden. Sprinkle seeds on eggplant just before serving.

Preparation: 20 min.   Easy   Serves: 4-6
Cooking: 40 min.   Can do ahead

Mrs. Herman S. Harvey, Jr.

MUSHROOM SUPREME

"A super side dish for steak or hamburger"

6 slices bacon
4 onions, chopped
1 lb. mushrooms, sliced
½ tsp. salt
¼ tsp. pepper
1 tbsp. Worcestershire sauce

Cut bacon into pieces and cook. Drain. To 2 tablespoons of fat, add onion, mushrooms, cooked bacon pieces, salt and pepper and sauté. Add Worcestershire sauce and stir to mix. Cover and keep warm until serving.

Preparation:	15 min.	Easy	Serves: 6
Cooking:	15 min.	Can do ahead	

Mrs. J. Stewart Urban

MUSHROOM ASPARAGUS CASSEROLE

4 cups fresh mushrooms, halved
1 cup onions, chopped
4 tbsp. butter or margarine
2 tbsp. all-purpose flour
1 tsp. instant chicken bouillon
½ tsp. salt
dash pepper
½ tsp. ground nutmeg
1 cup milk
2 8-oz. pkgs. frozen cut
   asparagus, cooked & drained
¼ cup pimento, chopped
1½ tsp. lemon juice
¾ cup soft bread crumbs
1 tbsp. butter or margarine, melted

Cook mushrooms and onions, covered, in 4 tablespoons butter until tender, 10 minutes. Remove vegetables and set aside, leaving butter in skillet. Blend in flour, chicken bouillon, salt, dash pepper and nutmeg. Add milk. Cook and stir until bubbly. Stir in mushrooms and onions, cooked asparagus, pimento and lemon juice. Turn into 3 quart casserole; combine crumbs and melted butter and sprinkle over top. Bake in 350° oven for 35-40 minutes.

Preparation:	30 min.	Easy	Serves: 8-10
Baking:	35-40 min.	Can do ahead	

Kathleen Pritchard

HARVEST BAKED ACORN SQUASH

"A delicious pineapple nut stuffing"

3 large acorn squash
1 cup water
1 13½-oz. can crushed
   pineapple, drained
1½ cups apple, unpeeled & diced
1 cup celery, chopped
½ cup walnuts, chopped
½ cup butter
½ cup brown sugar
½ tsp. cinnamon
¼ tsp. salt

Cut squash in half so edges are scalloped; clean out seeds. Place in pan with 2″ water. Bake, cut side down, at 350° for 45 minutes or until tender. Combine remaining ingredients; spoon into squash centers. Remove water from pan. Bake, cut side up, 15 minutes.

Preparation:	15 min.	Easy	Serves: 6
Cooking:	1 hour		

Barbara Gaudio

SPINACH CASSEROLE

"Excellent for a brunch"

2 10-oz. pkgs. frozen chopped
    spinach
2 cups cottage cheese
1 tsp. salt
½ cup Parmesan cheese, grated
3 eggs

Cook spinach and drain thoroughly. Combine spinach with cottage cheese, salt, Parmesan cheese and eggs and blend thoroughly. Pour into a greased shallow casserole or 7 x 11" baking pan. Bake at 350° for 30-40 minutes.

Preparation: 15-20 min.   Easy   Serves: 6
Cooking: 30-40 min.   Can do ahead

Mrs. John G. Zimmerman, Jr.

SPINACH AND ARTICHOKE CASSEROLE

"Serve this at your next dinner party"

2 small jars marinated artichoke
    hearts
3 10-oz. pkgs. frozen chopped
    spinach
1 8-oz. pkg. cream cheese,
    softened
4 tbsp. margarine
6 tbsp. milk
Parmesan cheese
red pepper

Arrange artichokes and marinade evenly on bottom of 9" baking pan. Drain and squeeze spinach well and arrange over the artichokes. In a small mixing bowl, blend the cream cheese, margarine and milk. Spoon the cream cheese mixture over the spinach. Sprinkle with Parmesan cheese and red pepper. Let stand 24 hours in the refrigerator. Bake at 350° for 40 minutes.

Preparation: 20 min.   Easy   Serves: 8-10
Baking: 40 min.   Must do ahead

Mrs. Francis J. Sullivan

STIR-FRIED SPINACH WITH MUSHROOMS

"Get out your wok and go to work"

1 tsp. lemon juice
1 tsp. salt
1 tsp. sugar
⅛ tsp. nutmeg
3 tbsp. peanut oil
1 cup fresh mushrooms, sliced
1 med. onion, chopped
1-2 cloves garlic, chopped
1 lb. fresh spinach, washed

Combine lemon juice, salt, sugar and nutmeg and set aside. Pre-heat wok or pan on medium-high setting, pour in oil. Add mushrooms, onions and garlic; stir-fry 3 minutes. Add spinach and stir-fry 3 minutes. Add lemon juice mixture. Serve immediately.

Preparation: 10 min.   Easy   Serves: 4
Cooking: 6 min.

Mrs. K. B. Mellon

SPINACH-STUFFED ONIONS

1 10-oz. pkg. frozen chopped
   spinach
1 3-oz. pkg. cream cheese,
   softened
1 egg
½ cup soft bread crumbs, about
   1 slice bread
¼ cup Parmesan cheese, grated
¼ cup milk
¼ tsp. salt
dash pepper
1 large flat white onion

Cook spinach according to package directions; drain well and set aside. Beat cream cheese with egg, add crumbs, Parmesan cheese, milk, salt and pepper; mix well. Stir in spinach. Peel onion and cut in half crosswise. Separate layers to form shells; place in 9" baking dish. Fill in base of shells with smaller onion pieces, if needed. Spoon spinach mixture into shells. Cover with foil and bake at 350° for 35-40 minutes or until onion shells are tender and filling is set.

Preparation: ½ hour   Easy   Serves: 6-8
Cooking: 40 min.   Can do ahead

Mrs. Malcolm Hay, Jr.

BROILED TOMATOES

tomatoes
butter
parsley
Thomas' English Muffins
Romano or Parmesan cheese,
   grated
salt, to taste
lemon-pepper marinade, to taste

Slice tomatoes crosswise into thick slices. Place on teflon cookie sheet. In blender, make bread crumbs using muffins, grated cheeses, salt and lemon-pepper. Top each slice with dot of butter, a sprinkle of parsley, and sprinkle of fine bread crumbs. Broil 5-8 minutes, until bubbly on top.

Preparation: 15 min.   Easy
Cooking: 8 min.

Carol Anne Boumbouras

TOMATO CASSEROLE

1 med. onion, chopped
2 tbsp. butter
4 med. ripe tomatoes, sliced
1 cup sharp cheese, shredded
1 cup fine soft bread crumbs
2 eggs, beaten
1 cup sour cream
½ tsp. salt

Sauté onions in butter until tender. Place ½ of the tomatoes in 8 x 8" baking dish and top with half of the onions, cheese and crumbs. Repeat layers. Mix remaining ingredients and pour over casserole. Cover and bake at 350° for 30 minutes. Uncover and bake 10 minutes. Can prepare first 5 ingredients ahead and refrigerate.

Preparation: 15 min.   Easy   Serves: 6
Baking: 40 min.   Can do ahead

Kathy Stewart

GREEN ZUCCHINI SOUFFLÉ

"Red pimentos and green zucchini - a Christmas casserole"

4 cups zucchini, unpeeled,
   shredded & loosely packed
1 tsp. salt
1 cup sharp Cheddar cheese,
   shredded
1 tsp. onion, minced
¼ cup parsley, chopped
⅛ tsp. garlic powder
2 tbsp. green pepper, chopped
¼ cup Bisquick
3 red pimentoes, chopped
4 eggs, beaten

Add salt to shredded zucchini and set aside for 1 hour; squeeze excess water from zucchini. Mix with next 7 ingredients; add the 4 beaten eggs and mix. Place in a buttered 1½ quart casserole. Bake 45 minutes at 325° or until done. *Note:* 4-6 medium zucchini equal 4 cups.

Preparation: 45 min.   **Easy**   Serves: 8
Cooking: 45 min.

Mrs. Louis Steup

ZUCCHINI BOATS

"A three cheese triumph"

6 zucchini, about 6″ long &
   straight
2 eggs, well beaten
6 oz. sharp Cheddar cheese,
   grated
½ cup small curd cottage
   cheese
3 tbsp. parsley, chopped
½ tsp. salt
freshly ground pepper, to taste
2 tsp. Worcestershire sauce
dash Tabasco
Parmesan cheese
butter
paprika

Trim zucchini and boil in salted water until tender, but firm. Refresh under cold water. Cut each zucchini in half lengthwise and scoop out pulp, leaving ½″ wall. Drain shells on paper towels. Mix the eggs, cheeses, parsley and seasonings and fill each shell with this mixture, adding zucchini pulp if necessary. Dust top with Parmesan cheese, dot with butter and sprinkle with paprika. Bake, uncovered, in a greased dish, for 15-20 minutes at 350° until heated; brown briefly under the broiler.

Preparation: 25 min.   **Easy**   Yield: 12
Cooking: 20 min.   **Can do ahead**

Mrs. Edward A. Montgomery, Jr.

ZUCCHINI PIZZA

"No one will guess it's zucchini"

4 lbs. zucchini, grated
salt
2 tbsp. oil
1 egg
½ cup Cheddar cheese, grated
pepper, freshly ground
1 med. onion, finely chopped
½ cup tomato sauce
1 tsp. oregano
½ cup Parmesan cheese, grated
½ cup Mozzarella cheese,
   shredded
1 green or red pepper, cut in
   strips

Cut ends off zucchini and grate. Put in colander and sprinkle with salt. Let stand for 30 minutes. Squeeze water out of zucchini with hands. When quite dry, sauté in oil for 5 minutes. Cool. Mix 2 cups zucchini with egg, cheese, onion, salt and pepper. Press mixture into an 8″ pie pan. Bake at 400° for 10 minutes. Cool. Cover with tomato sauce; sprinkle with oregano. Top with cheeses and arrange pepper strips over all. Bake at 350° for 20 minutes.

Preparation: 20 min.   Easy   Serves: 4
Cooking: 30 min.

Mrs. Frank R. Stoner, III

BOB'S FAVORITE ZUCCHINI CASSEROLE

"Cheese and chilies sharpen the flavor"

8 slices Pepperidge Farm bread,
   trimmed
¼ cup butter, scant
1 1-lb. can whole corn, drained
2 cups zucchini, thinly sliced
1 4-oz. can green chilies, seeded
   & chopped
½ lb. Monterey Jack cheese,
   shredded (2 cups)
½ cup sharp Cheddar cheese,
   shredded
4 eggs
2 cups milk
1 tsp. salt
⅛ tsp. pepper

Butter the bread and put in a 9 x 13″ flat casserole, butter side down. Cover bread with layered corn, zucchini, chilies and finally, the cheese. Mix eggs, milk, salt and pepper together. Pour over the vegetables. Let sit 4 hours. Bake for 25 minutes at 375°. Let rest 10 minutes before serving.

Preparation: 20 min.   Easy   Serves: 8
Cooking: 25 min.   Must do ahead

Claudia Irwin

POTATOES

HEAVENLY POTATOES
"Give yourself plenty of time—3 days"

15 med. Idaho potatoes	Day 1: Parboil potatoes for 20
1 med. onion, grated	minutes. Cool and refrigerate
1 cup butter, melted	overnight.
½ pt. whipping cream	Day 2: Peel and grate potatoes
1 pt. half & half	into a shallow 3 quart casserole.
1 cup milk, only as needed	Mix in onions, handling as little
salt & white pepper	as possible. Pour butter, creams
paprika	and milk over all, season to taste
	and stir gently. Cover and chill.

Day 3: Remove casserole from refrigerator 2 hours before baking.
Sprinkle with paprika and bake at 325° for 1 hour.

Preparation: 45 min.	Easy	Serves: 12-16
Cooking: 1 hour	Must do ahead	

Mrs. William S. Pampel, Jr.

POTATOES SOUTH
"Wonderful for the holidays"

12 to 14 med. red skin potatoes	Parboil potatoes for 20 minutes,
salt	chill. Do this one day ahead.
pepper	In morning, peel and grate
1½ pints whipping cream	potatoes into casserole. Salt and
	pepper to taste, pour cream over

potatoes and chill 6 hours. Bake at 350° for 1 hour. Do not use a
food processor when grating.

Preparation: 30 min.	Easy	Serves: 12
Cooking: 1 hour	Must do ahead	

Mrs. Furman South, III

MOM'S "ROTTEN" POTATOES

4 12-oz. boxes Ore-Ida frozen
    hash brown potatoes
1 qt. half & half
1 stick butter
2 tbsp. frozen chives
salt & pepper
Parmesan cheese
paprika

Place first 5 ingredients in large pot and stir until consistency of pudding. Reduce heat after thawing begins to avoid scorching. Place potato mixture in a greased 3 quart casserole. Sprinkle with Parmesan cheese and paprika and bake, loosely covered, for 20 minutes. Uncover and bake for 25 minutes at 350°.

Preparation: 45 min.   Easy   Serves: 10-12
Cooking: 45 min.   Can do ahead

Mrs. George Reed

PATRICIAN POTATOES

4 cups mashed potatoes, freshly
    cooked
3 cups cream-style cottage
    cheese
¾ cup sour cream
1½ tbsp. onion, grated
salt & pepper
butter, melted
½ cup almonds, toasted &
    chopped

Mash potatoes thoroughly, but do not use any liquid. Whirl cottage cheese in blender until smooth; mix with warm potatoes. Add sour cream and onion; salt and pepper to taste. Spoon into buttered shallow 2 quart casserole. Brush melted butter on top. Bake at 350° for 30 minutes. Sprinkle with almonds.

Preparation: 30 min.   Easy   Serves: 8
Baking: 30 min.   Can do ahead

Mrs. Edgar Fraser Sadd

SWEET POTATO APPLE CASSEROLE
"This turns out like a soufflé"

3 1-lb. cans sweet potatoes,
    drained
1 1-lb. can apple pie filling
1 cup milk
½ cup butter, melted
⅓ cup brown sugar
¼ cup molasses
3 eggs
½ tsp. cinnamon
½ tsp. nutmeg
⅔ cup dark raisins

In large bowl, beat potatoes and apple filling until smooth. Add remaining ingredients and mix well. Bake in 2 quart casserole for 50-60 minutes at 350°.

Preparation: 20 min.   Easy   Serves: 10
Cooking: 1 hour   Can do ahead

Marge Dixon

STELLAR SWEET POTATO CASSEROLE
"Very sweet and rich"

1 large size can sweet potatoes
2 eggs
½ cup sugar
1 cup canned milk
½ tsp. cinnamon
½ tsp. cardamon
5 tbsp. butter or margarine

Combine potatoes with next 6 ingredients and beat well. Spread in a greased pan and bake at 400° for 15 minutes. Remove from oven. Mix topping ingredients together, spread over potatoes and return to oven for 15 minutes.

Topping:
1 cup corn flakes, crushed
½ cup brown sugar
5 tbsp. butter, melted
½ cup walnuts

Preparation: 10 min. Easy Serves: 8
Cooking: 30 min. Can do ahead

Susan Kilmartin

POTATOES FOR THE GRILL
"So easy and so good"

6 med. baking potatoes, sliced
12 or more pats of butter
4 tbsp. chives
salt to taste, about 2 tsp.

Place potato slices on heavy duty aluminum foil which has been brushed with butter. Distribute butter, chives and salt evenly over the potatoes. Wrap tightly and cook on grill for 45 minutes or until the potatoes are tender. These can be baked for 40 minutes in a 375° oven or for 20 minutes in a microwave on high setting. Potatoes should not be peeled.

Preparation: 10 min. Easy Serves: 6
Cooking: 45 min.

Mrs. William H. Logsdon

MASHED POTATO CASSEROLE
"An easy do ahead dish"

½ cup sour cream
2 tsp. prepared mustard
½ tsp. sugar
salt, to taste
2 tbsp. green onions, chopped
4 servings instant potatoes, prepared
paprika

Heat sour cream, but do not boil. Add mustard, sugar and salt and mix into hot potatoes along with onions. Immediately turn into casserole and sprinkle with paprika. Bake 10 minutes at 350°.

Preparation: 15 min. Easy Serves: 4
Cooking: 10 min. Can do ahead

Dolores Cercone

159

WALNUT RICE

8 cups cooked rice
1½ cups walnut halves
2 tsp. butter
2 tsp. Worcestershire sauce
1 tsp. salt
¼ tsp. pepper

Cook rice. Heat butter and Worcestershire sauce in skillet; add nuts and toss lightly, 4-5 minutes until glazed. Drain on paper towel. Season hot rice to taste and add walnuts.

Preparation: 10 min.   Easy   Serves: 8-10
Cooking: 20 min.

Dorothy Hartley

RISOTTO ALLA ZANETTI

"Light and fluffy rice"

1 med. onion, minced
½ stick butter
1 4-oz. can mushrooms, drained
1 cup long grain rice
2 cups liquid: 1⅔ cups water or
   stock and ⅓ cup white wine
salt, to taste
2 tsp. Spice Islands chicken
   stock, optional

Sauté the onion in butter. When lightly browned, add the mushrooms and sauté a few minutes longer. Add rice, liquid, salt and chicken stock. Put mixture in a casserole, cover and bake at 350° for 45 minutes or until liquid is absorbed.

Preparation: 15 min.   Easy   Serves: 4
Cooking: 50 min.   Can do ahead

Mrs. Donald Brewster

PERSIAN RICE
"Dried fruits and nuts add a special touch"

¾ cup rice
2 cups water
1 tsp. turmeric
1 onion, chopped
½ cup dried apricots
½ cup raisins
¼ cup water chestnuts, sliced
¼ cup almonds, toasted
salt, to taste
pepper, to taste

Cook the rice in water with the turmeric until tender: drain, if necessary. Fry the onion until golden. Mix the onion and remaining ingredients with the rice. Serve immediately.

Preparation:	30 min.	Easy	Serves: 4
Cooking:	25 min.		

Carolyn S. Hammer

RICE AND BROCCOLI CASSEROLE
"A perfect party vegetable"

1½ cups rice, cooked
½ cup onion, chopped
½ cup celery, chopped
¼ cup butter
2 pkgs. frozen chopped broccoli,
   cooked
1 can cream of chicken soup
1 can cream of mushroom soup
1 small jar cheese spread
Parmesan cheese, grated

Preheat oven to 350°. Form rice into a crust in a large greased casserole. Sauté onion and celery in butter; combine with broccoli, soups, and cheese spread. Pour over rice and sprinkle with Parmesan cheese. Bake 20-25 minutes or until bubbly and lightly browned.

Preparation:	30 min.	Easy	Serves: 6-8
Cooking:	25 min.	Can do ahead	

Donna Young

BROWN RICE CASSEROLE
"Walnuts give a nice texture"

½ stick butter
1 cup brown rice
1 large onion, minced
½ cup celery, chopped
2 chicken bouillon cubes
2½ cups water
½ cup walnuts, chopped
1 8-oz. can mushrooms
¼ tsp. poultry seasoning
¼ tsp. salt
¼ tsp. pepper

Sauté rice, onion and celery in hot butter for 5 minutes, stirring constantly. Add bouillon cubes and water and bring to a boil. Reduce heat, cover and simmer 45 minutes or until all liquid is absorbed. Add remaining ingredients, stir to blend and heat thoroughly.

Preparation:	15 min.	Easy	Serves: 6-8
Cooking:	50 min.	Can do ahead	

Susan Gasparich

RICE ALICANTINA

1 lb. raw shrimp in the shell
pinch oregano
¼ tsp. saffron
1½ tsp. salt
1 or 2 cloves garlic, crushed
1 med. onion, thinly sliced
¼ cup olive oil
2 pimentos, cut in strips
1 cup long grain rice
2½ cups shrimp stock
1 tsp. parsley, minced
1 pkg. artichoke hearts, partially
   thawed or 1 can, drained,
   halved or quartered

Shell and devein shrimp; place shells in 3 cups boiling water with oregano, saffron and salt and boil 15 minutes. Strain and reserve 2½ cups stock.

In a large skillet, sauté the shrimp with the garlic and onion in hot oil until shrimp begin to turn pink; remove shrimp. Add pimento and cook until onion is tender. Add rice and stir to coat with oil. Add boiling hot shrimp stock, artichoke hearts and parsley. Bring to a boil and cook, uncovered, 10 minutes; replace shrimp, cover and keep in a warm place or place in a 325° oven for 20 minutes, or until liquid is absorbed. *Note:* Rinse artichoke hearts several times if using canned.

Preparation: 35 min.   Easy   Serves: 4
Cooking: 30 min.   Can do ahead

Mrs. Richard K. Foster

FRIED RICE

¼ cup salad oil
2 cups cooked rice
2 tbsp. salad oil
½ cup bamboo shoots
½ cup water chestnuts, sliced
3 scallions, sliced
3 eggs, beaten
2-3 bacon slices, cooked &
   crumbled
1½-2 tbsp. soy sauce
⅛ tsp. pepper
parsley

Sauté rice in hot oil until golden, 5 minutes. Sauté vegetables in 2 tablespoons oil in separate skillet, 5 minutes. Stir eggs into rice; cook, stirring constantly, 3 minutes. Add the bacon, vegetables, soy sauce and pepper and stir until blended. Garnish with parsley.

Preparation: 30 min.   Easy   Serves: 4
Cooking: 15 min.

Chappy's Choice

PASTA

LASAGNE FLORENTINE

Sausage Sauce:
1 tbsp. oil
1 lb. Italian sweet sausage
3 15½-oz. jars Marinara sauce
1¼ cups water
½ cup dry red wine
¼ tsp. sugar

¾ lb. lasagne noodles, cooked
   according to package
   directions

Ricotta Mixture:
2 cups Ricotta cheese
2 eggs, beaten
1 10-oz. pkg. frozen chopped
   spinach, thawed
¼ tsp. salt
⅛ tsp. pepper, freshly ground
⅛ tsp. nutmeg
1 tbsp. fresh parsley, chopped
2 cups Mozzarella, coarsely grated
¾ cup Parmesan cheese, grated

Brown sausage in hot oil and drain. Stir in remaining sauce ingredients and simmer 10-15 minutes, stirring occasionally. Mix Ricotta, eggs, spinach and seasonings together. Blend grated cheeses together. Spread 2 cups of sausage sauce in 3 quart oblong dish and cover with a single layer of noodles. Spread with half of Ricotta mixture and one-third of grated cheeses. Repeat layers and top with remaining sauce and grated cheese. Bake at 350° for 40 minutes and let stand 10 minutes before cutting.

Preparation: 30 min.   Easy   Serves: 12
Cooking: 40 min.   Can do ahead

Chappy's Choice

FETTUCINI CASSEROLE

"This is delicious with chicken or beef"

2 leeks, finely chopped
3 tbsp. butter
1 cup chicken broth
1 cup coffee cream
1 cup sour cream
¼ cup Parmesan cheese
2 tbsp. chives, chopped
½ lb. fettucini noodles, cooked
pignolia nuts, optional
crumbs for topping

Cook leeks in butter and broth 5 minutes. Remove from heat and stir in cream. Mix with next 5 ingredients and pour into a greased 1 quart casserole. Put crumbs on top and bake at 300° for 30 minutes. Do not overcook. If refrigerated, cook a while longer.

Preparation: 15 min.	Easy	Serves: 6-8
Cooking: 30 min.	Can do ahead	

Laura Y. Theis

SPAGHETTI WITH PARMESAN CHEESE AND EGGS

"Different and delicious"

6 slices bacon
¼ to ⅓ cup dry white wine
1 lb. spaghetti
2 tbsp. butter
3 eggs
⅔ cup Parmesan cheese

Cook bacon until crisp. Add wine and reduce until wine has evaporated. Drain and crumble bacon. Cook spaghetti in boiling water 7-8 minutes. Drain. Return spaghetti to pot and coat with butter. Beat eggs and cheese together in a measuring cup and mix well with spaghetti. Add bacon bits and toss to blend. Freshly ground pepper may be added.

Preparation: 20 min.	Easy	Serves: 4-6
Cooking: 15 min.		

Carolyn S. Hammer

NOODLES WITH ZUCCHINI AND MUSHROOMS

"Fresh Parmesan and fresh nutmeg make this special"

½ lb. noodles
salt, to taste
4 tbsp. margarine, unsalted
3 cups mushrooms, thinly sliced
3 cups zucchini, thinly sliced
freshly ground pepper, to taste
½ cup heavy cream
¼ tsp. nutmeg, grated
½ cup Parmesan cheese, freshly
  grated
⅓ cup almonds, toasted

Cook noodles in boiling, salted water. Drain. Meanwhile, sauté vegetables in hot butter until crisp-tender; do not overcook. Salt and pepper the noodles to taste; add the vegetables, cream and nutmeg, cheese and nuts. Place over low heat and toss until ingredients are blended and heated.

Preparation: 30 min.	Easy	Serves: 4
Cooking: 10 min.		

Mrs. Thomas M. Garrett

MEATLESS LASAGNE
"Vegetarians love this"

2 15-oz. cans tomato sauce
1 cup onion, minced
1 tbsp. seasoned salt
1½ tsp. Italian herb seasoning
¼ tsp. garlic powder
3 eggs, beaten
1 16-oz. carton Ricotta cheese
1 8-oz. carton small curd cottage
    cheese
1 lb. lasagne noodles, cooked
2 lbs. Mozzarella cheese, thinly
    sliced
½ cup Parmesan cheese, grated

In a bowl, combine tomato sauce, onion, seasoned salt, Italian seasoning and garlic powder; set aside. Blend eggs, Ricotta and cottage cheese in small bowl. Spoon a little sauce into a 14 x 11 x 2″ glass pan to coat the bottom. Arrange in layers half of each of the cooked noodles, Ricotta mixture, sauce mixture and Mozzarella cheese slices. Repeat layers; sprinkle with Parmesan cheese. Bake at 375° for 40 to 45 minutes. Let stand 10 minutes before cutting.

Preparation: 30 min.   Easy   Serves: 10-12
Cooking: 45 min.   Can do ahead

Woodene B. Merriman

GNOCCHI A LA ROMAINE
"A nice alternative to potatoes"

1 cup milk
½ cup butter
1 cup grits, slow cooking style
1 tsp. salt
1 cup Gruyere cheese, grated
⅓ cup butter, melted
1⅓ cups Parmesan cheese,
    grated

Bring milk to a boil; add ½ cup butter and gradually stir in grits. Boil slowly, stirring constantly, until mixture thickens and has the appearance of cream of wheat. Remove from heat, add salt and beat with electric beater until mixture creams. Pour into a 9 x 13 x 2″ casserole and allow to set. Cut into rectangular pieces. Place pieces like rows of fallen dominoes in a buttered shallow casserole. Pour ⅓ cup melted butter over grits and sprinkle with the grated cheese. Bake in 400° oven about 30 minutes, then run under broiler a few minutes to brown. Serve with veal sour cream or veal picatta.

Preparation: 30 min.   Easy   Serves: 4
Cooking: 30 min.   Can do ahead

Mrs. Furman South, III

LINGUINE WITH FRESH BROCCOLI
"Garlic lovers should add more garlic"

1 bunch fresh broccoli
1 clove garlic, mashed
⅓ cup olive oil
1 cup Parmesan cheese, freshly grated
salt & freshly ground pepper, to taste
1 lb. linguine, cooked & drained

Cook trimmed broccoli in boiling, salted water until crisp-tender. Sauté garlic in oil until golden; remove garlic, add broccoli and sauté 10 minutes, stirring to brown lightly. Season to taste. Toss broccoli with hot linguine and grated cheese. Serve immediately.

Preparation: 30 min.   Easy   Serves: 4
Cooking: 20 min.

Mrs. Thomas M. Garrett

MUSHROOM CLAM SAUCE
"Lovely over linguine"

2 tbsp. butter
2 tbsp. margarine
2 cups onions, thinly sliced
1 lb. mushrooms, quartered
2 cans minced clams, undrained
1 cup dry Sherry
3 tbsp. fresh basil, minced
3 tbsp. fresh parsley, minced
1 tsp. salt
freshly ground pepper, to taste
3 tbsp. Parmesan cheese, grated
3 tbsp. butter, softened
3 tbsp. flour
½ cup sour cream

Melt butter and margarine together in a large skillet. When sizzling, add onions and mushrooms and cook until golden, stirring occasionally. Add clams, Sherry, basil, parsley, salt, pepper and cheese. Stir to blend, reduce heat, cover and simmer 30 minutes, stirring occasionally.

Cream the butter and flour together. Slowly add butter-flour mixture to sauce, stirring and incorporating well after each addition. When sauce is thickened, add sour cream and stir to blend. Do not boil. Serve over pasta.

Preparation: 15-20 min.   Easy   Serves: 4-6
Cooking: 35 min.   Can do ahead

Gemma Nestor

SALADS

ROTUNDA · PENNSYLVANIA RAILROAD STATION

The circular, vaulted vehicular concourse—or cabstand!—of the Pennsylvania Railroad Station (once Union Station) is a charming example of Neo-Baroque architecture. Influenced by the then fashionable Art Nouveau, the rotunda was constructed during 1901-02 under the guidance of the Chicago architectural firm of Daniel Hudson Burnham & Co.

Additional illustrations in this section:

Carnegie Institute Relief — dedicated to the memory of John Wesley Beatty, the first Director of Fine Arts, Carnegie Institute.

Pittsburgh lead glass pieces - Historical Society of Pittsburgh - 1815-1840.

All types of boats taking part in the Three Rivers Regatta, a three-day river festival celebrating the important part Pittsburgh's three rivers play in our lives.

SALADS

FISHERMAN'S AVOCADOS

"A super luncheon dish"

4 large avocados, halved
5 tbsp. lemon juice
¼ cup mayonnaise
2 tbsp. chili sauce
1 tsp. onion, minced
4 tsp. chives, minced
2 6½-oz. cans crabmeat,
    drained

Cut avocados in half lengthwise; scoop out some of the pulp. Mix pulp with remaining ingredients and refill avocado shells.

Preparation: 15 min.   Easy   Serves: 8
    Can do ahead

Peggy Standish

STUFFED AVOCADO SALAD

"An unusual looking salad"

2-3 med. avocados
2 tbsp. lemon juice
1 3-oz. pkg. cream cheese
1 tsp. onion juice
4 stuffed olives, chopped
2 tbsp. nuts, finely chopped
salt & pepper, to taste
lettuce leaves
French dressing

Cut avocados in half lengthwise, peel and remove seed. Scoop out 1 tablespoon pulp from each avocado half, enlarging seed cavity. Dip avocados in lemon juice. Blend together with fork until smooth: the avocado pulp, cream cheese, onion juice, lemon juice; add olives and nuts. Season with salt and pepper.

Fill cavities of avocados, then press together, matching halves and wrap in foil. Chill 3-4 hours. To serve: cut avocados in rings and place on lettuce leaves. Drizzle with French dressing.

Preparation: 20 min.   Easy   Serves: 4-6
    Must do ahead

Lois Pugh

ORIENTAL SALAD

4 envs. Knox gelatine
1 cup cold water
1½ cups boiling water
1 cup lemon juice
1 cup sugar
1 cup canned pineapple, drained
 & finely chopped
1½ cup drained cucumber,
 finely cut
1-1½ cups grapefruit & juice,
 canned or fresh
1 cup blanched almonds, split
 lengthwise
1½ cups avocado, coarsely
 chopped
vinegar
salt

Add gelatine to cold water, then dissolve in boiling water with lemon juice and sugar. Cook 2 minutes. Cool. Add pineapple, cucumber, grapefruit and juice, almonds and avocado. Add vinegar and salt to taste. Turn into an oiled, chilled 8 cup mold. Serve with mayonnaise mixed with whipped cream; can add grated orange peel and juice. Cheese straws are a nice accompaniment.

Preparation: 30 min.   Easy   Serves: 6-8
                         Must do ahead

Dorothy Hartley

VEGETABLE MOLD

"A colorful addition to a buffet"

Mold:
peanut oil
1 tbsp. parsley, minced
12 cherry tomatoes, halved
8 olives, halved
2 cans Campbell's bouillon,
 undiluted*
2 envs. Knox gelatine
juice of 1 lemon
3 tbsp. Sherry
1 tbsp. chives, minced
2 stalks celery or small
 cucumbers, chopped
*or 1 can bouillon and 1 can
 Madrilene

Dressing:
3 tbsp. sour cream
2 cups mayonnaise
3 tbsp. wine vinegar
1 tbsp. fresh basil, or ½ tbsp.
 dried
1 tbsp. fresh rosemary or ½
 tbsp. dried

Combine dressing ingredients thoroughly and refrigerate.

Oil a 1 quart mold with peanut oil. Arrange parsley, tomatoes and olives in it. Heat bouillon to boiling and dissolve gelatine in ½ cup of bouillon. Remove from heat and add all other ingredients. Chill until partially set, add gelatine mixture and refrigerate until firm. Unmold and serve with dressing. This is a "dry," not a sweet, flavored salad.

Preparation: 20 min.   Easy   Serves: 4-6
                         Must do ahead

Katherine W. Wilbert

MOLDED BORSCHT SALAD
"This is good with lamb"

1 1-qt. bottle borscht
2 3-oz. pkgs. lemon jello
1 tsp. unflavored gelatin
2 tsp. horseradish
½ cup celery, chopped
1 1-lb. can beets, drained &
   chopped

Dressing:
1 cup sour cream
horseradish, to taste

Oil 2 quart mold. Heat half of borscht and stir in lemon jello. In ½ cup cold borscht, soften plain gelatin. Combine both mixtures and stir well. Add remaining ingredients and pour into oiled mold. Chill until firm, unmold, and serve with dressing.

Preparation: 15 min.   Easy   Serves: 12
Cooking: 5 min.   Must do ahead

Mrs. Jon E. McCarthy

SPECIAL TOMATO ASPIC
"Easy and good - a great gazpacho-type aspic"

1 1-lb. can Del Monte stewed
   tomatoes, undrained
1 3-oz. pkg. lemon jello
1 cup boiling water
2 tbsp. green pepper, finely
   chopped
2 tbsp. green onion, chopped
1 tbsp. vinegar
sugar, salt & pepper, to taste

Mash large tomato pieces before mixing with mixture of jello and water. Add remaining ingredients and chill in oiled 4 cup ring mold.

Preparation: 15 min.   Easy   Serves: 6
                           Must do ahead

Melissa Booth Moore

RASPBERRY-CRANBERRY WINE SALAD

1 6-oz. pkg. raspberry gelatin
2 cups boiling water
1 16-oz. can whole cranberry
   sauce
1 cup crushed pineapple,
   undrained
½ cup Burgundy
⅓ cup walnuts, chopped

Dissolve gelatin in 2 cups boiling water. Stir in cranberry sauce, pineapple and Burgundy. Chill until partially set, about 1 hour. Stir in nuts. Pour into 6 cup mold, chill several hours until set. Unmold.

Preparation: 30 min.   Easy   Serves: 10-12
Cooking: 5 min.   Must do ahead

Mrs. Joseph J. Ladik, Jr.

CURRIED TURKEY CHUTNEY SALAD ON CANTALOUPE

3½-4 lb. turkey breast
1½ cups celery, thinly sliced
1 cup mayonnaise
2 tsp. curry powder
¾ cup mango chutney, drained
   & chopped
salt
pepper
cantaloupe

Condiments:
½ cup scallions, minced
½ lb. cashews, toasted
½ lb. bacon, cooked &
   crumbled
¼ lb. golden raisins
¼ cup green pepper, chopped

Poach turkey breast for approximately 40 minutes until tender or bake according to package directions. Cool, discard skin and bones. Cut turkey into ½" cubes.

In a large bowl, combine turkey, celery, mayonnaise mixed with curry powder, and mango chutney. Salt and pepper to taste. Cover and chill. Slice cantaloupe into 2" rounds, remove seeds and fill with turkey mixture. Pass condiments in separate bowls.

Preparation: 15 min.	Easy	Serves: 6
Cooking: 40 min.	Must do ahead	

Mrs. Roger Brown, Jr.

MOLDED GAZPACHO SALAD WITH AVOCADO DRESSING
"Very special and very good"

2 envs. unflavored gelatin
3 cups tomato juice
⅓ cup red wine vinegar
1 tsp. salt
dash Tabasco sauce
2 small tomatoes, peeled & diced
½ med. bell pepper, diced
¼ cup onion, chopped
1 tbsp. chives, chopped
¼ cup celery, chopped

Dressing:
1 ripe avocado
1 tbsp. lemon juice
½ cup light cream
½ cup sour cream
1 clove garlic, minced
⅛ tsp. sugar
½ tsp. salt, or to taste
1 tbsp. onion, grated
dash cayenne pepper

Sprinkle gelatin over tomato juice and stir over low heat until dissolved. Remove from heat and add vinegar, salt and Tabasco. Stir. Chill until partially set. Add vegetables and stir. Pour into 1½ quart mold or pan. Refrigerate until ready to serve.

Dressing: Peel and mash the avocado with the lemon juice. Stir light cream into sour cream and blend; add seasonings. Stir in the avocado and chill.

Preparation: 1 hour	Easy	Serves: 6-8
	Must do ahead	

Mrs. William W. Morris

CURRIED EGG AND SPINACH
"A good combination with poached fish"

1 lb. spinach
1 heaping tbsp. Knox gelatine
¼ cup cold water
3 cups chicken broth, heated
1 cup mayonnaise
1-2 tsp. curry powder, to taste
salt & pepper, to taste
Accent
6 hard-boiled eggs, sliced

Cook spinach and set it aside to drain and cool. Chop coarsely. Soften gelatine in water; add hot broth and stir until dissolved. Mix in mayonnaise and seasonings. Gently stir in spinach and eggs. Turn into 1½ quart mold and chill until firm. Unmold and serve.

Preparation: 30 min.

Easy
Can do ahead

Serves: 8-10

Mrs. Robert B. Appleyard

COLESLAW

1 head cabbage, shredded
½ pt. coffee cream
½ cup sugar
1 cup Hellmann's mayonnaise
dash cider vinegar
salt & pepper, to taste

Mix all ingredients together, varying ingredients if you like it soupy or sweeter or more sour.

Preparation: 5-10 min. with
processor

Easy
Can do ahead

Serves: 6-8

Josephine Arrigo
Allegheny Country Club

CHERRY PORT WINE SALAD
"Pretty at Christmastime."

1 20-oz. can pitted black
cherries
1 cup cherry juice
1 3-oz. pkg. lemon gelatin
1 cup Port wine
¼ cup mayonnaise
⅓ cup cream, whipped or 1 carton
small curd cottage cheese

Drain cherries; reserve juice. If necessary, add water to juice to make 1 cup. Bring juice to boiling point; add gelatin; stir until dissolved. Cool. Add wine and chill until thickened. Add cherries, pour into mold and chill. Fold whipped cream into mayonnaise and serve as

dressing. Remove mold from tin and put on crisp lettuce or make a ring mold and serve with cottage cheese in center.

Preparation: 10 min.
Cooking: 5 min.

Easy
Must do ahead

Serves: 6-8

Mrs. Lloyd Booth, Jr.

MARINATED CARROTS

"Mr. Roger's favorite"

2 lbs. carrots, sliced
1 med. sweet onion, chopped
1 small green pepper, chopped
1 can tomato soup
½ cup cooking oil
1 cup sugar
¾ cup vinegar
1 tsp. hot mustard
1 tsp. Worcestershire sauce
1 tsp. salt
1 tsp. pepper

Cook carrots until tender; drain and cool. Add onions. Mix remaining ingredients and marinate at least 12 hours.

Preparation: 15 min.   Easy   Serves: 10-12
                          Must do ahead

Fred Rogers

DILL SLAW

"Easy to make for a crowd"

1 med. head cabbage
⅓ cup onion, chopped
⅓ cup stuffed, green olives, chopped
¾ cup mayonnaise
⅓ cup sour cream
¼ cup milk
1 tbsp. vinegar
1 tsp. dill weed
½ tsp. celery seed
salt & pepper, to taste
tomatoes, garnish

Finely grate cabbage, add chopped onions and olives. Mix the remaining ingredients for dressing and toss gently with the cabbage mixture. Chill before serving and garnish with tomatoes.

Preparation: 15 min.   Easy   Serves: 6-8
                          Must do ahead

Mrs. Donald D. Wolff, Jr.

DEUTSCH VEGETABLE SALAD

"Sweet and sour"

1 16-oz. can peas
1 16-oz. can shoepeg corn
1 16-oz. can green beans
1 med. onion, chopped
½-1 green pepper, chopped
½ cup celery, chopped
½ cup salad oil
½ cup vinegar
¾ cup sugar
1 tsp. salt
½ tsp. pepper

Drain all vegetables and set aside. Combine the oil, vinegar, sugar, salt and pepper and heat to boiling. Pour over vegetables, mix well and refrigerate 1 day before serving. Keeps refrigerated for 2 weeks.

Preparation: 20 min.   Easy   Serves: 6-8
                          Must do ahead

Carmella Pennetti

KANSAS CITY SALAD

"Try this with red onion rings for color"

1 head cauliflower
1 bunch broccoli tops
5-6 scallions, including tops
1 10-oz. pkg. frozen peas,
  defrosted
½ cup sour cream
½ cup Hellmann's mayonnaise
1 tbsp. horseradish
salt & pepper, to taste

Cut cauliflower, broccoli and scallions into small pieces: toss with peas. Combine dressing ingredients until blended. Mix with the vegetables and refrigerate. Prepare several hours or a day in advance.

Preparation: 40 min.

Easy
Must do ahead

Serves: 8-10

Jemele Sanderson Hudson

PORTUGUESE SALAD

"A sophisticated salad"

1 lb. salt cod, prepared for
  cooking
3 med. Idaho baking potatoes,
  boiled, unpeeled & warm
3 hard-boiled eggs, sliced
1 bunch scallions, thinly sliced,
  or 1 small red onion, thinly
  sliced
salt & freshly ground pepper, to
  taste
4 tbsp. wine vinegar
1 cup olive oil
tomatoes, cut in wedges & kept
  at room temperature
black & green olives
fresh parsley, chopped

To prepare cod, soak it in water to cover at room temperature for 24 hours, changing the water three or four times. Bring the fish slowly to a boil in fresh water, drain immediately and pat dry on paper towels. There should be no trace of salt left, and the texture should be similar to fresh fish except for a slight tendency to shred.

Put the prepared salt cod in fresh water, bring to a simmer and cook very slowly for 10 minutes. Drain and flake the fish. Peel the warm potatoes and slice them, about ¼" thick, into a bowl. Add the flaked salt cod, hard-boiled eggs, onions, a pinch of salt and plenty of freshly ground pepper, and toss with the vinaigrette, made from mixing together the vinegar and olive oil. Do not add all the vinaigrette at once, as it may be too much. Season to taste. Minced garlic can be added, if desired. To serve, heap on plate, surrounded by tomatoes, olives and a sprinkle of parsley. Do not refrigerate before serving.

Preparation: 45 min.
Cooking: 20 min.

Serves: 4-8

Teresa Heinz

ORANGE ONION ENDIVE SALAD

"The dressing makes this a superlative salad"

1 lb. Endive or Bibb lettuce
1 head Boston lettuce
1 bunch watercress
4 large navel oranges, peeled & sliced*
1 med. red onion, thinly sliced
*or 2 11-oz. cans mandarin oranges

Clean all salad greens and chill. Arrange in bowl, top with orange and onion slices. Toss with orange-sour cream dressing, see page 180.

Preparation: 20 min.

Easy
Can do ahead

Serves: 4-6

Mrs. R. S. Richards, Jr.

SOUTHERN POTATO SALAD

2 lbs. potatoes
1 cup celery, sliced
1 4-oz. can pimentos, drained & diced
2 tbsp. onion, diced
¼ cup sweet pickles, drained & diced
2 tbsp. sweet pickle juice
2-3 tsp. prepared mustard
½ cup mayonnaise
salt
white pepper

Cook potatoes in skins, drain, chill and cube. Mix with celery, pimento, onion and pickle. Blend the juice and mustard in a small bowl; gradually stir in the mayonnaise and mix thoroughly. Add to first mixture and toss lightly, but thoroughly. Season to taste with salt and pepper. Chill, covered, several hours or overnight.

Preparation: 45 min.
Cooking: 30 min.

Easy
Must do ahead

Serves: 6

Mrs. Vincent A. Cortese

MEDITERRANEAN POTATO SALAD

"Get the zucchini from your garden"

6 small potatoes, cooked
¼ cup onion, finely chopped
3 cups zucchini, diced
12 cherry tomatoes, halved
4 tbsp. lemon juice
4 tbsp. salad oil
2 tsp. basil leaves
1½ tsp. salt
¼ tsp. garlic powder
½ tsp. pepper

Cook potatoes; drain and chill. Cube potatoes and combine with onions, zucchini and tomatoes and toss lightly. Combine remaining ingredients in separate bowl and blend. Pour dressing over potato mixture and toss gently. Refrigerate.

Preparation: 20 min.

Easy
Must do ahead

Serves: 6

Doris H. Paul

HOT GREEN BEAN POTATO SALAD
"Potato salad for winter time"

4 med. potatoes, cooked & diced
1 1-lb. can cut green beans, drained
2 tbsp. bacon fat
2 tbsp. lemon juice
1 tbsp. sugar
1 tsp. salt
¼ tsp. pepper
⅛ tsp. garlic powder
¼ tsp. dry mustard
6 slices bacon, cooked & crumbled
2 tbsp. onion, minced
⅓ cup Hellmann's mayonnaise

Mix first 9 ingredients together. Put into a 2 quart casserole and heat, uncovered, at 325° for 20 minutes or until heated through. Add bacon, onion and mayonnaise and toss before serving.

Preparation: 30 min.   Easy   Serves: 5-6
Cooking: 20 min.   Can do ahead

Ann Selck

SPINACH SALAD

1 egg, beaten
⅔ cup sugar
½ cup apple cider vinegar
½ cup water
1 tsp. salt
1 lb. spinach, torn into bite-sized pieces
1 med. onion, sliced
½-1 lb. mushrooms, sliced
10-12 slices bacon, cooked

In saucepan, combine first 5 ingredients. Heat to boiling, stirring constantly. Cool. Toss dressing with spinach, onion and mushrooms. Garnish with crumbled bacon.

Can do dressing and salad ahead, separately, and combine just before serving.

Preparation: 15-20 min.   Easy   Serves: 6-8
Cooking: 5 min.   Can do ahead

Mona Fossee

SPINACH SALAD

1 10-oz. pkg. fresh spinach
2 hard-boiled eggs, sliced
6-8 slices bacon, cooked & crumbled
1 small red onion, sliced
¼ pkg. Pepperidge Farm stuffing mix

Dressing:
⅓ cup sugar
1 cup oil
⅓ cup vinegar
1 tsp. mustard
½ tsp. salt
¼ tsp. pepper
1 med. white onion, chopped
1 tsp. celery seed

Wash spinach thoroughly. Break into bite-sized pieces and combine with the next 4 ingredients. Mix all dressing ingredients well. Pour over salad and toss thoroughly.

Preparation: 30 min.   Easy   Serves: 4

Mrs. George B. Angevine

SPINACH ORANGE SALAD
"Outstanding"

Salad:
1 lb. spinach
1 4-oz. can water chestnuts,
  thinly sliced
1 16-oz. can mandarin oranges,
  drained
½ 8-oz. can bean sprouts,
  drained
½ red onion, sliced
3 eggs, hard-boiled
5 slices bacon, cooked &
  crumbled

Dressing:
½ cup salad oil
½ cup red wine vinegar
3 tbsp. ketchup
¼ cup sugar
1 tsp. salt

Clean spinach and tear into bite-size pieces. Toss with other ingredients ½ hour before serving. Crumble bacon over top.

Combine dressing ingredients, pour over salad and toss gently.

Salad and dressing can be prepared ahead, then tossed together immediately before serving.

Preparation: 20-30 min.   Easy   Serves: 6
                             Can do ahead

Mrs. Daniel Driscoll

SUPER SALAD
"A summer shrimp salad supper"

Dressing:
1 cup oil
⅓ cup red wine vinegar
⅛ tsp. pepper
1¼ tsp. salt
⅛ tsp. oregano

Salad:
1 cup Iceberg lettuce
1 cup Romaine lettuce
1 cup shrimp, cooked & diced
1 can artichoke hearts,
  quartered
1 can hearts of palm, sliced
¼ cup scallions, sliced
2 med. tomatoes, cubed
5 large, ripe olives, sliced
1 avocado, cubed

Combine dressing ingredients in jar and shake well. In large bowl, combine bite-sized pieces of lettuces with other salad ingredients. Pour dressing over all and let mellow for 1 hour or longer.

Preparation: 15 min.   Easy   Serves: 6-12
                            Can do ahead

Linda Payne

SPINACH AND PEA SALAD

1 pkg. fresh spinach
½ lb. bacon, cooked &
   crumbled
1 head lettuce
1 10-oz. pkg. peas, thawed &
   drained
1 red onion, thinly sliced
1 can water chestnuts, drained
   & sliced
1½ cups sour cream
1½ cups mayonnaise
1 pkg. Hidden Valley dressing
½ tsp. sugar
Parmesan cheese

Layer vegetables in order given in glass bowl. Combine the sour cream, mayonnaise, dressing and sugar and spread over the vegetables. Sprinkle generously with cheese. Cover tightly with plastic wrap and refrigerate 12 or more hours.

Preparation: 30 min.   Easy   Serves: 12
                             Must do ahead

Helga Freymark

TOMATOES FINES HERBES

"Simple and attractive"

8 large, firm, ripe tomatoes
8 tbsp. parsley, finely chopped
4 tbsp. onion, finely chopped
1 tbsp. garlic, minced
2 tbsp. basil, minced
2 tbsp. tarragon, minced
6 tbsp. salad oil
3 tbsp. wine vinegar
salt
pepper

Cut tomatoes into even slices. Mix herbs, onion, oil and vinegar; add salt and pepper to taste. Drizzle dressing over tomatoes or reform tomatoes with dressing in between slices.

Can be served as salad or vegetable. If serving as a vegetable, top with Parmesan cheese, run under broiler to brown and bake at 350° for 10 minutes.

Preparation: 20 min.   Easy   Serves: 8-12
Cooking: 10 min.   Must do ahead

Chappy's Choice

SALAD DRESSINGS

ORANGE SOUR CREAM DRESSING

peel of ½ orange, cut in very thin strips
2 tbsp. water
4 tbsp. sugar
½ cup salad oil
4 tsp. Dijon mustard
2 eggs yolks
4 tbsp. sour cream
1 tsp. chives

Put orange peel strips in a pan with water and sugar. Cook over very low heat until orange peel is translucent. Cool. Combine remaining ingredients in blender until thoroughly blended. Add orange mixture and continue blending.

Preparation: 20 min. | **Easy** | **Yield: 1 cup**
Can do ahead

Mrs. R. S. Richards, Jr.

CREAMY MUSTARD SALAD DRESSING

"Best if made one or two days ahead"

2 eggs
3 tbsp. olive oil
3 tbsp. tarragon vinegar
1 tbsp. plus 1 tsp. Dijon mustard
2¼ tsp. lemon juice
1½ tsp. garlic powder
1¼ tsp. sugar
1 tsp. salt
¾ tsp. dry mustard
⅛ tsp. pepper
½ cup plus 1 tbsp. vegetable oil
3 tbsp. heavy cream

Place all ingredients except vegetable oil and cream in blender or food processor. Blend until smooth, about 30 seconds. Gradually blend in the oil and cream; blend until smooth, about 30 seconds.

Preparation: 10 min. | **Easy** | **Yield: 1½ cup**
Must do ahead

Mrs. Francis J. Sullivan

HONEY KETCHUP DRESSING

½ cup honey
⅓ cup ketchup
⅓ cup vinegar
½ tsp. salt
1 tbsp. onion, minced
1 tbsp. Worcestershire sauce
1 cup salad oil

Mix all ingredients, except the salad oil, well. Add oil gradually, then beat until well blended. Serve over crab, shrimp or green salads.

Preparation: 5 min.   Easy   Yield: 1 pint
                          Can do ahead

Mrs. Joseph Dury, Jr.

ROQUEFORT DRESSING

"Tasty - keeps well in the refrigerator"

1 garlic clove
2 small onions
2 sprigs fresh parsley
½ lb. Roquefort or Blue cheese
1 pt. Hellmann's mayonnaise
juice of 2 lemons
½ cup sour cream

Put garlic, parsley and onions through a blender or food processor or chop finely. Crumble cheese in bowl; add other ingredients. Mix. This dressing keeps well in refrigerator. More cheese may be added, if desired.

Preparation: 10 min.   Easy   Yield: 3 cups
                          Can do ahead

Mrs. William H. Genge

GREEN GODDESS DRESSING

½ cup parsley, finely chopped
3 tsp. green onion, minced
¾ tsp. garlic, minced
1 tsp. sugar
1½ tbsp. anchovy paste
2 cups Hellmann's mayonnaise
⅓ cup corn oil
8 oz. sour cream
4½ tbsp. tarragon vinegar
1½ tbsp. fresh lemon juice
¼ tsp. salt
pepper, freshly ground
2-4 drops green food coloring

Combine all ingredients and mix well. Can be done in a blender.

Preparation: 10 min   Easy   Yield: 3 cups
                         Can do ahead

Mrs. Robert A. McKean, Jr.

HONEY DRESSING

"Try this over lettuce, orange sections and Bermuda onion slices."

⅔ cup sugar
1 tsp. dry mustard
1 tsp. paprika
¼ tsp. salt
1 tsp. celery seed
⅓ cup honey
5 tbsp. white vinegar
1 tbsp. lemon juice
1 small onion, quartered
1 cup oil

Put first 9 ingredients in blender and blend well. Add oil in a slow steady stream, whirling constantly. Good with greens and fruit salads.

Preparation: 10 min.   Easy
Can do ahead   Yield: 1½ cups

Mrs. Furman South, III

LEMON SALAD DRESSING

¼ cup sugar
juice of 2 lemons
2 egg yolks
dash salt
2 tsp. basil
1-1¼ cups vegetable oil

Beat the sugar and lemon juice until thoroughly combined. Add the egg yolks, salt and basil. Mix. Slowly beat in the vegetable oil.

Preparation: 10 min.   Easy   Yield: 2 cups

Ralph Wilson
"Willow Inn"

WHITE FRENCH DRESSING

"Tastes like Stouffer's"

3 tbsp. cornstarch
¼ cup cold water
½ cup boiling water
¼ tsp. paprika
¼ tsp. hot water
½ cup sugar
2 tbsp. salt, or to taste
1 tsp. dry mustard
2¾ cups salad oil
1 cup cider vinegar
½ tsp. onion juice
¼ tsp. fine herbs (salad herbs)
1 clove garlic on toothpick

Dissolve cornstarch in cold water. Add boiling water and cook until thickened, stirring constantly: it usually thickens immediately. Dissolve paprika in hot water and add to cornstarch mixture. Add sugar, salt and mustard. If lumpy, strain. Whip on high speed of electric mixer, gradually adding oil alternately with vinegar. By hand, mix in onion juice, herbs and garlic clove. Let stand 24 hours before removing garlic clove.

Preparation: 30 min.   Easy   Yield: 5 cups
Must do ahead

Cathy Beard

SWEETS

TROLLEY

The Black and Gold Steeler Trolley traveling through the city—past The Bank Center on Fourth Avenue—symbolizes Pittsburghers' pride in their home-town team.

Additional illustrations in this section:

Restored Victorian home in Manchester.

Leaded glass panel in Renaissance pictorial tradition—from Odd Fellows Hall in Bellvue, courtesy of the Pittsburgh History and Landmarks Foundation, Old Post Office Museum Collection.

Memorial to Stephen Collins Foster in Oakland.

Heinz Stoneware Crock from the Pittsburgh History and Landmarks Foundation, Old Post Office Museum Collection.

Imaginarium player entertains children at the annual Three Rivers Arts Festival. The Three Rivers Arts Festival began in 1960 and has steadily grown until the juried visual show now accepts over 650 artists, welcomes one-quarter million visitors and encompasses 165 performing events in various locations throughout the city. The children's activities have been financially supported by Child Health for many years, and since 1978 C.H. has also provided close and thorough guidance over this area of the Festival.

Free blown covered urns, circa 1860.*

General Store at Fort Pitt Museum in Point State Park.

*All glassware is early Pittsburgh unless otherwise indicated.

CAKES

VICTORIAN ORANGE PEEL CAKE
"Would be a good 'bake ahead' for Christmas"

Cake:
peel of 3 large oranges
1 cup raisins
1 cup sugar
½ cup butter, room temperature
2 eggs
¾ cup buttermilk
2 cups flour
1 tsp. baking soda
½ tsp. salt
½ cup walnuts, chopped

Orange syrup:
1 cup fresh orange juice
½ cup sugar
2 tbsp. dark Rum

Preheat oven to 325°. Grind orange peels and raisins together 3 times or place in food processor and chop finely. Cream sugar and butter thoroughly. Add eggs and buttermilk and mix well. Sift together flour, baking soda and salt and stir into batter. Mix in ground peel, raisins and walnuts. Pour into well greased 9 or 10" springform or tube pan. Bake 45 to 50 minutes, or until done. While cake is baking, heat orange juice, sugar and Rum together until sugar is completely dissolved.

When cake is done, let stand 10 minutes, then remove from pan. Invert and slowly pour orange juice mixture, a tablespoon at a time, over cake. Allow to stand overnight or better, several days. Store at room temperature if cake will be eaten in a few days or refrigerate for longer storage. *Note:* Best not to use bundt pan with a dark lining because cake gets too brown.

Preparation: 15-20 min.   **Easy**   **Serves:** 10-12
Baking: 45-50 min.   **Must do ahead**

Mrs. Herman S. Harvey, Jr.

185

CHOCOLATE CHEESECAKE
"Even has a chocolate crust - Heaven!

1½ cups chocolate wafers, crushed
⅓ cup margarine
8-oz. pkg. cream cheese
¼ cup sugar
1 tsp. vanilla
2 egg yolks, beaten
6-oz. chocolate chips, melted
2 egg whites
¼ cup sugar
1 cup heavy cream, whipped
¾ cup pecans, coarsely chopped

Combine wafers and margarine. Press into a 9″ springform pan. Combine the cheese, sugar and vanilla and beat until smooth. Add egg yolks and chocolate chips. Make a soft meringue of egg whites and sugar; fold into the chocolate mixture. Fold the cream and pecans into the chocolate meringue mixture. Pour into springform pan and freeze. Thaw 15-30 minutes before serving.

Preparation: 30 min.   Easy   Serves: 8-10
                          Must do ahead

Barbara Johns

PUMPKIN CHEESECAKE
"A melt in your mouth cheesecake"

Crust:
1½ cups graham crackers
⅓ cup butter, melted
⅓ cup sugar

Combine crust ingredients and press into a greased 10″ springform pan. Bake at 325° for 5 minutes. Cool.

Filling:
2 8-oz. pkgs. cream cheese, softened
1 cup coffee cream
1 cup pumpkin
¾ cup sugar
4 egg yolks
3 tbsp. flour
½ tsp. vanilla
1 tsp. cinnamon
½ tsp. ginger
¼ tsp. nutmeg
½ tsp. salt
4 egg whites

Mix all filling ingredients together, except egg whites. Beat the egg whites until stiff and fold into mixture. Pour into crust and bake at 325° for 1 hour.

Combine sour cream, sugar and vanilla. Pour over warm cheesecake and bake another 5 minutes. Chill overnight, remove from pan and serve.

Topping:
1 cup sour cream
2 tbsp. sugar
½ tsp. vanilla

Preparation: 30-35 min.   Easy   Serves: 18
Baking: 1 hour   Must do ahead

Melissa Booth Moore

ITALIAN CREAM CAKE

"This cake will get raves at your next dinner party"

1½ cups sugar
1 stick butter
½ cup Crisco
5 eggs, separated
2 cups flour
1 cup buttermilk with 1 tsp. baking soda added
1 cup Angel Flake coconut

Frosting:
1 8-oz. pkg. cream cheese
1 stick margarine
1 lb. confectioners' sugar
1 tsp. almond extract
½ cup walnuts or pecans, ground

Cream sugar, butter and Crisco. Add egg yolks one at a time, beating well. Alternately add flour and buttermilk; beat well. Add coconut. Beat egg whites until stiff and fold into batter. Bake in 4 greased and floured 8″ pans at 350° for 25-35 minutes. Layers will be thin.
Frosting: Cream the cheese and margarine; add the confectioners' sugar, almond extract and nuts. Mix until smooth. Frost cake.

Preparation:	30 min.	Easy	Serves: 12
Baking:	25-35 min.	Can do ahead	Can freeze

Cathy Beard

CHOCOLATE CHEESE CUPS

"A bit of heaven for chocolate lovers"

Cream Cheese mixture:
1 8-oz. pkg. cream cheese
1 egg
⅓ cup sugar
pinch salt
6 oz. chocolate chips

Chocolate batter:
3 cups flour
2 cups sugar
½ cup cocoa
2 tsp. baking soda
1 tsp. salt
2 cups water
⅔ cup cooking oil
2 tbsp. vinegar
2 tsp. vanilla

slivered almonds
sugar

Combine first 4 ingredients and stir in chocolate chips. In another bowl, sift dry ingredients, then add liquid ingredients. Place paper baking cups in muffin tins and fill half full with chocolate batter. Top with 1 heaping teaspoon of cream cheese mixture. Sprinkle with slivered almonds and sugar. Bake at 350° for 30-35 minutes.

Preparation:	20 min.	Easy	Yield: 3 doz.
Baking:	30-35 min.	Can do ahead	Can freeze

Mrs. Daniel H. Brooks

ORANGE NUT BUTTER CAKE

"Super moist, good even without icing"

Cake:
¾ cup butter, softened
1 cup sugar
1 tbsp. orange rind, grated
1 tsp. vanilla
3 eggs
1 cup orange marmalade
3 cups cake flour
1¼ tsp. baking soda
1 tsp. salt
½ cup orange juice
½ cup evaporated milk
1 cup nuts, chopped

Frosting:
1 cup heavy cream
2 tbsp. sugar
1 tbsp. orange rind, grated

Cream butter thoroughly. Add sugar, orange rind and vanilla. Beat until mixture is light and fluffy. Add eggs one at a time, beating well after each addition. Blend in marmalade. Sift flour, baking soda and salt together. Combine orange juice and evaporated milk. Add dry ingredients alternately with juice-milk mixture. Stir in chopped nuts and blend. Turn into well buttered tube pan. Bake in preheated 350° oven for 50-55 minutes. Cool in pan 10 minutes and remove. Serve warm or cool. Beat heavy cream until stiff and blend in sugar and rind. Frost cake when cool.

Preparation:	25 min.	Easy	Serves: 10-12
Baking:	55 min.	Can do ahead	

Mrs. Louis D. Ruscitto

PUMPKIN CAKE

"Sort of a cake, sort of a pie — unusual"

Cake mixture:
1 box yellow cake mix, reserve
　　¾ cup
1 stick butter, melted
1 egg, lightly beaten

Pumpkin mixture:
1 large can pumpkin
3 eggs, lightly beaten
½ cup brown sugar
¼ cup white sugar
⅔ cup evaporated milk
1½ tsp. cinnamon
½ tsp. ginger
½ tsp. ground cloves

¾ cup cake mix
½ cup white sugar
¼ cup butter, softened
½-1 cup nuts, chopped, optional

Blend the butter and egg into the cake mix and press into a greased and floured 9x13x2″ pan. Use the back of a tablespoon to pat this mixture evenly over the bottom and 1″ up the sides of the pan.

Gently mix the pumpkin, eggs, sugars, milk and seasonings. Pour over unbaked mixture. Blend the reserved cake mix with sugar and butter. Roll into walnut-sized balls and place over the pumpkin mixture. Sprinkle with nuts, if desired. Bake at 350° for 55 minutes.

Preparation:	20-30 min.	Easy	Serves: 18 2x3″ squares
Baking:	55 min.		Can freeze

Mrs. James Rankin Duncan, J

ONE-STEP POUND CAKE

"Second step is to serve with sherry at tea"

Cake:
2¼ cups flour
2 cups sugar
½ tsp. salt
½ tsp. baking soda
1 tsp. vanilla
1 8-oz. carton pineapple yogurt
　or 1 cup sour cream
3 large eggs
1 tbsp. lemon peel, grated, or
　2-3 tbsp. poppy seeds
1 cup margarine

Combine cake ingredients in a bowl and beat at low speed for 3 minutes. Bake in greased and floured 12 cup tube pan at 325° for 60-70 minutes. Cool.

Glaze: Combine 1 cup powdered sugar with 3 tablespoons lemon juice. Glaze cooled cake.

Preparation: 5 min.	Easy	Serves: 10
Baking: 60-70 min.		Can freeze

Ann Scott Sawhill

COCONUT POUND CAKE

"A variation on a classic cake"

6 eggs, separated
1 cup Fluffo or Crisco
½ cup margarine
3 cups sugar
½ tsp. almond extract
½ tsp. coconut extract
3 cups cake flour, sifted
1 cup milk
2 cups Baker's coconut
confectioners' sugar

Let egg whites warm to room temperature, about 1 hour. Preheat oven at 300°. Grease 10″ tube pan.

Using high speed of electric mixer, beat egg yolks with shortening and margarine until well blended. Gradually add sugar, beating until light and fluffy. Add extracts. At low speed, beat in flour, ⅓ at a time, alternating with milk. Add coconut and beat until blended. Beat egg whites just until stiff. Gently fold whites into batter until well combined. Turn into prepared pan.

Bake 2 hours or until a toothpick comes out clean. Cool in pan 15 minutes; remove from pan. Cool and dust with confectioners' sugar. Wrap well in plastic wrap - store in refrigerator overnight. Cake will be white using Crisco, golden using Fluffo.

Preparation: 20 min.	Easy	Serves: 12-16
Baking: 2 hours	Must do ahead	

Mrs. Gary H. McQuone

RAW APPLE CAKE

"You won't be able to stop with just one bite"

Cake:
½ cup shortening
2 cups sugar
2 eggs
2 cups flour
½ tsp. salt
2 tsp. soda
2 tsp. cinnamon
4 cups apples, sliced
1 cup raisins
½ cup walnuts

Fluffy Lemon Sauce:
½ cup sugar
2 tbsp. cornstarch
⅛ tsp. nutmeg
1 cup boiling water
1 tbsp. butter
2 tsp. grated lemon rind
4 tbsp. lemon juice
1 egg, well beaten

Cream together shortening, sugar and eggs. Sift together flour, salt, soda and cinnamon. Add apples, raisins and walnuts to creamed mixture; then add sifted dry ingredients. Bake at 350° for 60-70 minutes in a greased 9x13" pan.

Fluffy Lemon Sauce: Mix sugar, cornstarch and nutmeg together in saucepan. Gradually stir in boiling water. Boil 1 minute, stirring constantly. Stir in butter, lemon rind and juice. Very gradually add beaten egg. Pour over warm cake.

Preparation: 20 min.	Easy	Serves: 12-16
Baking: 60-70 min.	Can do ahead	

Patricia Turner

BLUEBERRY UPSIDE-DOWN CAKE

"Lovely texture - stays fresh and light"

Berry Mixture:
2 cups blueberries
2 tbsp. lemon juice
½ cup sugar
1 tbsp. flour or cornstarch
1-2 tbsp. butter

Batter:
½ cup butter, softened
1 cup sugar
1 egg
¾ cup milk
2 cups cake flour
2 tsp. baking powder
¼ tsp. salt
1 tsp. vanilla

whipped cream

Wash berries and turn into a buttered 8x12" pan. Sprinkle with lemon juice. Combine sugar and cornstarch and sprinkle over top of berries. Dot with butter.

Batter: Gradually add sugar to butter and cream thoroughly. Add egg and beat until light and fluffy. Sift flour once, then measure and sift 3 times with baking powder and salt. Add flour alternately with milk, a small amount at a time, beating after each addition until smooth. Add vanilla. Pour mixture over blueberries in pan and bake in 350° oven for 50 minutes until done. Invert and serve warm with whipped cream

Preparation: 30 min.	Easy	Serves: 12
Baking: 50 min.	Must do ahead	Can freeze

Mrs. Louis D. Ruscitt

HAWAIIAN CARROT CAKE
"Topped with a tart but sweet icing"

Cake:
3 med. carrots, peeled
1 cup sugar
½ cup vegetable oil
2 eggs
1 tsp. baking powder
1 tsp. baking soda
1 tsp. cinnamon
1 tsp. salt
¼ tsp. mace
1½ cups flour
1 8¼-oz. can crushed
   pineapple, undrained

Frosting:
1 3-oz. pkg. cream cheese
2-3 tsp. lemon juice
2 tbsp. butter or margarine
1½ cups confectioners' sugar
¼ tsp. mace

Shred carrots in food processor. Add sugar, oil, eggs, baking powder and soda, cinnamon, salt and mace and mix. Add flour and mix thoroughly. Add pineapple and combine until just mixed. Turn into a greased and floured 9" square baking pan. Bake at 350° for 30-35 minutes until cake springs back when lightly touched in center. Cool and remove from pan.

Frosting: Cream the cheese; add the lemon juice and butter. Mix. Add the sugar and mace and mix until smooth. Frost cake.

Preparation:	20 min.	**Easy**	**Serves: 8-10**
Baking:	35 min.	**Can do ahead**	

Mrs. James H. Morgens

SPICE CAKE WITH SEAFOAM ICING
"No wonder mother won prizes with this"

Cake:
2¼ cups cake flour, sifted
1 tsp. baking powder
1 tsp. baking soda
½ tsp. salt
1 tsp. cinnamon
1 tsp. nutmeg
½ tsp. cloves
½ cup shortening
1½ cups sugar
2 eggs
1 cup buttermilk

Seafoam Icing:
1½ cups light brown sugar
3 tbsp. water
2 egg whites

Preheat oven to 375°. Sift first 7 ingredients together twice. Cream shortening, add sugar and beat thoroughly. Add eggs, one at a time, and beat at high speed until mixture is light. Turn beater to lowest speed. Fold in flour mixture and buttermilk, alternately, as quickly as possible, blending thoroughly. Spread in 2 greased and floured 9" cake pans and bake for 30 minutes. Cool 10 minutes and remove from pans to rack to cool completely.

Heat icing ingredients in double boiler and beat at high speed until stiff peaks form. Frost cake.

Preparation:	30 min.	**Easy**
Baking:	30 min.	**Can do ahead**

Mrs. Robert E. Boyd

PRAIRIE BEER CAKE

"Moist and tasty - even better several days later"

1 cup shortening
2 cups brown sugar, firmly packed
2 eggs, well beaten
3 cups flour, sifted
½ tsp. salt
2 tsp. baking soda
1 tsp. cinnamon
½ tsp. allspice
½ tsp. ground cloves
1 cup walnuts or pecans, chopped
2 cups dates or prunes, finely chopped
2 cups beer

Preheat oven to 350°. Cream shortening until soft in a large bowl. Gradually add sugar, creaming until light and fluffy. Add eggs and mix well. Sift flour, salt, soda, and spices together. Reserve about 2 tablespoons. Beat the rest into the batter. Slowly add beer and blend thoroughly; it may foam while beating. Using reserved flour-spice mixture, toss fruits and nuts until lightly coated. Fold into batter, blending thoroughly.

Pour batter into a greased and floured 10" tube pan. Bake at 350° for 1 hour and 15 minutes, or until cake tester comes out clean. Cool in pan for 10 minutes; then carefully turn out of pan to cool completel Cover and refrigerate overnight. Serve plain, dusted with powdered sugar or with a lemon glaze.

Preparation:	20-25 min.	Easy	Serves: 12
Baking:	75 min.	Must do ahead	Can freeze

Julie Pitcava

WALNUT CREAM CAKE ROLL

Cake:
4 egg whites
pinch salt
2 tsp. vanilla
½ cup sugar
4 egg yolks
¼ cup flour
½ cup walnuts or pecans, coarsely chopped

Filling:
1 cup heavy cream
2 tbsp. confectioners' sugar
2 tsp. vanilla

Beat egg whites, salt and vanilla until slightly stiff. Gradually add the sugar, beating well between additior Beat egg yolks and fold into whites; carefully fold in flour and nuts. Line jellyroll pan w waxed paper. Pour cake batt in and spread to edges. Bake 375° for 12 minutes. Remove and cool 5 minutes. Sprinkle towel with powdered sugar a turn cake out on towel; peel the waxed paper. Cool slight Roll cake and towel jellyroll fashion; refrigerate 1 hour. Whip cream adding the vanilla and powdered sugar. Reserve some cream. Unroll cake and spread with whipped cream. Roll into log and decorate with reserved cream and nuts and cherries.

Preparation:	30 min.	Moderately difficult	Serves: 8
Baking:	12 min.	Must do ahead	

Mrs. F. Owen B

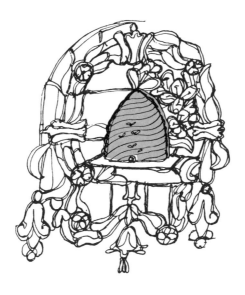

DESSERTS

STRAWBERRY CREAM CREPES

"You'll feel like a French chef serving these"

Basic dessert crepe:
1¼ cups flour
2 tbsp. sugar
pinch of salt
3 eggs
1½ cups milk
2 tbsp. butter, melted
½ tsp. lemon, Rum or Brandy
　　extract, optional

French cream filling:
½ pt. whipping cream
1 8-oz. pkg. cream cheese
2 cups confectioners' sugar
1 tsp. vanilla

Strawberry glacé:
½ cup sugar
2 tbsp. cornstarch
¾ cup water
1 tbsp. lemon juice
1 tsp. strawberry flavoring
¼ tsp. red food coloring
1 qt. fresh strawberries, sliced

Crepes: Place all ingredients in blender or mixer and beat well. Let batter stand 1 hour for more perfect crepes. Prepare crepes according to preferred method.

Filling: Whip cream; set aside. Soften cream cheese and blend in confectioners' sugar with vanilla. Blend in whipped cream with mixer at low setting. This recipe should fill 14-16 crepes. Assemble before serving.

Glacé: Combine sugar and cornstarch in small saucepan. Gradually add water, lemon juice, flavoring and food coloring. Cook over medium heat until thickened and clear. Cool to lukewarm. Spoon over berries. Pour sauce over filled crepes.

Preparation: 30 min.　　Moderately difficult　　Serves: 12
Cooking:　　20-25 min.　　Can do ahead

Jean Denuzzio

STRAWBERRY RHUBARB MOUSSE

"A Spring special"

1 lb. rhubarb, cut into
  1″ pieces, 3 cups
¾ cup cold water
1½ cups sugar
2 envs. unflavored gelatin
1 pt. strawberries
2 egg whites
1 cup heavy cream, whipped
red food coloring, optional

Place rhubarb, ¼ cup water and 1¼ cups sugar in saucepan and heat to boiling. Reduce heat, cover and simmer 10 minutes, until rhubarb comes apart into strings. Soften gelatin in remaining ½ cup water for 5 minutes. Add to hot rhubarb mixture and stir until gelatin is dissolved. Mash strawberries or purée in blender. Add to gelatin mixture. Chill, stirring occasionally, until mixture mounds slightly when dropped from a spoon.

Beat egg whites until soft peaks form. Add remaining ¼ cup sugar gradually, continuing to beat until egg whites are stiff and glossy. Fold in gelatin mixture and whipped cream. Add a few drops food coloring, if desired. Turn into a 2 quart mold. Chill until firm. Unmold. Serve with additional strawberries and whipped cream.

Preparation: 30 min.   Easy   Serves: 10-12
Cooking: 10 min.   Must do ahead

Dorothy Speak

SABAYON

"So sweet and satisfying"

10 egg yolks
½ cup dry Sherry or Marsala
  wine
2 tbsp. Grand Marnier or Triple
  Sec
¼ tsp. vanilla extract
dash salt
dash nutmeg
¾ cup powdered sugar, sifted

Combine egg yolks and all liquids with a whisk in a stainless steel mixing bowl. Add salt, nutmeg and sugar. Place in a hot, but not boiling, water bath, beating steadily in one direction. Remove from heat when the mixture becomes thick and fluffy and continue beating until bowl cools. Serve hot or chilled in wine glasses. If serving chilled, garnish with whipped cream, shaved chocolate and cherries.

Preparation: 15-20 min.   Easy   Serves: 6
    Can do ahead

Byron J. Bardy
Heinz

BRANDIED PEACH MOUSSE

"That little bit of brandy won't hurt the kids"

½ **pt. whipping cream**
2 **cups canned peaches, drained**
½ **cup syrup from peaches**
⅓ **cup sugar**
½ **cup peach Brandy**
⅛ **tsp. almond extract**

Whip cream. Blend all other ingredients in blender. Fold into cream. Fill 6 small soufflé dishes. Freeze overnight.

Preparation: 5-10 min.   Easy   Serves: 6
                          Must do ahead   Must freeze

Helga Freymark

CHOCOLATE MOUSSE

"So rich it will make your teeth itch"

1 **6-oz. pkg. semi-sweet chocolate bits**
6 **egg yolks, lightly beaten**
2 **tbsp. Cognac**
6 **egg whites, beaten**
dash salt
whipped cream, garnish

Melt chocolate bits in double boiler over hot water. Add chocolate, a little at a time, to egg yolks and Cognac and blend well. Beat egg whites stiff and fold into custard. Add the salt. Pour into glass dish or sherbet dishes and chill overnight. Garnish with whipped cream.

Preparation: 10 min.   Easy   Serves: 4-6
Cooking: 10-15 min.   Must do ahead

Mrs. Roger E. Wright

SLIM PEACH MELBA

"This would also be fabulous on fruit salad"

2 **fresh peaches, peeled & halved**
½ **cup low-fat yogurt**
2 **tsp. honey**
several dashes nutmeg
½ **cup fresh strawberries or raspberries, chopped**
lime peel, grated

Arrange 1 peach half in each of 2 sherbet glasses. Purée a peach half, yogurt, 1 teaspoon honey and nutmeg in blender. Chop last peach half and add to sauce, but do not blend. Pour into glasses. Blend berries with remaining honey and spoon into glasses. Sprinkle with lime peel.

Preparation: 15 min.   Easy   Serves: 2
                        Can do ahead

Mrs. W. H. Krome George, Jr.

CHERRY COTTAGE PUDDING

"Is there anyone who doesn't love cherries?"

1 cup sugar
¼ cup butter
1 egg, beaten
⅔ cup sweet milk
1½ cups flour
1 tsp. baking powder
¼ tsp. salt
¼ tsp. almond extract
1 pt. cherries, pitted
flour, to coat cherries

Cream the sugar and butter; add the beaten egg, milk, dry ingredients, sifted together, and the extract. Beat thoroughly. Stir in the cherries which have been well coated with flour. Bake in an 8 x 8" pan for 40 minutes at 350°.

Preparation: 20 min.
Cooking: 40 min.

Easy
Can do ahead

Serves: 6

Eleanor Thomson

STRAWBERRY MOUSSE

1 10-oz. pkg. frozen sliced strawberries, thawed
½ cup sugar
2 tbsp. lemon juice
1 cup sour cream

Sprinkle thawed strawberries with sugar, add lemon juice and fold in sour cream. Pour into serving bowl. Stir twice while freezing. Garnish with whole strawberries.

Preparation: 5 min.

Easy
Must freeze

Serves: 6

Mrs. W. H. Krome George, Jr.

ORANGE CREAM IN ORANGE CUPS

"Orangatangs even eat the orange cups"

8 large navel oranges
1⅓ cups sugar
2 tbsp. Cognac
2 envs. unflavored gelatin
½ cup cold water
1½ cups heavy cream
unsweetened chocolate, grated

Cut a thick slice from navel end of orange. Flute edges with a knife. Scoop out the pulp with a grapefruit spoon. Mash the pulp and strain the juice into a 1 quart measuring cup. There should be 3 cups of juice. If necessary, add additional orange juice. Stir Cognac and sugar into juice. Sprinkle the gelatin over the cold water in top of a double boiler. Place over simmering water and heat until gelatin is dissolved. Pour into bowl. Slowly stir juice mixture into gelatin. Stir in ¾ cup heavy cream and ladle into orange cups. Chill until firm. Before serving, whip remaining cream and spoon onto each serving. Top with chocolate.

Preparation: 40 min.

Moderately difficult
Must do ahead

Serves: 8

Mrs. Richard H. Greene

PEACH TREAT
"Better than a cobbler"

2 cups fresh peaches, sliced
1 ¼ cups sugar, divided
⅔ stick butter or margarine
¾ cup flour
¾ cup milk
2 tsp. baking powder
pinch salt

Mix peaches with ¾ cup sugar. Set aside. Put butter in a deep baking dish and set in 350° oven to melt. Combine ½ cup sugar and remaining ingredients to make batter. Remove pan with melted butter from oven. Pour in batter. Do not stir. Top with peaches. Do not stir. Batter will rise. Bake 1 hour at 350°. Serve warm or cold.

Preparation: 15 min.   Easy   Serves: 6-8
Cooking: 1 hour

Mrs. Arthur Dufala

FRESH PEACH OR APPLE KUCHEN
"A magician's dream, it disappears so fast"

Crust:
1 ¼ cups flour
¼ cup sugar
¼ tsp. salt
¼ tsp. baking powder
¼ cup margarine
1 egg
1-2 tbsp. cream

Peach filling:
1 ½-2 lbs. peaches, peeled & sliced
1 tbsp. flour
½ cup sugar
2 tbsp. margarine
¾ tsp. cinnamon

Apple filling:
¼ cup sugar
4-6 apples, peeled & sliced
grated rind & juice of ½ lemon
2 tbsp. butter
¼ cup sugar
½ tsp. cinnamon
2 tbsp. bread crumbs

Mix crust ingredients together and press into cake pan, bottom and edges. Lay peaches in bottom of uncooked crust. Mix flour and sugar and sprinkle over peaches. Dot surface with margarine and sprinkle with cinnamon. Bake at 450° for 15 minutes, reduce to 375° for 30 minutes. Serve warm or cold. Good with ice cream.

Apple filling: Place apples in rows like peaches. Dribble lemon juice and rind over apples. Sprinkle with sugar, dot with butter. In a skillet, mix sugar, cinnamon and bread crumbs. Sprinkle over everything. Follow baking instructions for peach filling.

Preparation: 25 min.   Easy   Serves: 4-6
Cooking: 45 min.   Can do ahead

Elizabeth Dithrich

FRUIT CRISP

"A refreshing summer dessert"

4-5 cups fresh fruit: apples,
   peaches, pears or plums
1 ½ oz. Grand Marnier, optional
1 ½ oz. Amaretto, optional
1 cup unbleached flour
1 cup sugar
¼ tsp. salt
1 tsp. cinnamon
½ cup butter, softened
whipping cream, whipped

Wash fruit and peel. Slice fruit into lightly greased 9 x 13" baking dish. Sprinkle Grand Marnier and Amaretto on fruit, if desired. Sift flour and mix with sugar, salt and cinnamon in medium size bowl. Cut in soft butter with a pastry blender until mixture resembles coarse cornmeal. Sprinkle mixture evenly over fruit. Bake 45 minutes in preheated 375° oven until topping is golden. Serve warm with whipped cream.

Preparation: 20 min.   Easy   Serves: 8-10
Cooking: 45 min.   Can do ahead

Cordelia Jacobs

PEARS IN ORANGE SABAYON

"Sybaritic"

6 ripe pears, Bosc preferred
acidulated water (water with a
   few drops of lemon juice)
3 cups water
1 ½ cups sugar
1 vanilla bean
1 whole cinnamon stick
½ cup candied fruit, finely
   diced & soaked in orange
   liqueur

Orange Sabayon:
4 large egg yolks
¾ cup orange liqueur
⅓ cup sugar
1 cup whipping cream

Garnish: candied violets,
mint leaves, raspberries

Carefully peel pears and drop immediately into large bowl of acidulated water. If you wish to fill pears with optional candied fruit, core and halve before placing in water. Combine 3 cups water, sugar, vanilla bean and cinnamon stick in 3-quart saucepan; bring to a boil over high heat. When sugar is dissolved, add pears. Reduce heat to medium and poach until tender, about 25 minutes. Allow pears to cool in their poaching liquid. Poaching may be done the day before serving. Drain pears and arrange on platter; chill. If desired, fill halves with candied fruit.

Orange Sabayon: Combine yolks, liqueur and sugar in top of double boiler and whisk until well blended. Place over simmering water and whisk constantly until mixture thickens and coats a metal spoon, about 20 minutes. Do not boil or mixture will curdle. Transfer to bowl and cool. Whip cream and fold thoroughly into cooled Sabayon.

Preparation: 40 min.   Moderately difficult   Serves: 6
Cooking: 30 min.   Can do ahead

Guen Larson

LEMON SOUFFLÉ WITH RASPBERRY SAUCE GRAND MARNIER
"Absolutely elegant"

2 envs. gelatin
½ cup cold water
8 eggs, separated
2 cups sugar, divided
1 cup lemon juice
½ tsp. salt
1 ½ tsp. lemon rind, grated
1 ½ pt. heavy cream

Sauce:
1 10-oz. pkg. frozen raspberries
sugar, to taste
2-3 tbsp. Grand Marnier or
   Cointreau

Sprinkle gelatin over water and let stand. Beat egg yolks with 1 cup sugar until light and fluffy. In a double boiler, combine the egg yolk mixture, lemon juice and salt; cook, stirring constantly, over boiling water until thickened and custard-like. Add gelatin and lemon rind, stirring constantly. Turn into a large bowl to cool slightly. Beat egg whites until stiff, add ¾ to 1 cup sugar and beat until firm peaks form. Fold into custard.

Whip cream and fold into custard. Refrigerate. Best if served within 10 hours. Sauce: Defrost raspberries. Blend berries with liqueur and sugar in blender. Strain. Pass in sauce bowl.

Preparation: 1 hour   Can do ahead   Serves: 12

Mrs. Joseph Vales

PEACH MELBA CREPES
"Rave reviews from children and adults"

Crepes:
6 eggs, well-beaten
½ tsp. salt
⅓ cup sugar
⅓ cup milk
1 tsp. vanilla, or other flavoring
1 cup flour

Crepe filling:
1 10-oz. pkg. frozen raspberries
   or 8 oz. raspberry syrup
⅓ cup currant jelly
3 tbsp. butter
¼ tsp. almond extract
1 16-oz. can peach slices,
   drained
10 scoops vanilla ice cream
10 cooked crepes
¼ cup almonds, sliced or
   slivered

Crepes: Add salt and sugar to beaten eggs and mix well; add milk and mix. Blend flour into above ingredients. Let stand 20-30 minutes. Mix again and strain. Prepare crepes according to preferred method.
Filling: Thaw raspberries; force through strainer. Combine purée or syrup, jelly, butter and extract. Bring to a boil over moderate heat. Add peaches, set aside and cool 5 minutes. Place scoop of ice cream in each crepe, fold over, spoon peaches and sauce over crepes. Sprinkle with almonds. Serve immediately while sauce is still warm.

Preparation: 30 min.   Moderately difficult   Serves: 10
Cooking: 15-20 min.

Russell Ebert
Wonderful Wanda's

STRAWBERRIES IMBROVNEV

1 pt. large fresh strawberries,
   with stems
½ cup Grand Marnier
½ cup sour cream
½ cup brown sugar
½ cup powdered sugar

Wash berries and pat dry. Pile in small bowl and place in center of large platter. Surround berries with small bowls filled with Grand Marnier, sour cream, brown and powdered sugars. To eat: Dip strawberry in the liqueur, then roll in powdered sugar; next dip in the sour cream, and then in brown sugar.

Preparation: 5 min.   Easy   Serves: 4

Woodene B. Merriman

ALMOND CHOCOLATE ICE CREAM TORTE

½ cup butter, melted
¾ cup almonds, slivered
½ cup sugar
1 cup flour
1 qt. chocolate ice cream
1 cup cold whipping cream
2 tsp. rum extract

Melt butter in heavy skillet. Add almonds, stirring constantly over medium heat until lightly toasted. Add sugar and flour, stirring constantly until mixture is golden and crumbly, 10 minutes or less. Do not let it burn! Remove from heat and cool slightly. Reserve ¾ cup for topping. Pat remaining mixture in bottom of a buttered 8″ springform pan. Freeze 2 hours.

Soften ice cream in a large mixing bowl; set aside. Using small chilled mixing bowl, whip cream until soft peaks form. Gently fold whipped cream into the ice cream, add rum extract and blend. Spoon over prepared crust. Sprinkle with reserved crumbs. Freeze until firm, at least 4 hours, or up to several weeks.

Preparation: 30 min.   Easy   Serves: 10-12
                          Must do ahead   Must freeze

Mrs. Frank H. Traupman

FRUIT PIZZA

Crust:
2½ cups flour
1 cup butter, softened
6 tbsp. sugar

Topping:
2 8-oz. pkgs. Philadelphia
   cream cheese
⅔ cup sugar
½ tsp. vanilla extract
assorted fresh or canned fruits,
   sliced
½ cup orange marmalade
2 tbsp. water

Blend crust ingredients and pat into jellyroll pan. Bake at 400° for 12-15 minutes. Let cool. Blend softened cream cheese, sugar and vanilla and spread over cooled crust. Arrange any combination of fresh or canned fruits on top in an attractive manner. Thin marmalade with water and coat fruit with mixture. Chill and serve.

Preparation: 30 min.   Easy   Serves: 12
Cooking: 12-15 min.   Must do ahead

Nancy Toomey

ICE CREAM TORTE

8 Heath bars, crushed
2 pkgs. lady fingers
1 qt. chocolate ice cream
1 qt. vanilla ice cream
1 qt. strawberry or peppermint
  ice cream
½ pt. heavy cream, whipped
  with vanilla and sugar

Crush Heath bars. Soften ice cream. Split lady fingers in ½ and line the bottom and side of 10" or 12" springform pan. Spoon layer of chocolate ice cream over lady fingers. Cover with ½ of crushed Heath bars. Add layer of vanilla ice cream. Cover with remaining Heath bars. Add top layer of strawberry ice cream. Freeze at least 8 hours. Unmold and top with sweetened whipped cream.

Preparation: 20 min.   Easy   Serves: 8-10
                          Must do ahead   Must freeze

Mrs. Frederick W. Okie, Jr.

RASPBERRY ICE

2 10-oz. pkgs. frozen
   raspberries
1 cup heavy cream

Cut partially thawed raspberries into 2" chunks or process using steel chopping blade. Pour cream through feed tube with machine running. Process only until smooth. Transfer to a shallow dish and freeze 45-60 minutes. Can be reprocessed through food processor. Serve with chocolate sauce.

Preparation: 5 min.   Easy   Serves: 4
                         Must freeze

Marlene Parrish

PEPPERMINT ICE CREAM

"Be aware that kids will want seconds and thirds"

3 cups crushed peppermints,
  divided
1 qt. half & half
4 eggs
1 cup sugar
2 tbsp. vanilla
1 tsp. peppermint oil, not
  extract
4 cups heavy cream
½ tsp. salt
1-2 cups milk

Soak 1½ cups crushed peppermints in half and half for several hours. Beat eggs until foamy, add sugar and beat until thickened. Add vanilla, peppermint oil, cream and salt and beat well. Add peppermint mixture and mix. Pour into 1 gallon ice cream freezer and add milk to fill line. Freeze, according to manufacturer's directions, until semi-hard — usually about 10 minutes. Add reserved 1½ cups crushed mints and continue freezing, about another 10 minutes.

Preparation: 35 min.   Easy   Yield: 1 gallon
                          Must do ahead

Carolyn S. Hammer

CREAM PUFFS OR ÉCLAIRS

"A fork is a must"

Puffs:
1 cup water
½ cup butter or margarine
¼ tsp. salt
1 cup flour, sifted
4 large eggs

Vanilla Custard:
1 cup sugar
2 tbsp. flour
2 tbsp. cornstarch
½ tsp. salt
3 cups milk
2 egg yolks, beaten
2 tsp. vanilla
¾-1 cup whipping cream,
  whipped

Chocolate Icing:
1½ oz. unsweetened chocolate,
  melted & cooled
¼ cup butter or margarine,
  softened
⅛ tsp. salt
1¼-1½ cups confectioners'
  sugar
⅓ cup cream
1 tsp. vanilla

Puffs: Heat water, butter and salt to full, rolling boil. Reduce heat and stir in flour all at once, mixing vigorously until mixture leaves sides of saucepan. With mixer, add eggs, one at a time, beating about ½ minute with each addition. Scrape bowl and beat another 30 seconds.

Drop dough from metal spoon onto greased cookie sheets, forming mounds 3″ apart. Puffs will at least double, so be careful. Bake at 400° for 10 minutes; lower heat to 350° and bake for 25 minutes until golden. Remove from oven and cut side of each puff; return to turned off oven and let stand, with door ajar, for 10 minutes. Cool on racks, slit tops and fill with custard. Sprinkle with confectioners' sugar.

Éclairs: Shape puffs with spatula into 16 éclairs 1 x 4″. Bake as above at 400° for 40-50 minutes. Remove and place on racks to cool. Split, fill with custard and top with chocolate icing.

Vanilla Custard: In saucepan, combine sugar, flour, cornstarch and salt. Stir well to blend. Gradually add milk; cook and stir until mixture thickens and boils. Cook 3 minutes longer. Stir small amount of hot mixture into egg yolks; return to hot mixture. Cook and stir just until mixture comes to a boil. Add vanilla. Cool. Beat smooth, will be lumpy after cooling, and fold in whipped cream. If a thicker custard is desired, reduce amount of whipped cream, or increase cornstarch.

Chocolate Icing: Place chocolate and butter in bowl; gradually add salt and sugar and beat at low speed for 2 minutes. Add cream as needed, a tablespoon at a time. Add vanilla. Beat until very smooth and creamy; it will thicken in refrigerator and is not a usual glaze for éclairs.

Preparation: 70 min.	**Moderately difficult**	**Serves: 12-16**
Cooking: 65 min.	**Must do ahead**	

Carolyn S. Hammer

PIES

MUM'S CHOCOLATE PIE

"A disappearing pie"

Crust:
2 cups pecans, finely chopped
5 tbsp. plus 1 tsp. brown sugar
5 tbsp. butter, chilled & cubed
2 tsp. dark Rum

Filling:
6 oz. semi-sweet chocolate
   morsels
½ tsp. instant coffee powder
4 eggs, at room temperature
1 tbsp. dark Rum
1 tsp. vanilla
1 cup whipping cream, whipped
½ cup cream, whipped

Crust: Blend all ingredients until mixture sticks together. Press into bottom and sides of pie pan. Freeze for 1 hour.

Filling: Melt chocolate and coffee in top of double boiler. Remove from heat and add a small amount to the beaten eggs; blend. Return to chocolate and add Rum and vanilla, whisking until smooth. Cool for 5 minutes. Take 2 cups of the whipped cream and gently fold into the chocolate mixture. Pour into crust and freeze. Remove from freezer 1 hour before serving.

Spread with half cup heavy cream, whipped, before serving. Can freeze for 3 months.

Preparation: 45 min.	Easy	Serves: 8
Cooking: 20 min.	Must freeze	

Sibby McCrady

BLUEBERRY TARTS

3 cups fresh blueberries
½ cup sugar
½ tsp. cinnamon
1 tbsp. cornstarch
pinch salt
1 cup water
2 tsp. lemon juice
6 tart shells, baked
whipped cream, garnish

Wash blueberries and drain well. Mix next 5 ingredients together in a saucepan. Cook and stir over medium low heat 4-5 minutes or until glaze mixture is clear and of medium consistency. Remove from heat and stir in lemon juice. Fill tart shells with blueberries and spoon the glaze over berries to cover. Chill until glaze is set. Serve with whipped cream.

Preparation: 15 min.   Easy   Yield: 6
Cooking: 5 min.   Must do ahead

Mrs. James H. Morgens

MRS. DELANEY'S IRISH COFFEE PIE

8″ pie crust
1 3½-oz. pkg. Dream Whip
2 tsp. instant coffee
½ cup milk
½ cup water
3 tbsp. Irish Whiskey
½ cup whipping cream,
  whipped

Combine Dream Whip and coffee powder. Add milk; beat at high speed 1 minute. Add water and Whiskey, beating for 2 minutes or until fluffy. Add whipped cream and blend. Pour into pie crust and allow to set 3-4 hours, refrigerated. Garnish with rosettes of whipped cream.

Preparation: 30 min.   Easy   Serves: 8
                          Must do ahead   Can freeze

Mrs. Stuart D. Moiles

FROZEN CRANBERRY VELVET PIE
"A dessert with a smooth but tart flavor"

1¼ cups fine vanilla wafer
  crumbs
6 tbsp. butter or margarine,
  melted
1 8-oz. pkg. cream cheese,
  softened
1 cup whipping cream
¼ cup sugar
½ tsp. vanilla
1 16-oz. can whole cranberry
  sauce

Combine crumbs and melted butter; press firmly into bottom and sides of 9″ pie plate. Chill until firm. Meanwhile, beat cream cheese until fluffy. Combine whipping cream, sugar and vanilla; whip until thickened but not stiff. Gradually add to the cream cheese, beating until smooth and creamy. Set aside a few whole cranberries for

garnish. Fold the remaining sauce into the whipped mixture. Spoon into chilled crust and freeze until firm. Remove from freezer 10-15 minutes before serving. To serve, top with additional whipped cream and cranberries.

Preparation: 20 min.   Easy   Serves: 6-8
                          Must freeze

Mrs. C. Taylor Marshal

WHIPPED KAHLUA PIE
"A heavenly Mexican dessert"

Crust:
½ pkg. chocolate wafers,
   crushed, (1¼ cups)
6 tbsp. butter, melted
½ cup nuts, finely chopped
1 tbsp. sugar

Filling:
1 qt. coffee ice cream
1 pt. whipping cream
1 tsp. vanilla
⅓ cup Kahlua
4 Heath bars, crushed

Crust: Crush chocolate wafers, using a food processor if possible, then add melted butter, nuts and sugar. Pat into large greased pie pan and bake at 350° for 10 minutes. Let cool.

Filling: Soften ice cream. Whip cream, adding vanilla and Kahlua. Gently fold crushed Heath bars into whipped cream. Gently combine the 2 mixtures. Pour into shell and freeze. Remove from freezer 15 minutes before serving.

Preparation: 30 min.	Easy	Serves: 8
Baking: 10 min.	Must freeze	

Mrs. Donald D. Wolff, Jr.

KEY LIME PIE
"Could also be put in a pastry crust"

Butter Crunch Crust:
½ cup butter
¼ cup brown sugar, packed
1 cup flour, sifted
½ cup pecans or walnuts,
   chopped

Filling:
1 can Eagle Brand sweetened
   condensed milk
4 egg yolks
½ cup key lime juice or ¼ cup
   lime & ¼ cup lemon juice
1 large egg white, beaten stiff

Meringue:
3 egg whites
6 tbsp. sugar
½ tsp. cream of tartar

Crust: Combine all ingredients and mix well. Spread in a 13x9" pan and bake at 400° for 12-15 minutes until golden. Stir immediately and press into a 9" pie pan and cool.

Filling: Combine milk, egg yolks and juice; fold in beaten egg white. Pour into crust.

Meringue: Beat egg whites; gradually add sugar and cream of tartar and beat until stiff and glossy. Cover filling with meringue. Bake pie at 350° until meringue browns.

Preparation: 30 min.	Easy	Serves: 8
Baking: 30 min.	Must do ahead	

Mrs. Jon E. McCarthy

KENTUCKY BLUEGRASS PIE

"You can bet on this one"

9″ pie shell, unbaked
2 eggs, lightly beaten
1 cup sugar
½ cup butter or margarine,
  melted
1 tsp. vanilla
1 cup walnuts or pecans,
  chopped
1 cup semi-sweet chocolate
  morsels, melted
½ cup flour
whipped cream, garnish

Combine the eggs, sugar, butter, vanilla, nuts and morsels in bowl. Mix well, add flour and mix again. Spread into unbaked pie shell and bake at 350° for 30 minutes. Garnish with whipped cream after cooling.

Preparation:	30 min.	Easy	Serves: 6-8
Baking:	30 min.	Must do ahead	Can freeze

Dorothy Speak

LIGHT AND HIGH LEMON PIE

graham cracker pie shell
1 8-oz. pkg. Cool Whip, thawed
1 small can frozen lemonade,
  thawed
1 14-oz. can sweetened
  condensed milk
candied lemon, garnish

Blend Cool Whip, lemonade and milk, pour into pie shell and chill. Garnish with candied lemon if desired.

Preparation: 10 min.	Easy	Serves: 6-8
	Must do ahead	

Mrs. Stephen W. Scott

LOU'S AUNT'S PIE

"A variation on an old theme"

1 cup walnuts
14 Ritz crackers
3 egg whites
1 cup sugar
1 tsp. vanilla
½ tsp. baking powder
whipped cream
chocolate, grated

Break nuts and crackers coarsely. Beat egg whites until stiff; gradually add sugar, vanilla and baking powder. Fold in nuts and crackers with a spatula. Line bottom of pie pan with brown paper. Pour mixture in pan and bake at 325° for 25-35 minutes. Cool. Top with cream and chocolate. Refrigerate until very cold.

Preparation:	15 min.	Easy	Serves: 8
Baking:	30 min.	Must do ahead	

Mrs. William Floyd

PEANUT BUTTER PIE

"Hooray for All American pie"

graham cracker crust
1 cup peanut butter
1½ cups confectioners' sugar
½ tsp. vanilla
1 8-oz. pkg. cream cheese, softened
2 cups whipped cream or whipped topping
whipped topping, garnish

Combine peanut butter, sugar, vanilla, cream cheese and whipped cream or topping and mix thoroughly. Pour into crust and freeze. Garnish with additional whipped topping, if desired.

Preparation: 15 min.	Easy Must freeze	Serves: 6-8

Chappy's Choice

PINEAPPLE PIE

"This has a lovely lemony flavor"

Crust:
3 cups flour
3 sticks margarine, softened
4 tbsp. cold water

Filling:
2 3-oz. pkgs. lemon pie filling
1 16-oz. can crushed pineapple, drained

Topping:
2 pkgs. Dream Whip, whipped
6-oz. cream cheese, softened

Blend flour and margarine with pastry cutter; add water and continue blending until crumbly. With floured hands, press into 11x17x1" cookie sheet, keeping sides high. Prick crust with fork and bake at 350° for 35-40 minutes or until golden brown. Cool shell while preparing filling. Prepare pie filling according to directions. Add pineapple and pour mixture into crust. Cool 1 hour before adding topping. Make topping according to directions, beat the cream cheese and fold into topping. Spread over filling and refrigerate.

Preparation: 20 min.	Easy	Serves: 18-20
Baking: 40 min.	Can do ahead	

Mrs. Larry Pryor

GINGER PEACHY PIE

pastry for 2 crust 10" pie, unbaked
4-5 cups fresh peaches, sliced
¼ cup flour
½ tsp. ground ginger
½ cup brown sugar, packed
2 tbsp. butter

Preheat oven to 400°. Line a 10" pie plate with half the pastry. Combine the peaches, flour, ginger and sugar. Turn into pie plate and dot with butter. Cover with remaining pastry and flute the edges. Make several slits in top for steam to escape. Bake 45-50 minutes or until browned. If frozen, bake at 365° for 1½ hours.

Preparation: 1 hour	Easy	Serves: 8-10
Baking: 45-50 min.	Can do ahead	Can freeze

Mrs. William H. Riley

PUMPKIN PIE WITH NO ROLL CRUST

Pastry:
1½ cups flour, sifted
1½ tsp. sugar
1 tsp. salt
½ cup vegetable oil
2 tbsp. cold milk

Filling:
1½ cups pumpkin
¾ cup brown sugar
2 eggs, beaten
1½ cups milk
½ tsp. vanilla
½ tsp. salt
1 tbsp. pumpkin pie spice

Place dry ingredients in pie plate. Combine oil and milk in measuring cup and whip with fork; pour over flour mixture all at once. Mix until moistened and press dough evenly with fingers to line bottom and sides of pan.

Filling: Mix ingredients in order given. Pour into pie shell and bake in a preheated oven, 400°, for 15 minutes. Reduce heat to 350° and bake for 30 minutes or until filling is firm.

Preparation: 15 min.   Easy   Serves: 6
Baking: 45 min.   Must do ahead

Mrs. Edwin H. Gott, Jr.

RASPBERRY RIBBON PIE

"Very rich - good luncheon dessert"

9″ pie shell, baked
1 3-oz. pkg. raspberry jello plus
   1 tsp. unflavored gelatin
¼ cup sugar
1 cup boiling water
2 10-oz. pkgs. frozen red
   raspberries
1 tbsp. lemon juice
1 3-oz. pkg. cream cheese,
   softened
⅓ cup powdered sugar, sifted
1 tsp. vanilla
dash salt
½ pt. heavy cream, whipped

Dissolve jello, gelatin and sugar in hot water. Add raspberries and lemon juice and stir until berries thaw. Chill until partially set. Prepare white layer by blending cheese, powdered sugar, vanilla, salt and a small amount of whipped cream. Fold in remaining cream. Spread ⅓ of cheese mixture over bottom of pie shell; cover with half of raspberry mixture. Repeat layers ending with cheese mixture. Chill. Make a day ahead to let flavors ripen. Can serve with additional whipped cream.

Preparation: 1 hour   Easy   Serves: 8
                          Must do ahead

Mrs. Stanley A. Walker

MILE HIGH STRAWBERRY PIE

9″ pastry shell, baked
1 cup sugar
2 egg whites
1 10-oz. pkg. frozen
   strawberries, partially thawed
1 tsp. vanilla
1 tbsp. lemon juice
pinch salt
1 cup heavy cream, whipped

Combine sugar, egg whites, strawberries, vanilla, lemon juice and salt in mixer bowl. Beat at high speed for 15 minutes until mixture is thick, fluffy and voluminous. Fold in whipped cream and pile mixture in pie shell. Freeze overnight. Wrap in foil or plastic wrap after freezing. May be decorated with fresh strawberries and rosettes of whipped cream. *Note:* This filling may not work well on a humid day.

Preparation: 30 min.   Easy   Serves: 8
                            Must freeze

Mrs. Francis J. Sullivan

ICE CREAM PUMPKIN PIE

1 qt. butter crunch or pecan ice
   cream
1 cup pumpkin
1 cup sugar
1 tsp. cinnamon
½ tsp. ginger
¼ tsp. nutmeg
½ tsp. salt
1 cup heavy cream, whipped

Line bottom and sides of a 9″ pie pan with ice cream. Mix remaining ingredients, except cream, and cook over low heat for 5 minutes. Cool. Fold in whipped cream. Turn into pie pan and freeze. Put in refrigerator for 1 hour before serving.

Preparation: 30 min.   Easy   Serves: 6-8
Cooking: 5 min.   Must do ahead   Must freeze

Mrs. Emerson M. Wickwire

SWEDISH APPLE PIE

5-6 apples, peeled, cored &
   sliced
1 tbsp. sugar
1 tsp. cinnamon
¼ tsp. nutmeg
1 tsp. lemon juice

Topping:
1 egg
¾ cup butter or margarine
½ cup sugar
½ cup walnuts or cashews,
   chopped
1 cup flour

Butter a deep dish pie plate and fill with apples approximately ¾ full. Sprinkle with sugar, cinnamon, nutmeg and lemon juice. Mix topping ingredients until soft and pliable. Spread over top of apple filling. Bake at 350° for 45 minutes.

Preparation: 30 min.   Easy   Serves: 6-8
Baking: 45 min.   Must do ahead

Michelle G. Smyser

RASPBERRY SAUCE

"Good over peaches and ice cream"

1 10-oz. pkg. frozen raspberries
2 tsp. cornstarch
1 tbsp. butter
¼ - ½ cup sugar
lemon juice

Combine first 4 ingredients in saucepan and bring to a boil. Cook until thickened and remove from heat. Add 1 wooden spoonful of lemon juice and stir. Allow to sit for flavors to blend, but reheat before serving.

Preparation: 15 min.   Easy   Yield: 1½ cups
                            Must do ahead

Mrs. Louis D. Ruscitto

BRITISH HARD SAUCE

¼ lb. butter, room temperature
2 cups confectioners' sugar
⅛ tsp. salt
½ tsp. vanilla
¼ tsp. ground nutmeg
¼ cup Cognac
½ cup heavy cream

Beat butter with electric mixer until creamy. Slowly sift sugar into the butter, beating constantly. Add salt, vanilla, nutmeg and Cognac. Finally add cream and beat until very smooth. Transfer to serving bowl and refrigerate overnight, covered with waxed paper. Serve directly from chilled bowl.

Preparation: 10 min.   Easy   Yield: 2 cups
                            Must do ahead

Mrs. Benjamin V. Smith, Jr.

CARAMEL SAUCE

1 stick butter or margarine
1 cup light Karo syrup
3 cups light brown sugar
2 tsp. vanilla
1 cup whipping cream

Combine butter, syrup and sugar. Bring to boiling point and cook 2-3 minutes. Remove from heat. When mixture stops foaming, add vanilla and cream. Cool and place in jar. Does not need to be refrigerated for brief storage.

Preparation: 15 min.   Easy   Yield: 1 qt.
                        Must do ahead

Mrs. William C. Crampton, Jr.

WALNUT CARAMEL SAUCE

2 tbsp. butter, melted
½ cup brown sugar, firmly
    packed
¼ cup light cream
2 tbsp. walnuts, chopped
½ tsp. vanilla

Add sugar to butter in saucepan, heating until sugar dissolves and is blended. Remove from heat and stir in cream. Return to heat, cooking and stirring for 1 minute. Pour into jar or serving bowl, add nuts and vanilla and stir to combine. Serve at room temperature.

Preparation: 5-10 min.   Easy   Yield: 1 cup
                         Can do ahead

Mrs. Joseph Yut

CHRISTMAS HOT FUDGE SAUCE

2 squares Baker's unsweetened
    chocolate
6 tbsp. water
½ cup sugar
dash salt
1 med. candy cane, crushed
3 tbsp. butter
½ tsp. vanilla

Melt chocolate in water over low heat, stirring until smooth. Add sugar, salt and candy cane. Cook and stir until slightly thickened. Add butter and vanilla. Stir and serve warm. When doubling this recipe, cut back on the vanilla and sugar.

Preparation: 10-15 min.   Easy   Yield: 1 cup
                          Can do ahead

Mrs. W. H. Krome George, Jr.

GRAND MARNIER SAUCE A LA GRENOUILLE

5 egg yolks
½ cup plus 2 tbsp. sugar
¼ cup Grand Marnier
1 cup heavy cream

Beat egg yolks and ½ cup sugar together in top of double boiler until well combined. Continue beating over simmering water until mixture is very pale yellow and thickened, 5-8 minutes. Remove from heat; stir in the Grand Marnier. Cool sauce to room temperature. Refrigerate, covered, until very cold. Beat the whipping cream with the 2 tablespoons of sugar until almost stiff. Fold into the egg yolk mixture: be sure to incorporate thoroughly. Refrigerate. Serve over fresh fruit.

Preparation: 20 min.   Easy   Serves: 8
                              Must do ahead

Mrs. Edward A. Montgomery, Jr.

LEMON SAUCE

½ cup sugar
1 heaping tbsp. cornstarch
¼ tsp. nutmeg
1 cup boiling water
2 tbsp. butter
2-4 tbsp. lemon juice, to taste

Blend sugar, cornstarch and nutmeg. Add boiling water, butter and juice and boil until thickened. Serve immediately over yellow cake.

Preparation: 5 min.   Easy   Serves: 4

Mrs. Robert C. Wright

CHOCOLATE FONDUE
"A delicious dip for your favorite fruits"

6 1-oz. squares unsweetened
      baking chocolate
1½ cups sugar
½ cup butter
1 cup light cream
½ tsp. salt
2 tbsp. Creme de Cacao
pieces of: fresh pineapple,
      bananas, strawberries, pound
      cake, angel food cake

Melt chocolate. Add sugar, cream, butter and salt. Stir constantly until slightly thickened. Remove from heat. Add liqueur. Pour into fondue pot and keep warm. Cut fruit and cake into bite-size pieces. Dip pieces of fruit and cake into fondue.

Preparation: 10 min.   Easy   Serves: 8-10
Cooking: 15 min.   Can do ahead

Mrs. Walter Gregg, Jr.

COOKIES

EASY MINT-GLAZED BROWNIES
"A perfect marriage of flavors"

1 family size pkg. Duncan Hines
   brownie mix
5 large York peppermint patties

Prepare brownies according to package directions. Bake in a well greased 13 x 9" pan. Split the peppermint patties horizontally into two patties. Place them chocolate side up on top of the still warm brownies. Return the brownies to the oven with the heat turned off and let the chocolate melt for 5 minutes. Swirl the chocolate with a knife to cover, then let cool completely before cutting.

Preparation: 10 min.   Easy   Yield: 24 squares
Baking: 25-30 min.   Must do ahead   Can freeze

Chappy's Choice

ITALIAN ALMOND COOKIES

1 stick sweet butter, softened
1 cup sugar
3 egg yolks
¼ tsp. almond extract
¼ tsp. vanilla extract
1 cup almonds, blanched &
   ground in blender until very
   fine
1½ cups all-purpose flour

Cream butter and sugar. Add egg yolks, one at a time, beating after each addition. Add extracts and mix well. Add ground almonds and flour and mix again. Shape dough into 1½" cylinder. Wrap in waxed paper and chill for several hours. Slice into ⅙" rounds and place on a greased cookie sheet. Bake at 325° for 20 minutes.

Preparation: 15 min.   Easy   Yield: 5 doz.
Baking: 20 min.   Can do ahead

Nancy Toomey

BROWNIES
"Hang on to your dentures - these are really chewy"

4 squares unsweetened chocolate	Beat eggs. Melt chocolate and butter together. Cool. Gradually
½ cup butter	add sugar to eggs, beating after
4 eggs	each addition. Blend in flour
2 cups sugar	and chocolate mixture. Add
1 cup flour	vanilla and nuts. Mix together.
½ tsp. salt	Spread into a greased 9″
1 tsp. vanilla	square pan. Bake at 300° for
1 cup walnuts, chopped	40-50 minutes.

Preparation: 15-20 min.	Easy	Yield: 20
Baking: 40-50 min.	Can do ahead	Can freeze

Ruth M. Debevoise

BUCKEYES
"Another treat for our good neighbors from Ohio"

1 lb. peanut butter	Blend peanut butter, sugar,
1½ lb. powdered sugar	margarine and vanilla in large
½ lb. margarine, softened	bowl. Shape into balls and chill
½ tsp. vanilla	in freezer until hard. Melt
2 12-oz. pkgs. chocolate chips	chocolate chips in double
	boiler. Dip balls in chocolate

with toothpick to look like buckeyes. Put on wax paper and freeze until chocolate is hard or refrigerate for 2 hours. Can store in freezer.

Preparation: 25-30 min.	Easy	Yield: 5 doz.
	Must do ahead	Can freeze

Beth Gates

SANDY'S BEST CHOCOLATE CHIP COOKIES
"These will keep several days if you want to hide them"

1 cup salad oil	Mix first 5 ingredients with
2 eggs	mixer at medium speed until
¾ cup brown sugar	blended. Mix in next 3
¾ cup sugar	ingredients; then fold in chips.
1 tsp. vanilla	Drop 2″ apart on greased
2 cups flour	cookie sheets by tablespoonsful.
1 tsp. salt	Bake at 350° until cookies puff
1 tsp. baking soda	up, then collapse—about
12 oz. chocolate chips	8 minutes.

Preparation: 10 min.	Easy	Yield: 5-6 doz.
Baking: 8 min.	Can do ahead	Can freeze

Mrs. Dana M. Friedman

CHOCOLATE ALMOND CRISP

"Especially nice for tea or luncheon"

1 cup butter
½ cup light brown sugar
½ cup granulated sugar
1 egg yolk
1 tsp. vanilla
1½ cups flour
¼ tsp. salt
8-oz. semi-sweet chocolate,
 melted
¾ cup almond slivers, toasted

Cream butter and sugars until light and fluffy. Add egg yolk, vanilla, flour and salt and mix well. Spread evenly in ungreased jellyroll pan and bake for 30 minutes at 350°. Remove from oven and cool 10 minutes. Melt chocolate and spread on top of cookies; sprinkle almonds over chocolate. Cool slightly and cut.

Preparation:	20 min.	Easy	Yield: 3 doz.
Baking:	30 min.	Can do ahead	

Mrs. Roger E. Wright

CHOCOLATE DELIGHT BARS

"The name says it all - absolutely delicious"

½ cup butter or margarine
1 egg yolk
2 tbsp. water
1¼ cups flour, sifted
1 tsp. sugar
1 tsp. baking powder
1 12-oz. pkg. Nestle's chocolate
 chips
2 eggs
¾ cup sugar
6 tbsp. butter or margarine,
 melted
1 tsp. vanilla
2 cups walnuts, finely chopped

Beat butter, egg yolk and water together. Sift and stir in flour, sugar and baking powder. Press mixture into greased 13x9" pan. Bake at 350° for 10 minutes. Remove from oven, sprinkle with chocolate chips and return to oven for 1 minute. Remove and spread the melted chocolate to cover top. Beat 2 eggs until thickened. Add sugar, then melted butter and vanilla; mix thoroughly. Add the walnuts and spread mixture over the chocolate. Bake for 30-35 minutes. Cut into squares.

Preparation:	20 min.	Easy	Yield: 48 squares
Baking:	40-45 min.	Can do ahead	Can freeze

Mrs. Philip Pugh

PEANUT BUTTER FILLED BARS

"Have fun with your cookie press"

Dough:
1 cup butter or margarine,
 softened
⅔ cup sugar
1 egg
1 tsp. vanilla
2½ cups flour

Filling:
1½ cups smooth peanut butter
1 cup confectioners' sugar,
 sifted

Cream butter and sugar until fluffy. Beat in egg and vanilla. Stir in flour and set aside. In a small bowl, thoroughly mix the peanut butter and sugar; set aside. Place half of the dough in a cookie press. Using ribbon plate, press strips on ungreased cookie sheets. Place small lines of peanut butter filling down the center of dough strips. Press remaining dough over the filling. Mark into 2″ squares. Bake at 375° for 10-12 minutes. Cut cookies immediately.

Preparation: 35 min.   Moderate difficulty   Yield: 4½ doz.
Baking: 10-12 min.   Can do ahead

Rose Gregg

AUNT NANA'S CINNAMON COOKIES

"A delicious old fashioned refrigerator cookie"

1 cup butter
1 cup sugar
1 cup light brown sugar
2 eggs, beaten
3½ cups flour, sifted
pinch salt
2 tsp. cinnamon
1 tsp. baking soda
1 cup pecans

Cream butter and sugars. Add eggs and mix. Add flour, salt, cinnamon and soda. Add nuts, then mix well and shape into 2 rolls. Refrigerate 2 to 3 hours or overnight. Slice very thinly, place on greased cookie sheet and bake at 375° for 8-10 minutes. Store in tin. Unbaked dough can be frozen for 1 week.

Preparation: 20-25 min.   Easy   Yield: 4 doz.
Baking: 8-10 min.   Can do ahead

Jean Sebolt

GINGERBREAD BOYS
"Gingerbread persons - decorations make the difference"

½ cup butter or margarine
½ cup brown sugar
1 3¾-oz. pkg. regular
  butterscotch pudding
1½ cups flour
½ tsp. baking soda
½ tsp. cinnamon
1½ tsp. ginger
1 egg

Mix ingredients together. Chill for several hours. Roll out to ¼" thickness for crisp cookies. Cut into gingerbread boys and place on ungreased cookie sheet. Bake at 350° for 6-8 minutes. Cool slightly. Ice, if desired, before removing from cookie sheet.

| Preparation: | 10 min. | Easy | Yield: 24 large cookies |
| Baking: | 6-8 min. | Must do ahead | Can freeze |

Debbie St. Martin

COCONUT BALLS
"A Miss America cookie - really beautiful"

½ lb. dates, chopped
1 cup sugar
¼ lb. butter or margarine
1 egg, lightly beaten
2 cups Rice Krispies
¼ cup walnuts, chopped
coconut, shredded

Melt butter or margarine in heavy saucepan. Add sugar and dates, then lightly beaten egg. Cook until dates are soft, stirring often. Remove from heat and add Rice Krispies and walnuts. Put pan in refrigerator to chill. Form into small balls and roll in shredded coconut.

| Preparation: | 20-30 min. | Easy | Yield: 5 doz. |
| Cooking: | 5 min. | Can do ahead | Can freeze |

Mrs. Joseph W. Blackhurst

QUINCE DROPS
"An exotic treat"

7-8 med. quinces
8 egg whites
juice & grated rind of 1 lemon
2½ lbs. powdered sugar

Boil quinces until tender. Cool and peel. Grate the pulp and set aside 1½-2 cups of pulp. Beat the egg whites until frothy; add lemon juice, rind and sugar and beat until stiff peaks form. Fold in quince pulp. Drop by teaspoonsful on wax paper-coated cookie sheet which has been sprinkled with powdered sugar. Set aside in warm room to dry. In dry weather, cookies will be ready in 4-5 days. Store in airtight tins. The pulp can be frozen ahead. *Note:* The meringue must stand in stiff, sharply pointed peaks to form cookies.

| Preparation: | 3 hours | Difficult | Yield: 6 doz. |
| | | Must do ahead | |

Mrs. John W. Todd, Jr.

LUSCIOUS PINEAPPLE SQUARES

2 eggs
2 cups sugar
1 20-oz. can crushed pineapple,
    undrained
2 cups flour
2 tsp. baking soda
1 tsp. vanilla extract
½ cup nuts, chopped

Frosting:
1 8-oz. pkg. cream cheese,
    softened
1 stick of butter or margarine,
    softened
1¾ cup confectioners' sugar
1 tsp. vanilla
½ cup nuts

Mix all ingredients, except nuts, together. Stir in nuts. Bake in greased 9 x 13" pan at 350° for 25-35 minutes. Will turn very brown; be sure to bake entire time indicated. Cool and frost.

Mix frosting ingredients, except nuts, together and spread on bars. Sprinkle with nuts.

Preparation:	10 min.	Easy	Yield: 54 squares
Baking:	35 min.	Can do ahead	Can freeze

Mrs. Jack A. Morrow

LEMON SOURS
"Three layers of lusciousness"

¾ cup flour
⅓ cup butter
2 eggs
1 cup brown sugar
¾ cup coconut
½ cup nuts, chopped
⅛ tsp. baking powder
½ tsp. vanilla

Topping:
⅔ cup confectioners' sugar
1½ tsp. lemon juice
1 tsp. lemon rind, grated

Crumble flour and butter together and sprinkle in a 7 x 11" baking pan. Bake at 350° for 10 minutes. Beat eggs, add sugar, coconut, nuts, powder and vanilla, mixing thoroughly. Spread over first mixture; return to oven and bake 20 minutes. Combine the sugar, lemon juice and rind until blended. Spread over coconut layer while still hot. Cool slightly and cut into squares.

Preparation:	50 min.	Easy	Yield: 25
Baking:	30 min.	Can do ahead	Can freeze

Mrs. James R. Phipps

SCOTCH SHORTBREAD
"Nice and thin and crispy"

1 cup butter, softened
⅝ cup sugar
1 tsp. vanilla
2½ cups flour, sifted

Cream the butter, sugar and vanilla together. Stir in flour; mix with hands. Chill dough. Roll out to ⅓ to ½" thickness. Cut into fancy shapes no bigger than one inch. Place on ungreased baking sheet. Bake in 300° oven for 20-25 minutes.

Preparation: 5-10 min.	Easy	Yield: 2 doz.
Baking: 25 min.	Must do ahead	Can freeze

Mrs. James L. Stuart, Jr.

POTATO CHIP COOKIES
"A different and delicious tea cookie"

1 lb. margarine
1 cup sugar
2 tsp. vanilla
1 cup potato chips, crushed
3½ cups flour
confectioners' sugar

Cream margarine until fluffy, add sugar and cream together. Add vanilla, potato chips and flour and mix well. Drop cookies from a teaspoon 2" apart on an ungreased cookie sheet. Bake in preheated 350° oven for 15 minutes. Sprinkle with powdered sugar while hot and place on paper towels to cool.

Preparation: 10 min.	Easy	Yield: 8 doz.
Baking: 15 min.	Can do ahead	Can freeze

Maureen G. Carroll

SUGAR COOKIES
"Makes you remember Mama"

1 cup margarine
2 cups sugar
3 egg yolks
2 cups flour
1 tsp. baking soda
1 tsp. cream of tartar
¼ tsp. salt
1 tsp. vanilla

Cream margarine and sugar. Add yolks, then remaining ingredients. Place tablespoon-size chunks of dough on ungreased cookie sheet. Bake at 350° for about 8 minutes. Cookies should be faintly brown at edges. They may be puffed up when removed from oven, but will fall as they cool.

Preparation: 5 min.	Easy	Yield: 6 doz.
Baking: 8 min.	Can do ahead	Can freeze

Mrs. R. H. Semple III

RAISIN-HONEY DROP COOKIES

"Will make you healthy for sure and maybe wealthy and wise"

¾ cup honey
¾ cup sugar
¾ cup margarine
1 egg
2 cups flour
1 tsp. salt
1 tsp. cinnamon
½ tsp. baking soda
2 cups quick rolled oats
1 cup raisins

Cream first 3 ingredients together. Add egg and mix. Sift flour, salt, cinnamon and soda together and add to creamed mixture. Stir in oats and raisins. Drop by teaspoonsful onto greased cookie sheet. Bake on upper shelf of oven at 375° for 10 to 12 minutes or until lightly browned.

Preparation: 10 min.   Easy   Yield: 4 doz.
Baking: 30 min.   Can do ahead   Can freeze

Mrs. Gary R. Bauer

MINT BARS

"Wow! Peppermint frosting"

½ cup margarine, melted
2 squares chocolate, melted
2 eggs
1 cup sugar
½ tsp. peppermint or vanilla
  flavoring
½ cup almonds, pecans, or
  walnuts, shredded
½ cup flour

Frosting:
2 tbsp. margarine
1 tbsp. milk or cream
1 cup confectioners' sugar
1 tsp. peppermint extract
1 square chocolate
1 tbsp. margarine

Melt margarine and chocolate together. Combine with eggs and sugar. Add peppermint flavoring, nuts and flour. Pour into a greased 9" pan and bake at 350° for 25-30 minutes. Cool.

Frosting: In a bowl, blend margarine and milk; then add the sugar and peppermint. Spread this mixture over the cooled brownies. Melt the chocolate and margarine together, then pour over the frosting and tilt pan so it will cover evenly.

Preparation: 30 min.   Easy   Yield: 36 squares
Baking: 30 min.   Can freeze

Mrs. Richard H. Green

220

OUTSTANDING OATMEAL COOKIES
"Super for 'CARE' packages"

¾ cup shortening
¾ cup granulated sugar
¾ cup brown sugar, packed
3 tbsp. water
1 egg
1 tsp. vanilla
1 cup flour
2 tsp. cinnamon
1 tsp. ground cloves
1 tsp. salt
½ tsp. baking soda
1 cup raisins, dates, or dried
   apricots, chopped
1 cup nuts, chopped
¾ cup coconut, freshly grated
3 cups quick cooking oats

Blend first 6 ingredients
together; cream thoroughly. Stir
in remaining ingredients. Drop
dough by rounded teaspoonsful
onto ungreased cookie sheets.
Bake 12 minutes in 350° oven.
Store in an airtight container.

Preparation: 15 min.	Easy	Yield: 4-5 doz.
Baking: 12 min.	Can do ahead	Can freeze

Marilynn Sebastian

KITTY SWATEK'S CONGO BARS
"What did we ever do before chocolate chips?"

1½ sticks butter or margarine
1 lb. box dark brown sugar
2¾ cups flour
2½ tsp. baking powder
½ tsp. salt
3 eggs
1 tsp. vanilla
1 12-oz. pkg. chocolate chips
1 cup nuts, chopped, optional

Place a 10 x 13″ pan over low
flame; add butter and melt.
Spread butter up sides. Remove,
add brown sugar, stir and cool
slightly. Sift flour, baking
powder and salt together.
Mix eggs and vanilla into brown
sugar, then the dry ingredients.
Stir in the chocolate chips and, if
desired, the nuts. Bake for 25
minutes at 350°. Cool before
cutting.

Preparation: 15 min.	Easy	Yield: 48 bars
Baking: 25 min.	Can do ahead	Can freeze

Diana Morrow

PRALINE GRAHAMS
"Great name for a cookie or a movie star"

40 split graham crackers
2 sticks butter*
½ cup white sugar
1 tsp. vanilla
1 cup pecans, chopped

*if using margarine, use 2
  sticks minus 2 tbsp.

Place graham crackers side by side on a 15 x 10" greased cookie sheet with 4 raised sides. Boil butter and sugar together for 2 minutes. Remove from heat; add vanilla and pecans. Spread over crackers. Bake at 350° for 10 minutes. Remove from oven, let settle a few seconds. Spoon excess onto crackers and remove individually to another cookie sheet to cool.

Preparation: 25 min.	Easy	Yield: 40 pieces
Baking: 10 min.	Can do ahead	Can freeze

Mrs. William H. Colbert

ORANGE COOKIES
"Topped with yummy icing"

1 cup sugar
1 egg
1 cup margarine
½ cup sour cream
2 cups flour
½ tsp. soda
½ tsp. baking powder
pinch salt
juice & grated rind of ½ orange

Mix all ingredients. Place by teaspoonful on greased cookie sheet and bake for 10 minutes at 350°. Combine icing to spreading consistency. Frost when cool.

Icing:
juice & grated rind of ½ orange
1 cup powdered sugar
1 tsp. butter

Preparation: 5 min.	Easy	Yield: 4 doz.
Baking: 10 min.	Must do ahead	

Mrs. John B. McElderr

CANDIES

CREOLE PRALINES
"A taste of the South"

cup brown sugar, firmly
  packed
cup sugar
 cup cream
tbsp. butter
½ cups pecan halves

Combine sugars and cream in a heavy saucepan; stir over low heat until sugar dissolves. Increase heat and cook rapidly, without stirring, until mixture registers 230-234° on candy thermometer or firm soft balls an be formed with fingers when a sample is dropped in a cup of cold ater. Stir in butter and pecans. Cook until mixture reaches 234°; cook 3 minutes and do not stir. Then stir to thicken and quickly drop by poonsful on buttered wax paper. Store in airtight container.

| eparation: | 2 min. | Easy | Yield: 20 |
| oking: | 10-15 min. | Must do ahead | |

Mrs. F. Owen Black

EASY CREAMY FUDGE
"True to its name"

4½ cups sugar
1 13-oz. can evaporated milk
½ lb. butter or 1 stick butter &
   1 stick margarine
3 6-oz. pkgs. chocolate chips
2 cups nuts, chopped
3 tsp. vanilla

In large kettle, mix sugar and milk, stirring until sugar dissolves. Cook 7½ minutes after mixture reaches a boil. Pour over butter, chocolate chips, nuts and vanilla in a large bowl, stirring until mixed. Pour in a cookie sheet or, for thicker fudge, in a 9x13″ pan. Let cool and cut into squares.

Preparation: 15 min.	Easy	Yield: 120 squares
Cooking: 10 min.	Do ahead	

Carmella Pennett

ROCKY ROAD FUDGE
"Full of comforting ingredients"

¼ cup milk
2 6-oz. pkgs. chocolate chips
2 cups miniature marshmallows
½ cup nuts, chopped

Heat milk and chocolate chips in saucepan over low heat until chips melt, stirring constantly. Remove from heat; stir in marshmallows and nuts: mixture will be lumpy. Spread the candy in a buttered 8 x 8 x 2″ pan with a spatula. Refrigerate 1 hour or until firm. Cut into 1″ squares.

Preparation: 15 min.	Easy	Yield: 64 1″ squares
	Must do ahead	

Stephen Schrot

CHOCOLATE PEANUT BUTTER SWIRLS
"Easy and quick—fun for kids to make"

1 cup peanut butter
½ cup confectioners' sugar
½ cup light corn syrup
2 cups Cheerios
1 6-oz. pkg. chocolate chips
2 tbsp. water

Mix peanut butter, sugar and corn syrup in medium bowl. St in cereal. Shape mixture into 1½″ balls; flatten slightly. Hea chocolate chips and water in saucepan over medium heat, stirring constantly, until melte

Cool. Dip tops of balls into chocolate. Place on waxed paper lined cookie sheet. Refrigerate until firm, about 30 minutes. Store in refrigerator.

Preparation: 20 min.	Easy	Yield: 2 doz.
Cooking: 10 min.	Must do ahead	

Stephen Schro

APRICOT BALLS

1 6-oz. pkg. dried apricots
3-oz. coconut, shredded
milk or cream
sugar

Chop apricots and coconut in food processor. Add just enough milk or cream to form balls. Make balls and roll in sugar. Chill in refrigerator. If sticky, roll in sugar again. Store in airtight container.

Preparation: 10 min.   Easy
                        Must do ahead   Can freeze

Mrs. Lloyd Booth, Jr.

DADDY'S PEANUT BRITTLE

2 cups sugar
⅔ cup light syrup
½ cup water
2 cups raw peanuts
1 tsp. baking soda

Mix first 3 ingredients in a 4 quart saucepan. Cook over medium high heat, stirring occasionally, to hard crack stage, 300° on candy thermometer. Add nuts all at once and stir rapidly to prevent burning. Continue cooking and stirring until syrup is amber and nuts begin to smell cooked. Remove from heat. Add soda, stirring rapidly for 10-15 seconds; mixture will foam and darken. Immediately pour into buttered pans or cookie sheet. Spread if thin brittle is preferred. When cool, break into small pieces and store in airtight container.

Preparation: 2 min.   Easy
Cooking: 15 min.   Must do ahead

Mrs. Earl L. Gadbery

TRUFFLES

1 lb. semisweet chocolate
½ lb. butter, room temperature
6 egg yolks
6 tbsp. dark Rum
½ cup confectioners' sugar
½ cup powdered cocoa

Heat oven to 200°. Put chocolate in heatproof bowl and put in oven until soft: watch carefully to keep from burning. Immediately beat in butter, egg yolks and Rum, using a whisk or mixer, until thickened. Let sit for mixture to thicken more. Shape into 1″ balls, roll in combined sugar and cocoa. Arrange on rack and let stand several hours in a cool place.

Preparation: 1 hour   Easy   Yield: 4-5 doz.
Cooking: 10 min.   Must do ahead   Must refrigerate

Mrs. James W. Wilcock

CURRIED PECANS
"Super special pecans"

½ stick margarine, melted
1½ tsp. curry powder
1 tsp. salt
1 lb. pecan halves

Combine margarine, seasonings and pecans. Spread on jellyroll pan and bake 10-12 minutes at 350°, stirring occasionally. Can be reheated and served warm.

Preparation:	5 min.	Easy	Yield: 2+ cups
Baking:	10-12 min.	Can do ahead	Can freeze

Mrs. Jon E. McCarthy

ICED ALMONDS
"With a mild toffee flavor"

1 cup whole blanched almonds
½ cup sugar
2 tbsp. butter or margarine
½ tsp. vanilla
¾ tsp. salt

Heat almonds, sugar and butter in heavy skillet over medium heat, stirring constantly, until almonds are toasted and sugar is golden brown. Stir in vanilla. Spread nuts on a sheet of aluminum foil; sprinkle with salt. Cool and break into 2 or 3 nuts per cluster. Other nuts such as walnuts or pecans can be used.

Preparation:	5 min.	Easy	Serves: 6
Cooking:	15 min.	Must do ahead	Can freeze

Jane Cricks

SUGARED WALNUTS
"A change from salted nuts"

1 cup sugar
½ tsp. vanilla
4 tbsp. water
1 tsp. salt
1 tsp. cinnamon
3 cups walnuts

Mix sugar, vanilla, water, salt and cinnamon and boil 5 minutes. Add walnuts and stir until thoroughly coated. Spread separated nuts on cookie sheet to cool.

Preparation:	10 min.	Easy	Yield: 3 cups
Cooking:	5 min.	Must do ahead	

Carolyn K. Kastroll

NATIONALITY
FAVORITES

LAWRENCEVILLE STREET

The people who call streets like this one in the Lawrenceville section of Pittsburgh "home," provide the character, strength and ethnic nobility to a city made rugged by its very terrain and the industry which propelled it into the 20th Century—Steel.

Additional illustrations in this section:

St. Alexander Nevsky Orthodox Church in Allison Park. The first Orthodox Church in the Greater Pittsburgh area, the parish was established in 1891 in the Woods Run section of the North Side. In 1972, the parish moved to its new church in Allison Park.

The Syria Temple Mosque in Oakland was designed by architects Jansen & Abbot, and dedicated in 1916. It is Pittsburgh's purest example of Arabic architecture.

"Calcite" and "Gypsum" are examples from the spectacular permanent exhibit in the Hillman Hall of Minerals and Gems at the Carnegie Museum of Natural History which opened in 1981.

Architectural details of some Pittsburgh churches.

NATIONALITY FAVORITES

GOTTO SPEISE
"A very rich Austrian dessert"

6 oz. fresh white bread crumbs
1 tsp. instant Nescafé
⅔ cup brown sugar
4½ oz. Nestle's Quik
2 cups heavy cream, whipped
cinnamon
4 oz. Brandy or Sherry
chocolate, grated

Combine first 4 ingredients. Whip cream until stiff. In a glass dish, layer the crumb mixture, sprinkle with cinnamon and brandy and top with whipped cream. Repeat layers until you have 6 layers, the final being cream. Top with grated chocolate. Chill.

Preparation: 15 min.   Easy   Serves: 4-6
                          Can do ahead

Mrs. Simon Beloe

DANISH COFFEECAKE

½ cup butter or margarine
1 cup water
1 cup flour
3 large or 4 med. eggs
8 oz. confectioners' sugar
1-2 tbsp. almond extract
milk
almonds, sliced

Boil water and butter. Beat in flour. Cool. Stir in eggs, one at a time. Form dough into a ring on an ungreased cookie sheet. Bake at 400° for 20-25 minutes. Mix sugar, extract and milk to make frosting of medium consistency. Drizzle over hot cake. Top with almonds. Cake falls when removed from oven.

Preparation: 15 min.
Baking: 20-25 min.   Easy   Serves: 6

Mrs. Jon W. Fay

FRIKADELLER—DANISH MEAT BALLS

"First cousin to Swedish meatballs"

½ lb. ground veal
½ lb. ground pork
3 tbsp. flour
½-1 cup club soda
1 egg, beaten
1 tsp. salt
¼ tsp. pepper
1 med. onion, coarsely chopped
4 tbsp. butter
2 tbsp. oil

In large mixing bowl, vigorously beat the flour into the ground meats. Gradually beat in the club soda, a few tablespoons at a time, and continue to beat until light and fluffy. Beat in egg, salt, pepper and onion. Cover bowl and refrigerate 1 hour. Form into 4 x 3 x 1" oblong patties. Melt butter and oil; when foam subsides, cook patties over moderate heat, 6-8 minutes on each side. Cook only 4 or 5 at a time.

Preparation: 20 min.   Easy   Yield: 8-10 patties
Cooking: 30 min.   Must do ahead   Can freeze

Mrs. Jon W. Fay

JEAN'S FLAPJACKS

"Make your own granola bars"

1 stick butter
⅔ cup brown sugar, firmly
  packed
1 tbsp. Golden Syrup or honey
6 oz. Quaker Oats, quick or old-
  fashioned
raisins, optional
nuts, optional

Melt butter, sugar and syrup in saucepan. Add oats and stir to combine. Add raisins and chopped nuts as desired. Spread in a greased 9 x 13" pan and bake at 350° for 25-30 minutes until golden brown. Cut into bars while warm.

Preparation: 5 min.   Easy   Yield: 18-24 bars
Baking: 25-30 min.   Can do ahead

Susan P. Perin

SCOTCH CURRANT SQUARES
"Interesting - not too sweet"

1 12-oz. pkg. currants
3 tbsp. cornstarch
1 tbsp. lemon juice
1 cup sugar
pastry
powdered sugar

Place currants in saucepan; add enough water to cover. Add sugar and bring to a boil. Mix cornstarch with a little water and add to currants. Add lemon juice. Boil for 15 minutes, stirring, then cool. Line a 9 x 13" pan with pastry; spread with currant mixture. Top with second layer of pastry. Prick and bake at 425° for 30 minutes, or until lightly browned. Cut in squares when cool and sprinkle with powdered sugar. *Note:* We recommend using the short crust pastry on page 232.

Preparation:	45 min.	Easy	Yield: 48 squares
Baking:	45 min.	Can do ahead	

Mrs. Joseph W. Blackhurst

MARDI'S CHRISTMAS PUDDING
"This is a do ahead pudding - two or three months ahead"

1 lb. flour
1 lb. beef suet, finely chopped
1 lb. raisins
1 lb. golden raisins
1 lb. currants
1 lb. brown sugar
½ lb. fresh bread crumbs
½ lb. candied peels: lemon, citron, orange
¼ lb. blanched almonds, sliced
½ tsp. cinnamon
½ tsp. ground cloves
½ tsp. mace
¼ tsp. nutmeg
pinch salt
8 eggs, or more

Mix all ingredients, except eggs, together in a very large bowl. Add enough beaten eggs so mixture is similar to cake dough. Do not add milk or pudding will not keep. Divide between 3-4 well greased 1½ quart pudding bowls of china, pyrex or stainless steel with lip or handles. Allow 1-2" air space at the top of each bowl for expansion. Put together 1 piece of wax paper and 1 piece of tin foil; make a pleat in middle and cover bowl with the foil on top. Tie down tightly with string under the handles so puddings are sealed. Place a piece of string across top to facilitate lifting out of steam pot. Place in pot(s) with boiling water halfway up sides of pudding bowls. Cover and steam 3-3½ hours. Check water level. Store in cool dry place for 2-3 months before Christmas to mellow. Do not refrigerate. To serve: steam again for 1 hour. Turn onto warmed serving plate. Cover with flaming Brandy and serve with whipped cream or hard sauce.

Preparation:	1 hour	Easy	Serves: 3 puddings serving
Cooking:	4-4½ hours	Must do ahead	12 each

Susan P. Perin

ENGLISH MINCE PIES WITH SHORT CRUST PASTRY

Pastry:
2 tsp. powdered sugar, sifted
1 lb. flour
6 oz. butter
6 oz. Crisco
pinch of salt
ice water, to mix

English no-meat mincemeat,
** recipe following**
whipped cream
hard sauce

Sift dry ingredients together in a bowl. Chop butter into bowl. With a motion of lifting hands about a foot above, lightly rub flour mixture across tips of fingers with thumbs to keep mixture cool. Rub in Cricso. Add water to make mixture stick together but not sticky. The less water, the smoother the pastry. Refrigerate dough when not in use. Divide in 3 or 4 pieces. Roll 1 piece very thin. Use cookie cutter to cut rounds and line tart or muffin tins. Spoon a little mincemeat in each muffin, being sure to keep edges of pastry clean. Cut more pastry rounds; dampen edges with water and place on top of each tart, carefully sealing edges with rounded handle of spoon. Prick tops. Bake 25 minutes at 425° or until pale golden. Serve warm or cold with whipped cream or hard sauce.

To prepare tart shells for use with a cooked filling, prick bottoms with a fork and bake at 400° for 10 minutes. Cool before filling.

Preparation:	1½ hours	Can freeze	Yield:	36-48 English tarts
Baking:	25 min.	Moderate difficulty		12 American tarts

Susan P. Perin

JEAN'S MINCEMEAT

1 lb. apples, peeled & chopped
1 lb. currants
¾ lb. beef suet, finely chopped
¾ lb. raisins
¾ lb. sugar
grated rind & juice of 3 lemons
¼ lb. candied peel: lemon,
** citron, orange, finely chopped**
½ tsp. cinnamon
½ tsp. cloves
½ tsp. mace
½ tsp. nutmeg
½ pt. Brandy, or to taste

Mix all ingredients together. Refrigerate in a tightly closed container at least 2 weeks to allow mincemeat to mellow. Will keep several months refrigerated.

Preparation: 30 min.	Easy	Yield:	4-6 American pies
	Must do ahead		15 doz. English pies

Susan P. Perin

LEMON OR ORANGE CURD

Lemon curd:
3 large eggs
3 large lemons, rind & juice
3 oz. butter
9 oz. sugar

Orange curd:
4 eggs
2 oranges, rind & juice
1 lemon
2 oz. butter
8 oz. sugar
whipped cream
tart shells

Lightly whip eggs in top of double boiler. Add grated rind, juice, butter and sugar. Stir constantly until butter has melted. Continue to cook and stir 5-10 minutes, until thickened and smooth. Use baked pastry tarts, page 232, or your favorite pastry shells. Fill with curd and top with whipped cream. *Note:* May prefer to cook over direct heat.

Preparation: 15 min.   Easy   Yield: 36-48 tassie tarts
Baking: 10 min.

Susan P. Perin

ELEANOR'S NASIGORENG

"What fun to tell the kids they're having Nasigoreng for dinner"

1 lb. Uncle Ben's rice, cooked
2 lbs. ground beef
4 tbsp. onion, chopped
2 tsp. sambal oelek
4 tbsp. soy sauce
salt, to taste

In a skillet, fry meat, onions and sambal in oil until meat is cooked. Add soy sauce and rice; heat thoroughly and salt to taste. Serve with your choice of condiments. This recipe is good without the ethnic spices.

Suitable condiments are: fried or raw bananas, cucumber or tomato slices, chopped hard-boiled egg, kroe toek or fried coconut. To prepare coconut, heat 1 tablespoon oil, sauté 4 ounces of coconut with 2 tablespoons of salted peanuts and 1 tablespoon sugar. Store in jar and serve cold.

Preparation: 25 min.   Easy   Serves: 4-8
Cooking: 20 min.

Nell Tabor Hartley

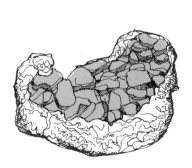

KOTOPITA

"It's fun to work with phyllo — Try these Greek chicken rolls"

Rolls:
10 sheets phyllo dough
1 cup celery, chopped
¾ cup onion, chopped
½ lb. butter
2 cups chicken, cooked & cubed
½ cup chicken broth
2 tbsp. parsley
¼ tsp. nutmeg
½ tsp. salt
⅛ tsp. pepper
3 eggs

Béchamel Sauce:
2 tbsp. butter
2 tbsp. flour
2 cups hot chicken broth
3 egg yolks, beaten
4 tsp. lemon juice
¼ tsp. salt

cooked rice

Thaw phyllo dough. Cook celery in 1 stick of the butter for 5 minutes. Add onions, cook until tender. Add chicken and broth and simmer until the broth is absorbed. Cool, add parsley, nutmeg, salt and pepper. Beat eggs until frothy and add to chicken mixture. Melt the second stick of butter. Brush one sheet of phyllo with butter, fold in half and brush again with butter. Spread 1 tablespoon of chicken mixture across the short edge. Fold in the long sides and roll as for jellyroll. Place seam side down on lightly buttered pan and brush each roll with butter. Bake at 350° for 40 minutes until rolls are golden and crisp. Serve with Béchamel sauce.

Béchamel Sauce: Melt butter, add flour and stir until thickened. Add broth and stir until bubbly; add seasonings. Combine yolks and lemon juice. Stir a little of the hot sauce into yolks, return to pan and cook, stirring, 2-3 minutes. Arrange chicken rolls on bed of rice and spoon sauce over them.

Preparation: 45-50 min.   Can do ahead   Serves: 5 of 2 rolls each
Baking: 40 min.

Holy Cross Ladies Philoptochos Society

ROAST LEG OF LAMB WITH FETA CHEESE

"A wonderful, different way to cook lamb"

1 leg of lamb, boned
¾ lb. feta cheese, crumbled
1 tsp. oregano
½ tsp. salt
½ tsp. pepper
juice of ½ lemon

Bone lamb and fill with cheese, pepper and oregano. Tie meat and place in baking pan. Rub with salt, pepper and juice of half a lemon. Bake at 350° for 3 hours, or until done — about 28-30 minutes per pound.

Preparation: 20 min.   Can do ahead   Serves: 8
Cooking: 3 hours   Can freeze

Julia Pahountis

SAUERBRATEN WESTPHALIAN
"A classic four day German recipe, so think ahead"

7 lb. rump roast
equal amounts of water & cider
   vinegar
2 tsp. salt
2 tbsp. sugar
2 tbsp. whole pickling spices
3 bay leaves
6 cloves
2 med.-large onion, chopped
25 gingersnap cookies
water
½-¾ cup sugar
1 tsp. salt

Day 1: Combine pickling spices, bay leaves and cloves and put in a cheesecloth bag. Cut the roast into two pieces and put in a large container. Do not use aluminum containers in any stage of recipe. Pour equal quantities of water and cider vinegar over the roast until level is 1" above the meat. Chop onions and add along with salt and sugar. Immerse spice bag and refrigerate overnight.

Day 2: Turn meat over in liquid. Later, turn again.

Day 3: Turn meat over again in morning. In the evening, put meat, liquid and spice bag in large pot. Bring to a boil and reduce heat until liquid is at a high simmer; cover pot. Check occasionally to see that the liquid level has not dropped. If it does, add equal parts water and vinegar. Continue simmering for 2-3 hours until meat is done, but do not overcook so that meat falls apart. When done, remove and retain spice bag, and drain liquid into a separate container. Cool. When the spice bag has cooled, squeeze the juice out of it into the liquid and discard it. Refrigerate meat and liquid, separately, overnight.

Day 4: Skim fat from refrigerated liquid and heat liquid slowly in a saucepan. Crumble gingersnaps and place in bowl. Add water and mix until gingersnaps dissolve into a thick paste. After liquid begins to simmer, slowly add gingersnap paste. Add sugar; salt to taste. Cook slowly until all is dissolved and gravy thickens. Remove from heat: *Note:* At all times after sugar has been added, be very careful not to overheat mixture or let it cook without stirring, because the sugar will make it scorch very easily. Slice meat about ½" thick and arrange in container. Pour gravy over meat and let stand at room temperature for 4 hours. Stir mixture every half hour to make sure all pieces of meat are well-coated with gravy. That evening, heat meat and gravy mixture; be careful not to scorch it. Stir often. Fill tureen with meat and gravy; serve remaining gravy separately. Serve with potato pancakes or noodles.

Cooking: 4-5 hours   Must do ahead   Serves: 16

Cam Allen

235

SCALLOPS ITALIENNE

"Try scallops French one week and Italian the next"

3 tbsp. butter
1 tbsp. shallot or scallion, minced
2 tsp. garlic, minced
½ cup mushrooms, chopped
1 tbsp. parsley, minced
¼ tsp. oregano or basil
½ cup dry white wine
2 tomatoes, peeled, cored & seeded
salt & pepper
¼ cup bread crumbs
⅓ cup mixed Romano & Parmesan cheeses, grated
1 lb. bay scallops

Sauté shallots and garlic in hot butter until soft. Add mushrooms, parsley and oregano and cook briskly until water evaporates, about 2 minutes. Add wine and cook briskly until reduced by half. Add tomatoes, mixing well. Salt and pepper to taste. Add scallops and stir until heated through. Sprinkle with crumbs and cheese. Broil 3" from heat until brown and bubbly. Serve immediately.

Preparation: 25 min.   Easy   Serves: 4
Broiling: 3-5 min.   Can do ahead

Mrs. J. A. Raub

KERRY CREAM

"An Irish recipe with soy sauce???"

1 8-oz. pkg. cream cheese
1 oz. sesame seeds
soy sauce

Press seeds into cream cheese on all sides and place on serving dish. Pour soy sauce over cheese until sauce covers bottom of dish. Let sit at room temperature 2 hours. Serve with assorted crackers.

Preparation: 2 min.   Easy   Must do ahead

Mary A. Kenny

JENNY'S PIZZELLES

"To make a long rainy afternoon brighter, make pizzelles"

1 lb. margarine or butter, melted & cooled
12 eggs
2 cups sugar
3 oz. Whiskey
2 tbsp. butternut flavoring or 1 tbsp. orange, lemon or vanilla
4 cups flour
½ tsp. salt

Beat eggs and sugar. Add cooled margarine or butter; continue beating on slow speed. Add Whiskey and flavoring, then slowly add salt and flour. Batter will be the consistency of pancake batter. Preheat pizzelle iron. Use 1 teaspoon of batter per cookie. Time according to pizzelle iron directions. Store in airtight container to maintain crispness.

Preparation: 10 min.   Easy   Yield: 80-90 cookies
Cooking: several hours   Can freeze

Mary Kay Russo

ROAST CHICKEN VOLHYNIAN STYLE

"Stuffing has delicious soufflé-like quality."

3 lb. chicken
salt & ground pepper
1 cup day-old bread, cubed
¼ cup milk
2 cups parsley leaves, loosely
 packed
1 chicken liver, raw
6 tbsp. butter, softened
2 eggs, separated
juice of ½ lemon

Preheat oven to 425°. Sprinkle chicken inside and out with salt and pepper. Soak bread in milk and work into a mush with fingers. Chop the liver with parsley leaves until fine. Cream 4 tablespoons butter and egg yolks. Add bread and parsley mixture to eggs. Salt and pepper to taste. Fold in stiffly beaten egg whites and stuff bird and neck cavities. Truss bird. Melt remaining butter, add lemon juice and coat chicken. Roast chicken at 425° for 10 minutes, reduce heat to 375° and roast 80 minutes. Baste every 10-15 minutes. Can make a day ahead to serve cold, but do not freeze.

Preparation: 20 min.   Easy   Serves: 2-3
Cooking: 1½ hours   Can do ahead

Mrs. A. M. Aksoy

TORTE COUNTESS KRASINSKA

*"Topped with orange sauce and whipped cream —
a royal Polish treat"*

½ cup unsalted butter
¼ cup shortening
1 cup sugar
2 eggs
2½ cups cake flour, sifted
½ tsp. salt
½ tsp. baking soda
1½ tsp. baking powder
1 cup yogurt, or ½ cup sour
 cream diluted with ½ cup
 water
1 cup dates, chopped
½ cups walnuts
1 tbsp. orange peel, grated
⅔ cup orange juice
1 cup sugar
whipped cream

Cream shortening, butter, and sugar until light and fluffy. Add eggs to butter mixture and beat well. Sift dry ingredients together and add to butter mixture alternately with liquid. Beat well after each addition. Stir in dates, nuts and peel. Pour into greased and floured 9" springform pan. Bake at 350° for 1 hour. Cool 15 minutes. While cake is cooling, simmer orange juice with sugar until sugar dissolves. Pierce cake several times with a sharp tester to permit greater absorption. Pour syrup over cake. Serve with unsweetened whipped cream.

Preparation: 20 min.   Easy   Serves: 8-10
Baking: 55-60 min.   Can do ahead

Mrs. A. M. Aksoy

237

CABBAGE SOUP
"Makes enough for two delicious dinners"

2½ lbs. soup meat, chuck or
   brisket
1 46-oz. can tomato juice
3-4 lbs. green cabbage, finely
   chopped
2 onions, diced
1 clove garlic
1 tbsp. salt
dash pepper
2 tbsp. molasses, optional
1 28-oz. can whole peeled
   tomatoes
juice of 1½-3 lemons, to taste
brown sugar, to taste
raisins, optional

Cube meat into bite-size pieces. Simmer in tomato juice for 1 hour until tender. Add remaining ingredients and cook 2 hours. If desired, serve with boiled potatoes and top with sour cream. Russian piroshki are also a nice accompaniment. This is a Russian recipe.

Preparation:	30 min.	Easy	Serves: 15-20
Cooking:	3 hours	Can do ahead	

Natasha Green

RUSSIAN TORTE
"Great because it is not too terribly sweet"

4 cups walnuts, ground
1 cup sugar
2 tsp. cinnamon

Dough:
1 pkg. dry yeast
¼ cup warm water
4 cups flour, sifted
3 sticks butter
4 egg yolks, lightly beaten
¼ cup milk
2 10-oz. jars Bakers apricot
   filling

Topping:
5 egg whites
10 tbsp. sugar

Combine first 3 ingredients and mix. Measure 1 cup and set aside for topping. Combine yeast with warm water. Set aside. Sift flour into bowl; add butter and blend until mealy in texture. Add egg yolks, milk and yeast mixture. Blend and stir batter until it pulls away from the bowl. Place on floured board and knead a few minutes. Divide dough into 3 sections. Roll first section to measure 15 x 10". If dough is difficult to handle, roll between waxed paper. Place in lightly greased 10x15" pan and work to sides for lining. Spread nut mixture over dough.

Roll and place second section over nuts. Spread apricot filling over the dough. Spread remaining dough over the filling. Bake at 350° for 45 minutes. During last 10 minutes of baking, beat egg whites and sugar until stiff. Spread mixture on torte and cover with reserved nut mixture. Return to oven until light golden brown. Cut diagonally into 1" squares.

Preparation:	1 hour	Must do ahead	Yield: 75 squares
Cooking:	50 min.		

Mrs. Robert L. Steup

238

TORTA ROLL

"This will make you two delicious Serbian rolls - one to eat,
one to freeze"

Roll:
6 egg yolks
6 tbsp. sugar
1 tsp. vanilla
4 rounded tbsp. cake flour
¼ tsp. salt
2 rounded tbsp. nuts, ground
6 egg whites

Filling:
4 eggs
4 heaping tsp. sugar
4 tbsp. Nestle's instant cocoa
¼ lb. nuts, ground
½ lb. sweet butter

confectioners' sugar

Roll: Ingredients listed are for one roll. Repeat for second roll. Beat egg yolks 10 minutes until lemon-colored. Add sugar and beat well, 5 more minutes. Add vanilla. Sift flour with salt and add to above mixture. Add nuts and set aside. Beat egg whites until stiff but not dry. Fold into first mixture. Grease 11 x 15" jellyroll pan and line with wax paper. Grease paper. Pour in batter and bake at 325° for 25 minutes. While first roll is baking, make another batter for second roll. Sprinkle a tea towel with powdered sugar. When cake is done, remove from oven and immediately invert it onto tea towel. Remove wax paper, roll cake and set aside until filling is made.

Filling: (sufficient for two rolls). Put eggs and sugar in double boiler; beat thoroughly until foamy, making sure eggs do not cook. Add cocoa and mix well again. Remove from stove; add nuts and cool. Add refrigerated butter to cooled mixture and beat 10 minutes or until light and fluffy. Place in refrigerator to chill. Spread on cooled rolls and reroll. Store filled rolls in plastic wrap. Sprinkle with powdered sugar before serving.

Preparation: 20-30 min.   Moderately difficult   Yield: 2 rolls
Baking: 25 min.   Can freeze

Kathleen Cabraja

ALMOND SALAD DRESSING

"An exotic dressing - give it a try"

8 almonds, blanched
1 or 2 cloves garlic
½ tsp. salt
1 cup olive oil
¼ cup white wine vinegar

Crush almonds and garlic to a paste; work in salt. Slowly beat in olive oil, then vinegar until blended. Good on any green salad. This is a Spanish recipe.

Preparation: 5 min.   Easy   Yield: 1¼ cups

Mrs. Richard K. Foster

SPANISH SPINACH SAUCE
"Especially good with salmon"

½ lb. spinach or ½ 10-oz. pkg.
  frozen spinach, thawed
1 green pepper, diced
2 tbsp. onion, chopped
4 tbsp. olive oil
¼ tsp. salt
1 tsp. vinegar

Coarsely chop spinach in blender. Add pepper and onion and purée. Slowly add olive oil and last, salt and vinegar. This is a thick sauce and could be thinned for other uses. Excellent with fish.

Preparation: 10 min.   Easy   Yield: 1½ cups
                           Can do ahead

Mrs. Richard K. Foster

PAELLA VALENCIA
"You'll need your very largest casserole for this colorful dish."

2½ lbs. chicken
5 cups water
1 onion
½ tsp. saffron
1½ tsp. salt
1 tbsp. flour
½ tsp. salt
½ cup olive oil
1½ lbs. raw shrimp, shelled
1 cup ham, or garlic flavored
  hard pepperoni, chopped
1 med. onion, minced
2 or 3 cloves garlic, crushed
1 pimento, cut in strips
2 tomatoes, peeled & chopped
2 cups rice, uncooked
1 7-oz. can minced clams &
  juice
½ pkg. frozen peas
salt, to taste

Reserve chicken breast, drumsticks and wings. Use remaining chicken to make broth. Add 5 cups water, peeled onion, 1½ teaspoons salt and ½ teaspoon saffron to the chicken. Boil 30 minutes, then strain and reserve 4½ cups stock.

Meanwhile, cut chicken parts into small pieces and dust with flour, blended with ½ tsp. salt. Cook in hot olive oil until crispy brown. Remove chicken. Add shrimp and ham, or pepperoni, and cook until lightly browned. Remove to casserole. Add onion, garlic, pimento and tomatoes and cook until onion is tender. Add rice and stir to glaze. Add boiling hot chicken broth, clams and clam juice. Bring to a boil and cook 5 minutes. Add peas and cook 5 minutes longer, uncovered. Transfer to a large casserole and arrange some of the shrimp and chicken over top of rice. Cover casserole and cook over very low heat 15-20 minutes or bake at 300° until liquid is absorbed.

Preparation: 45 min.-1 hour   Can do ahead   Serves: 6
Cooking: 30 min.

Mrs. Richard K. Foste.

SPANISH STYLE STUFFING
"Try this when you want something unusual for a change"

3 cups rice, cooked
¼ cup ham, cooked & diced
2 chicken livers, chopped
6 almonds, chopped
1 tbsp. parsley, minced
2 tbsp. butter

Sauté livers and almonds in the butter; add remaining ingredients and stir to coat and combine thoroughly.

Preparation: 25 min.   Easy   Serves: 6

Mrs. Richard K. Foster

GREEN BEANS AND LAMB
"This is even better the next day"

1 lb. green beans
1½ lbs. lamb, cubed
butter
1 onion, diced
1 ʾbsp. salt
½ tsp. pepper
1 12-oz. can tomatoes
1-2 cups water

Steam beans, cut in half and rinse in cold water. Sauté lamb cubes in butter; add onion and brown. Add beans, salt and pepper. Cover and cook over low heat for 45 minutes, stirring occasionally. Add tomatoes and water and cook 15 minutes, uncovered. Serve over Syrian rice.

Preparation: 30 min.   Easy   Serves: 4
Cooking: 1 hour   Can do ahead

Evelyn Perkins

SYRIAN RICE
"Easily expanded or decreased"

2 cups long grain rice
2 tsp. salt
3 tbsp. butter
½ cup orzo or rose marina
4 cups chicken broth

Soak rice in hot water with 1 teaspoon salt for 1 hour; rinse rice and drain. Melt butter in 3 quart saucepan, add orzo and stir until browned. Add rice and stir gently for 2 minutes. Add chicken broth and 1 teaspoon salt. Cook over low heat for 20 minutes or until broth is absorbed.

Preparation: 5 min.   Easy   Serves: 8-12
Cooking: 30 min.

Evelyn Perkins

GRAPE LEAVES
"A favorite with Adam and Eve"

1 cup long grain rice
1 ½ lbs. beef or lamb, freshly
  ground
½ -1 tsp. salt
½ tsp. pepper
2 tbsp. butter, melted
grape leaves*
lemon juice, to taste

*can be purchased in specialty
  stores or home preserved

Soak rice in warm water for 10 minutes and drain. Combine all ingredients, except leaves, and mix well. Place 1 teaspoon of mixture in center of each grape leaf. Roll into long thin cigar shape. Use left-over leaves to line bottom of 3 quart pot. Arrange grape leaves close together, alternating the direction of the layers. Place inverted plate or a smaller pot lid over the grape leaves as a weight. Add water to cover. Simmer over low heat, 45 minutes to 1 hour. Before serving, add lemon juice to taste. Additional weight may be placed on the lid to avoid the splitting of the leaves.

Preparation: 1 hour   Easy   Yield: 80-90 stuffed leaves
Cooking: 45-60 min.   Can do ahead

Elizabeth Haddad

ROAST LEG OF LAMB
"Spices make this special Syrian lamb"

5 lb. leg of lamb
1 tsp. salt
2 garlic cloves, minced
¼ tsp. pepper
¼ bay leaf, crushed
¼ tsp. marjoram
¼ tsp. sage
¼ tsp. ginger
¼ tsp. thyme
1 tbsp. oil

onions, peeled
carrots, peeled
potatoes, peeled

Wipe lamb with damp cloth. Cut ¼ " gashes on top of lamb. Combine all ingredients, except oil, and rub well until gashes are filled. Coat lamb with oil. Sear in preheated oven at 500° for 15 minutes. Reduce to 350° and cook for 45 minutes. Add prepared raw vegetables and cook 45 minutes longer.

Preparation: 10-15 min.   Easy   Serves: 4-6
Cooking: 1 ¾ hours

Elizabeth Haddad

KIBBEE
"An exotic way to use ground beef"

1½ cups bulgar wheat
2 lbs. lean ground beef or lamb
salt & pepper, to taste
1 large onion, finely chopped

Filling:
½ lb. ground beef
½ small onion, finely chopped
3 tbsp. pine nuts
salt & pepper, to taste
½ cup butter, melted

Cover wheat with water and soak 5-10 minutes. Drain wheat, cup hands and squeeze out all moisture. Let wheat stand for 10 minutes to drain. Add remaining ingredients. Knead well; add ½ cup cold water to soften and knead again. Can be eaten raw with melted butter spooned over it.

Grease 8 x 11" glass baking pan. Spread half of mixture in bottom of pan. Spread filling over and cover filling with remaining mixture; spread evenly. Score deeply in triangles with knife. Loosen around edge of pan with a knife. Pour ½ cup melted butter over top. Bake at 350° for 25-30 minutes or until bottom appears golden. Mixture may also be formed into hamburgers and baked, broiled or fried.

Filling: Fry ground beef until done. Drain excess fat and add onion; salt and pepper to taste. Add pine nuts if desired. Blanched, slivered almonds may be substituted for pine nuts.

Preparation: 20 min.   Easy   Serves: 6-8
Cooking: 25-30 min.   Can do ahead

Elizabeth Haddad

TABOULEH
"A Middle Eastern salad"

1 cup bulgar, cracked wheat
1 bunch scallions
2 large bunches parsley
4 large tomatoes
juice of 4 lemons, or ½ cup
   lemon juice
½ cup oil
salt & pepper, to taste
3 tbsp. mint, chopped, optional

Rinse wheat several times in water and drain. Soak wheat in water to cover. While wheat is soaking, chop onions, parsley and tomatoes. Drain wheat; add the vegetables, seasonings, lemon juice and oil and mix well. Serve on fresh lettuce leaves or with yogurt. If preparing ahead, reserve tomatoes and add immediately before serving.

Preparation: 30 min.   Easy   Serves: 6
                           Can do ahead

Evelyn Perkins

TURKISH PILAF PIE

"A glorious rice dish"

3 tbsp. olive oil
2 cups long grain rice
⅓ cup onion, finely chopped
¼ cup currants
2 tbsp. pignolia nuts
½ tsp. salt
¼ tsp. allspice
chicken broth
6 sheets phyllo or strudel leaves
1 stick unsalted butter, melted

Cook onion in hot oil until soft. Add rinsed rice and stir to coat. Add nuts, currants, salt, allspice and chicken broth to cover rice. Bring to a boil, stir and reduce heat. Simmer, covered, 10 minutes. Test and adjust seasoning to taste.

While rice cooks prepare phyllo sheets. Butter a flameproof or metal mixing bowl; drape one sheet of phyllo across bottom and sides of bowl, letting ends hang over sides. Brush with melted butter. Arrange remaining sheets in same manner. When rice has absorbed liquid, pour into bowl and cover with the ends of phyllo to make a package. Turn over in bowl, brush top with butter and bake at 375° for 1 hour or until golden. Cut into wedges to serve.

Preparation: 1 hour   Moderately difficult   Serves: 8-10
Cooking: 45 min.

Mrs. A. M. Aksoy

SVIKLY

"This has to be super since it rhymes with Sewickley"

3 cups beets
½ cup horseradish, or more to taste
1 tbsp. vinegar
1 tbsp. brown sugar

Boil beets until tender. Drain and chill. Peel and shred finely; drain in colander if watery. Peel and shred horseradish. Mix vinegar and horseradish together and add to beets. Add sugar and mix well. Put in jar and refrigerate at least several days before serving.

Preparation: 30 min.   Easy   Yield: 3 cups
Cooking: 20 min.   Must do ahead

Mrs. John Lewicki

INDEX

247

251

MEASUREMENTS

dash	= less than 1/8 tsp.
1 tbsp.	= 3 tsp.
2 tbsp.	= 1 oz.
4 tbsp.	= ¼ cup
5⅓ tbsp.	= ⅓ cup
8 tbsp.	= ½ cup
16 tbsp.	= 1 cup
8 oz.	= 1 cup
16 oz.	= 1 lb.
2 cups	= 1 lb./1 pt.
2 pints	= 1 qt./4 cups
4 quarts	= 1 gallon
8 quarts	= 1 peck
4 pecks	= 1 bushel

METRIC CONVERSION

VOLUME

1 tsp.	=	5 ml.
1 tbsp.	=	15 ml.
2 tbsp.	=	30 ml.
1 cup.	=	240 ml.
1 pint	=	480 ml.
1 quart	=	960 ml.

WEIGHT

1 oz.	=	28 gm.
1 lb.	=	454 gm.
2.2 lbs.	=	(1 Kg.) 1,000 gm.

LENGTH

1 in.	=	2.54 cm.
39.37 in.	=	1 meter

EQUIVALENTS

Apples	4 oz.	=	1 cup sliced
Bread	1 slice	=	⅓ cup dry crumbs
Butter	1 oz.	=	2 tbsp.
	¼ lb. = ½ cup	=	1 stick
	1 lb.	=	2 cups
Cheese, dry	1 lb.	=	4 cups
grated	1 lb.	=	4-5 cups
cottage	½ lb.	=	1 cup
cream	3 oz.	=	6 tbsp.
Chicken	3½ lbs. drawn	=	2 cups cooked, diced
Coconut, flaked	3½ oz.	=	1⅓ cups
Cream, heavy	1 cup	=	2 cups whipped
Eggs, whole	5	=	1 cup
whites	8-10	=	1 cup
yolks	10-12	=	1 cup
Flour,	1 lb.	=	4 cups
for thickening	5 tsp.	=	2 tsp. arrowroot
	2 tbsp.	=	1 tbsp. cornstarch
	1 tbsp.	=	2 tsp. quick-cooking tapioc
Gelatin	¼ oz. env.	=	1 tbsp. (gels 2 cups)
Herbs	⅓-½ tsp. dried	=	1 tbsp. fresh
Lemon	1	=	2-3 tbsp. juice
		=	2 tsp. rind
Meat, cooked	1 lb.	=	3 cups minced
Mushrooms	1 lb. fresh = 5 cups sliced	=	6 oz. canned
Nuts	1 lb. in shell = ½ lb. kernels	=	3-4 cups
Orange	1 med.	=	6-8 tbsp. juice
			1-2 tbsp. rind
Potatoes	1 lb. raw	=	2 cups mashed
Raisins, seedless	1 lb.	=	2 cups
Rice	2-2½ cups (1 lb.)	=	8 cups cooked
Sugars, brown	1 lb.	=	2¼ cups packed
confectioners'	1 lb.	=	4 cups
white	1 lb.	=	2 cups

To place an order or to receive current pricing, please call Child Health Association at 412.741.3221, email us at childhealth@comcast.net, or visit www.childhealthassociation.org/threeriverscookbooks.php

Mail-in Order form (please complete using current pricing):

Three Rivers Cookbook:

Volume I (red)   Qty _____ x Unit Price _____ = Total _____
Volume II (green)   Qty _____ x Unit Price _____ = Total _____
Volume III (blue)   Qty _____ x Unit Price _____ = Total _____
Volume IV (green hardcover)   Qty _____ x Unit Price _____ = Total _____
Collection   Qty _____ x Unit Price _____ = Total _____
(Volumes I, II and III in a decorative sleeve)

Subtotal $_____
Shipping charges $_____
PA sales tax *(Books shipped to PA address)* $_____
Total Payment Due $_____

Mail form and payment information to: Child Health Association of Sewickley
108 Ohio River Boulevard, Suite 802, Sewickley, PA 15143

Make check payable to Child Health Association, or include credit card information below:

Visa ❑ Mastercard: Account # ☐☐☐☐☐☐☐☐☐☐☐☐☐☐☐☐ Exp. Date: ☐☐/☐☐

Name on Card: _____ Phone #: _____

Billing Address: _____

Shipping address if different from above:

_____

Allow 2-3 weeks processing time.

- -

To place an order or to receive current pricing, please call Child Health Association at 412.741.3221, email us at childhealth@comcast.net, or visit www.childhealthassociation.org/threeriverscookbooks.php

Mail-in Order form (please complete using current pricing):

Three Rivers Cookbook:

Volume I (red)   Qty _____ x Unit Price _____ = Total _____
Volume II (green)   Qty _____ x Unit Price _____ = Total _____
Volume III (blue)   Qty _____ x Unit Price _____ = Total _____
Volume IV (green hardcover)   Qty _____ x Unit Price _____ = Total _____
Collection   Qty _____ x Unit Price _____ = Total _____
(Volumes I, II and III in a decorative sleeve)

Subtotal $_____
Shipping charges $_____
PA sales tax *(Books shipped to PA address)* $_____
Total Payment Due $_____

Mail form and payment information to: Child Health Association of Sewickley
108 Ohio River Boulevard, Suite 802, Sewickley, PA 15143

Make check payable to Child Health Association, or include credit card information below:

Visa ❑ Mastercard: Account # ☐☐☐☐☐☐☐☐☐☐☐☐☐☐☐☐ Exp. Date: ☐☐/☐☐

Name on Card: _____ Phone #: _____

Billing Address: _____

Shipping address if different from above:

_____

Allow 2-3 weeks processing time.

To place an order or to receive current pricing, please call Child Health Association at 412.741.3221, email us at childhealth@comcast.net, or visit www.childhealthassociation.org/threeriverscookbooks.php

Mail-in Order form (please complete using current pricing):

Three Rivers Cookbook:

Volume I (red)	Qty _____ x Unit Price _____ = Total _____
Volume II (green)	Qty _____ x Unit Price _____ = Total _____
Volume III (blue)	Qty _____ x Unit Price _____ = Total _____
Volume IV (green hardcover)	Qty _____ x Unit Price _____ = Total _____
Collection	Qty _____ x Unit Price _____ = Total _____
(Volumes I, II and III in a decorative sleeve)	

Subtotal $_____

Shipping charges $_____

PA sales tax *(Books shipped to PA address)* $_____

Total Payment Due $_____

Mail form and payment information to: Child Health Association of Sewickley
908 Ohio River Boulevard, Suite 802, Sewickley, PA 15143

Make check payable to Child Health Association, or include credit card information below:

❏ Visa   ❏ Mastercard: Account # [ ][ ][ ][ ][ ][ ][ ][ ][ ][ ][ ][ ][ ][ ][ ][ ]   Exp. Date: [ ][ ] / [ ][ ]

Name on Card: _____   Phone #: _____

Billing Address: _____

Shipping address if different from above:

_____

Allow 2-3 weeks processing time.

- -

To place an order or to receive current pricing, please call Child Health Association at 412.741.3221, email us at childhealth@comcast.net, or visit www.childhealthassociation.org/threeriverscookbooks.php

Mail-in Order form (please complete using current pricing):

Three Rivers Cookbook:

Volume I (red)	Qty _____ x Unit Price _____ = Total _____
Volume II (green)	Qty _____ x Unit Price _____ = Total _____
Volume III (blue)	Qty _____ x Unit Price _____ = Total _____
Volume IV (green hardcover)	Qty _____ x Unit Price _____ = Total _____
Collection	Qty _____ x Unit Price _____ = Total _____
(Volumes I, II and III in a decorative sleeve)	

Subtotal $_____

Shipping charges $_____

PA sales tax *(Books shipped to PA address)* $_____

Total Payment Due $_____

Mail form and payment information to: Child Health Association of Sewickley
908 Ohio River Boulevard, Suite 802, Sewickley, PA 15143

Make check payable to Child Health Association, or include credit card information below:

❏ Visa   ❏ Mastercard: Account # [ ][ ][ ][ ][ ][ ][ ][ ][ ][ ][ ][ ][ ][ ][ ][ ]   Exp. Date: [ ][ ] / [ ][ ]

Name on Card: _____   Phone #: _____

Billing Address: _____

Shipping address if different from above:

_____

Allow 2-3 weeks processing time.